P9-AFX-544

PRINCIPLES OF GRAMMAR & LEARNING

PRINCIPLES OF GRAMMAR & LEARNING

William O'Grady

THE UNIVERSITY OF CHICAGO PRESS
CHICAGO & LONDON

William O'Grady is associate professor of linguistics at
the University of Calgary.

The University of Chicago Press, Chicago 60637
The University of Chicago Press, Ltd., London
© 1987 by The University of Chicago
All rights reserved. Published 1987
Printed in the United States of America
95 94 93 92 91 90 89 88 87   54321

Library of Congress Cataloging-in-Publication Data

O'Grady, William.
   Principles of grammar and learning.

   Bibliography: p.
   Includes index.
   1. Grammar, Comparative and general.   2. Language
acquisition.   I. Title.
P151.O37   1987   415   86-11402
ISBN 0-226-62074-3

FOR MY PARENTS

CONTENTS

PREFACE

Some twenty-five years ago the discipline of linguistics embarked on a research program aimed at identifying the grammatical rules underlying human linguistic knowledge as well as the mental structures that make possible their acquisition. For the most part, this research has been based on two central assumptions: the view that grammatical notions are not constructed on a semantic base (the autonomy thesis) and the view that central components of the grammar are innate (nativism). In this book I will undertake to question the validity of each of these assumptions, proposing in their place an alternate conception of the nature of grammatical notions and of linguistic development.

There is an understandable tendency on the part of many linguists to dismiss this alternate type of research on the grounds that it has been tried many times and has always led to failure. This attitude deserves considerable sympathy. Many critiques of the autonomy thesis and nativism have been based on serious misunderstandings, and few have offered interesting counterproposals. However, it is also important to recognize that the lines of inquiry most likely to give fruitful results in the early stages of a discipline's development are those to which the largest number of people devote their energy, not necessarily those that are correct. Alternatives that are not seriously explored or given careful consideration should therefore not be simply dismissed out of hand as hopeless endeavors or inherently flawed research programs.

With these considerations in mind, I will attempt to sketch an approach to language and learning that exploits a set of ideas and assumptions substantially different from those currently dominating linguistic inquiry. I will begin in chapter I by arguing that the basic syntactic categories of language (N, V, Adj, etc.) can be derived from a set of fundamental semantic contrasts, although not those that have been considered in the traditional literature (i.e., agent, entity, action, event, etc.). The key notion underlying my proposal will be that of "dependency"—a concept that I will argue has its roots outside the language faculty. Accompanying this characterization of syntactic categories will be a theory of sentence formation that incorporates the basic insight of categorial grammars (namely, that combinatorial operations apply from the "bottom up," creating phrases from words and sentences from phrases). This line of inquiry will ultimately lead to the proposal that the basic syntactic operation for English can be stated simply as, "Combine elements."

In the chapters following this introduction to my version of categorial grammar, I will examine a number of central syntactic phenomena (extraction, anaphora, quantifier float, and extraposition, among others) and attempt to show that they can be characterized in terms of principles that exploit notions such as adjacency, precedence, continuity, and dependency, all of which have their roots outside the language faculty (contrary to the autonomy thesis). A recurring theme in these chapters will be the claim that principles formulated in this way can be acquired without the help of innate linguistic knowledge. This is not to say that the human language faculty is free of all innate structuring, only that the contribution of the genetic endowment is restricted to the specification of concepts and learning strategies that are required independent of language. We can distinguish this view, which I will call "general nativism," from the thesis that certain specifically linguistic principles and categories are biologically determined, which I will refer to as "special nativism."

The thesis of general nativism does not entail that linguistic categories and principles (e.g., NP, VP, constraints on anaphora, etc.) have counterparts in other cognitive domains. Although this idea has occasionally been explored, it seems to me to be entirely misguided and implausible. In what follows I consistently assume that the grammar forms a separate cognitive system and that language has its own set of categories and principles. Where my work differs from other theories is in the claim that the concepts out of which language learners construct syntactic categories and principles (i.e., dependency, adjacency, and so on) are not specifically linguistic in character and that none of the biologically determined mental structures involved in grammatical development are unique to the language faculty.

Two problems confront this type of thesis. First, it is necessary to identify the hypothetical general concepts in terms of which descriptively adequate grammatical rules can be formulated. Second, it must be determined how children come to realize that these are the concepts that they should use to construct a grammar in response to linguistic experience. These problems constitute a major concern of this book.

Ideally, the viability of general nativism would be established by proposing grammatical rules of obvious descriptive adequacy that clearly satisfy preestablished criteria for learnability. In practice, however, such definitiveness is often not feasible in the initial stages of a research program. The immediate goal of work in linguistics (or any other science) is not so much an exhaustive description of the known facts as a fundamental insight into the system of principles underlying them. The viability of linguistics as a scientific discipline is therefore not challenged by the indisputable fact that its principles do not attain descriptive perfection. Rather the success of an idea is quite properly judged on the basis of a somewhat less tangible quality—the promise of a conceptual advance that can provide a new insight into the functioning of the grammar or the language acquisition mechanism.

It would be unrealistic to think that the work of any one person could equal in descriptive coverage the combined effort of hundreds of people over a twenty-five-year period. A far more realistic expectation would be that alternatives to current lines of inquiry match the descriptive successes of their competitors at a comparable stage of development and that they point to promising directions for future research. Whether the proposals that I make below satisfy these more modest criteria is an open question, of course, but one that deserves careful consideration, given the importance of the conceptual and empirical issues at stake here.

ACKNOWLEDGMENTS

I would like to express my thanks to the following people for their comments on earlier versions of this manuscript: Donna Gerdts, Michael Dobrovolsky, Joyce Hildebrand, Matthew Dryer, Derek Bickerton, Gregory Lee, Patricia Lee, Ann Peters, David Stampe, Patricia Donegan, Henry Rosemont, James McCawley, and various anonymous reviewers. Thanks are also due to Lynda Costello for typing many earlier versions of this manuscript. Finally, and most of all, I wish to thank Sook Whan Cho for her constant encouragement and help during the preparation of this manuscript.

I

CATEGORIES AND PRINCIPLES

1.1 Introductory Remarks

The value of linguistics as a cognitive science lies largely in its potential for providing insights into the mental faculties involved in language use and acquisition. The major advance of the last quarter century has been the realization that theories in this branch of psychology must be formulated in terms of a grammar, a system of categories and rules that relates form to meaning in the sentences of a language. Like most work in linguistics, this book is intended as a contribution to the theory of grammar. What distinguishes this book from much recent and current work in the field is the particular grammar that I propose and its consequences for a theory of language acquisition. The key idea is that descriptively adequate grammars can be constructed from concepts and relations that are not specific to the language faculty and that the ontogeny of these grammars does not presuppose the existence of innate linguistic knowledge.

I will be primarily concerned in this chapter with outlining the basic categories and principles that make up the theory I wish to develop. The subsequent five chapters will be devoted to the analysis of a wide range of syntactic problems. My strategy throughout these chapters will be to outline the required descriptive principles and then to consider the relevant learnability issues. This practice reflects the very intimate relation between proposals about the grammar (the rule system that children must acquire) and theories of language acquisition. In the final chapter of this book, I will explore in some depth the broader implications of these proposals for our understanding of the language faculty and language learning.

Although the proposals that I will be outlining in this book break sharply with the dominant view in theoretical linguistics, the problem that I will be addressing is the familiar one of how children are able to construct a grammar for their language on the basis of relatively limited experience.

Moreover, the syntactic phenomena that I will be considering include many of the problems that are central to current inquiry in syntactic theory (e.g., anaphora and extraction). Because transformational grammar (TG) is in a sense the starting point for what follows, I will begin by briefly reviewing the principal conclusions and claims that the last twenty-five years of research in this framework have yielded.[1]

1.2 The Transformational Tradition

For the past several decades, syntactic theory in North America has concentrated on the study of the rules and principles involved in the formation of syntactic representations of the type exemplified in (1).

(1)

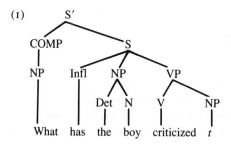

Such representations, called "S-structures," are generated with the help of two major rule systems. The first, consisting of the phrase structure rules exemplified in (2), specifies the initial organization of the syntactic relations underlying a sentence (producing a so-called deep structure).

(2) S'   →   COMP S

    COMP   →   {that, Ø}

    S   →   NP Infl VP

    NP   →   (Det) N

    VP   →   V (NP) (PP)

    PP   →   P NP

The deep structure of the sentence represented in (1) resembles (3), with *what* occurring after the verb (reflecting the fact that it is the direct object).

(3)

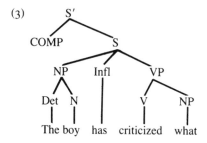

A second set of rules—called transformations—can modify deep structure, primarily by moving elements. In the case of (3), transformations invert the subject and auxiliary verb and move the *wh* word into the COMP position, leaving behind an empty category (called a trace) to yield the representation depicted in (1).

Various abstract principles constrain the formation of syntactic representations. One such principle, the Subjacency Condition of Chomsky (1977b, 1981), helps restrict the operation of movement transformations.

(4) *The Subjacency Condition:*
No transformation may involve positions *x* and *y*, where α and β are "bounding nodes" (for English, S or NP).
$\ldots x \ldots [_\alpha \ldots [_\beta \ldots y \ldots] \ldots] \ldots$

The Subjacency Condition is motivated in part by the ungrammaticality of sentences such as (5) and (6), in which the *wh* phrase has been moved to COMP from the position marked by *t*—over at least two bounding nodes.

(5) *[$_{S'}$ Who [$_S$ did you destroy [$_{NP}$ the book about *t*]]]

(6) *[$_{S'}$ Who [$_S$ did you hear [$_{NP}$ the rumor [that Sue liked *t*]]]]

It seems reasonable to assume that children are never informed that structures such as (5) and (6) are unacceptable, let alone that bounding nodes play a critical role in accounting for their ungrammaticality. (In fact, children appear not to receive systematic feedback about the grammaticality or ungrammaticality of any class of utterances.) If anything, experience might actually mislead language learners in this case since apparent violations of the Subjacency Condition (e.g., [7]) can be found. (I return to these cases in chap. 3.)

(7) [$_{S'}$ Who [$_S$ did you see [$_{NP}$ a picture of *t*]]]

The fact that the Subjacency Condition can apparently not be discovered on the basis of experience leads to the conclusion that it must be innate, via the "argument from poverty of stimulus" outlined by Chomsky (1977a, 65): "Suppose that we find a particular language has the property P. . . . Suppose, furthermore, that P is sufficiently abstract and evidence bearing on it sufficiently sparse and contrived so that it is implausible to suppose that all speakers, or perhaps any speakers, might have been trained or taught to observe P or might have constructed grammars satisfying P by induction from experience. Then it is plausible to postulate that P is a property of the language faculty, that languages conform to P as a matter of biological necessity." The system of putative innate principles to which languages conform as "a matter of biological necessity" makes up what is called Universal Grammar (UG).

In addition to being underdetermined by experience, the principles of UG typically exhibit a second property: they exploit notions (e.g., bounding node) that have no apparent counterpart outside the language faculty. This suggests not only that the language faculty is innately structured but also that at least some biologically determined notions are specific to language. As noted in the Preface, I will refer to this view as "special nativism," distinguishing it from the thesis that innate structuring is restricted to the specification of notions and principles that are relevant to nonlinguistic phenomena as well ("general nativism").

There is currently no compelling reason to rule out special genetic structuring of the language faculty (or the perceptual system or any other cognitive faculty). As is the case in science in general, proposed principles must be evaluated in terms of their empirical motivation, explanatory value, coherence, and so forth rather than some a priori standard of concreteness or learnability. This notwithstanding, there is also no reason to think that TG has exhausted the set of plausible hypotheses about the nature and development of grammatical knowledge. Since claims about the poverty (or the adequacy) of experience for language learning necessarily presuppose some conception of the adult grammar (the system being acquired), modifications to grammatical theory could obviously force quite radical revisions to current claims about the role of the genetic endowment in language development.

A major flaw in virtually all past and present attempts to avoid the conclusions about language and learning that have been drawn in TG is that specific alternatives are rarely offered. Rather reference is made to some still to be developed grammar exploiting an unspecified set of "learnable devices," or, alternately, an extremely fragmentary grammar is proposed and applied to a narrow range of simple structures of dubious relevance to claims about special nativism. While one can hardly expect any single work to provide a full-fledged alternative to a theory that has developed over a period of twenty-five years through the collaboration of hundreds of linguists, this cannot excuse the failure to offer serious counterproposals. Clearly, initial attempts at an alternative to current lines of inquiry must fall somewhere between the two extremes—an objective that I will now begin to pursue by outlining an alternate conception of syntactic rules and representations.

My position throughout this book will be that much can be learned from precisely formulated hypotheses, even when these turn out to be incorrect. Such a position has guided productive work within special nativism for many years. Within transformational grammar, for instance, the failure of a principle is taken not to undermine the entire research program but rather to point the direction in which future work must proceed. The immediate objective of a research program based on the thesis of general nativism must be a set of explicit proposals about the nature of the grammar and of the cognitive structures involved in its acquisition. This is also the goal of this book. While my discussion will, of necessity, leave various significant problems unresolved, it will provide the basis for considering the learnability of fundamental syntactic categories and rules. Moreover, despite its incomplete character, this description will also provide the foundation required for our examination of the more complex syntactic phenomena that constitute the subject matter of subsequent chapters.

1.3 Grammatical Categories

A natural starting point for any discussion of syntactic structure is with the nature of the categories that make up these representations. A variety of approaches to syntactic categories can be distinguished in the traditional and current linguistic literature, with most proposals falling into one or the other of two broad types—distributional and semantic. The former type is exemplified in its most extreme form by the American descriptivist tradition, which characterized syntactic categories in terms of their distribution, characteristic morphology, and so on. The treatment of syntactic categories dominating the transformational literature is an evolved form of the early descriptivist tradition, with more elaborate and refined tests for category membership but with a basic commitment to the view that syntactic categories are essentially formal entities that cannot be reduced to more primitive semantic notions. McCawley (1982b) discusses tests for category membership in TG at some length, pointing out various flaws in this approach and making a variety of new proposals.

The distributional approach to syntactic categories contrasts sharply with a number of proposals that have been made in the literature on formal logic and that seek to characterize syntactic categories in terms of the semantic objects they denote. This tradition, which is often associated with categorial grammar, includes contributions by Ajdukiewicz (1935), Bar-Hillel (1950), and proponents of Montague Grammar (Dowty, Wall, and Peters 1982). In what follows, I will develop an approach to syntactic categories that exploits the fundamental insights of categorial grammar, although I will make various innovations consistent with the overall objective of this book (the elaboration of a grammar consistent with the thesis of general nativism).

In a typical categorial grammar, two types of categories are recognized: "basic" categories—typically NP (nominal) and S (sentence)—and "functor" or "operator" categories, which apply to an expression of one category type to yield an expression of the same or a different type. An intransitive verb such as *arrive,* for instance, is often treated as a functor that applies to an NP to give an S (as in *Harry arrived*). An alternate way to express this is to say that an intransitive verb is a "function" from an NP to an S.

Categorial grammars commonly exploit the contrasts outlined below. (The "*x/y*" notation is read from right to left, with *y* representing the category to which a function applies and *x* the category that it yields.)

(1) *Basic categories:*
   C (common noun): *book, pencil,* etc.
   NP: *John, the book,* etc.
   S (sentence): *Bob left, Harry read the book,* etc.

   Functor categories:
   Adj: A function from C to C (i.e., C/C).
   Det: A function from C to NP (i.e., NP/C).
   IV (intransitive verb): A function from NP to S (i.e., S/NP).
   TV (transitive verb): A function from NP to IV (i.e., IV/NP).
   Adv: A function from IV to IV (i.e., IV/IV).

This system allows formation of structures such as (2).

(2)

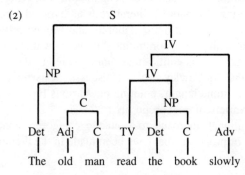

As readers can verify for themselves, each of the categories represented in (2) was formed in accordance with the definitions outlined in (1). Thus the Adj *old* applies to the C *man* to yield a larger phrase of the same type. The Det *the* then applies to this category to give an NP just as it does when it combines with the C *book*. Next, the TV *read* combines with the NP *the book* to yield an IV, in accordance with the definition given in (1). The adverb *slowly* can then combine with this phrase to give a larger phrase of the same type. Finally, this IV combines with the NP *the old man,* giving an S.

A Modified Categorial Grammar
In adapting categorial grammar to my purposes, I will make three basic innovations. First, I will attempt to define a set of subcategorial properties that will allow syntactic categories to be grouped into various natural classes. In the system I will develop, for instance, the categories of intransitive verb and transitive verb share a property not found in nominals. A second innovation that I will introduce relates to the formation of structural configurations such as (2). According to the traditional view, the constituents in such representations occur as products of the categorial definitions themselves. Thus there is a phrase *read the book* only because the definition of TV stipulates that it is a function that applies to an NP to yield a larger IV phrase. In contrast with this approach, I will attempt to derive the configurational properties of syntactic structure from general principles rather than from individual categorial definitions.

A third difference between the approach I will be developing and conventional categorial grammar has to do with the nature of the relation between syntactic and semantic categories. The traditional view (e.g., Marantz 1984; Williams 1983) maintains that there should be a straightforward correspondence between the two, with each syntactic category linked to a particular semantic type in intensional logic. The syntactic category "common noun," for instance, is often taken to correspond to the semantic type whose intension is a function from possible worlds to entities. (That is, a noun like *dog* would pick out, in all possible worlds, just those entities that are canines.) Although I will take the position that categorial distinctions in the syntax reflect semantic contrasts, I will not commit myself to the view that these are the same contrasts posited in orthodox intensional semantics. This is not to say that such contrasts cannot be exploited in the interpretation of sentences or in the drawing of inferences but only that they are not directly encoded in the syntactic representation.

A research program that seeks to avoid the usual conclusions about innate linguistic knowledge has good reason to be wary of the view that phrasal categories such as NP and VP are direct "projections" of semantic entities. As I will argue in greater detail below, it seems unlikely that experience could provide the child with the evidence needed to determine that in an SVO sentence, for example, there is a semantic entity corresponding to a verb and its object (i.e., a VP) rather than the verb and its subject. While it could naturally be argued that such knowledge is part of the genetic endowment, positing an innate set of semantic categories isomorphic with syntactic phrases would obviously threaten the thesis that there is no inborn linguistic knowledge (general nativism). For this reason, I will not adopt a projection theory for phrasal categories. Instead I will outline a projection theory for lexical categories and then propose a way to predict the category of a phrase from the properties of the lexical categories that compose it.

In what follows, I will be assuming a more or less traditional set of syntactic categories that includes the lexical classes noun (N), verb (V), adjective (Adj), adverb (Adv), and preposition (P) in addition to the phrasal categories NP, VP, AdjP, AdvP, and PP. The grammar that I will propose therefore assigns a syntactic structure resembling (3) to a sentence such as *The man left quickly.*

(3)
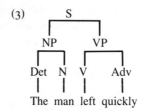

As (3) shows, my proposal does not differ from most work in TG in terms of either the assignment of individual words to lexical categories or the organization of phrasal categories. Where my proposal differs is in the way in which lexical categories are defined and the manner in which phrasal categories are formed, matters to which I now turn.

1.3.1 Lexical Categories

My major concern in this section will be with the characterization of the four "open" lexical categories of English—N, V, Adj, and Adv. As is common in work on categorial grammar, I will assume that certain of these categories name functions, that is, operations that apply to one category to yield a new category. Although these functions apply to syntactic categories rather than semantic entities, I will take the position that the type of predicate a word denotes determines its combinatorial properties. This can be stated as the Lexical Projection Principle.

(1) *The Lexical Projection Principle:*
   A word's predicate type determines its syntactic category.

The key notion underlying the categorial contrasts that I will be proposing is that of dependency, defined in (2).

(2) *x* depends on *y* if *x* names a function applying to *y*.

According to (2), then, a category naming a function that applies to a nominal (e.g., an intransitive verb) would be said to depend on that element.

   The most basic categorial contrast involving dependency distinguishes between independent and dependent elements as follows.

(3) *Dependent* elements name a function that applies to another linguistic category.

(4) *Independent* elements do not name a function that applies to another linguistic category.

Dependent Categories

An obvious candidate for inclusion in the set of dependent categories is the word class consisting of verbs, which express functions that apply to one or more nominal elements (according to the predicate type). I will assume that there are two types of verbal categories—intransitive verbs (V^i), which express "one-place" predicates and combine with one NP, and transitive verbs (V^{tr}), which express "two-place" predicates and depend on two NPs.[2] Another obvious example of a dependent word class consists of adjectives, which are typically assumed to express functions that apply to a type of nominal (e.g., common nouns). This dependency reflects the fact that these elements canonically denote properties of individuals and sets, the denotata of nominal elements.[3]

   Consider next the diverse class of elements that includes *very, extremely, often, quietly, intentionally,* and other modifiers that are traditionally categorized as adverbs. Although there are important differences in the syntax and semantics of these elements, they all exhibit the need to combine with a dependent category—an adjective, a verb, or another adverb (e.g., *very quiet, very quietly, leave quietly*). In conventional categorial grammar, this fact is captured by assuming that these elements express functions that apply to categories of the types just noted. In the terminology employed here, we would say that the adverbial elements in question "depend" on these other categories. This dependency can presumably be traced to the type of semantic object denoted by the words in question. *Quietly,* for example, denotes a property that must be predicated of the type of semantic object typically expressed by an action verb. Elements like *very*, on the other hand, cannot function as degree modifiers without the intensions associated with the class of adjectives denoting properties that can manifest themselves to different degrees (e.g., *tall, rich*, etc.).

An Independent Category

This leaves us with the problem of classifying nouns with respect to the notion of dependency. I will take the position that nouns do not as a matter of course exhibit an inherent dependency on another linguistic element; that is, they do not denote predicates that apply to a separate linguistically expressed argument. This proposal is most obviously applicable to proper nouns, which are usually taken to name individuals in the world rather than argument-taking predicates. However, I believe that this characterization is also appropriate for common nouns, which typically must be taken to denote predicates. Consider in this respect a sentence such as *Humans are mortal* or *Humans die*. Although it is plausible to assume that the predicate named by the adjective *mortal* or the verb *die* applies to the set of individuals denoted by *humans*, the predicate named by the noun does not apply to a separate linguistically expressed argument. (If anything, the property "human" is predicated of the individuals in the set picked out by the noun itself.) In the terminology employed here, we would say that nouns are instances of an independent category and do not express functions that apply to other elements in the sentence. In this, nouns would be distinct from verbs, adjectives, and adverbs.

A problem that arises at this point has to do with the status of "nominalizations" such as *Harry's destruction of the room*. Here it is tempting to suppose that the noun *destruction* denotes a predicate taking *Harry* and *the room* as arguments just as the verb *destroy* presumably does (cf. *Harry destroyed the room*). Although it is obviously necessary to account for the parallels between these two structures (which I will do in chap. 2), doing so need not undermine the proposed distinction between nouns and verbs. Particularly significant here is the fact that nouns cannot combine directly with other NPs. Thus there are no phrases such as (5b), paralleling (5a).

(5) a. Harry destroyed the room.
    b. *Harry destruction the room

Rather, the NPs combining with a noun must be accompanied by either a preposition or the genitive marker. I will take the position that such elements convert NPs into categories that express functions that apply to other nominal elements. In a phrase such as *Harry's arrival*, then, *Harry's* will depend on the noun *arrival* rather than vice versa. (A comparable position has been taken by Rappaport [1983]; see also Williams [1982] and Marantz

[1984, 67].) This allows us to maintain the view that nouns are independent and do not express functions that apply to other categories.

A second problem with the hypothesis that nouns are independent relates to the so-called predicative use of the second nominal in sentences such as *The boys are students*. Here it seems clear that a nominal element encodes a predicate that applies to a linguistically expressed argument (the subject *the boys*) and should therefore count as a dependent category, contrary to what I have been claiming. I will suggest below that the apparent dependent status of *students* in this sentence is brought about by a category-changing operation triggered by the copula verb. This allows us to maintain that nominal elements are inherently independent while still permitting their predicative use in a limited range of cases (e.g., copular constructions).

Before proceeding, three points must be clarified. First, I am obviously making some important assumptions about the nature of the semantics for natural language. For instance, I have assumed that verbs denote predicates that apply to entities normally expressed by NPs and that nouns denote predicates that are not applied to separate linguistically expressed arguments. These assumptions, while widely accepted (e.g., Chierchia 1985; Rothstein 1985), are of course not necessarily correct. In some theories, for example, NPs express functions that apply to verb arguments (the reverse of what I have proposed). Rather than attempting to resolve this controversy here, I will simply assume that the distinctions I have adopted are viable and proceed to explore their consequences for the theory of grammar and learning that I wish to develop.

Second, it is important not to confuse the notion of dependency that I have proposed with obligatory co-occurrence. It is quite possible in the theory I am advocating for an element to require a determiner or complement without depending on it in the technical sense. Thus a singular count noun in English must be accompanied by a determiner (e.g., *the book*), but this does not entail that *book* names a function that must apply to a determiner. Rather I will be proposing that *the* names a function that must apply to a nominal category. The obligatoriness of the determiner (a language-particular property of English) is taken to reflect facts about singular count nouns other than the function they name.

Finally, it is necessary to distinguish my use of the term "dependency" from that associated with work in so-called dependency grammar (e.g., Hudson 1984). In that theory, dependency involves a relation between syntactic categories and the head of the phrase in which they occur. Thus both an adverb and a direct object NP are said to "depend" on the verb since both are components of a phrase (VP) headed by that element. In the theory I have proposed, in contrast, adverbs and NPs have very different dependency properties since they name distinct predicate types. The advantages of this latter approach for a theory of syntactic categories will become evident as we proceed.

Further Contrasts

Thus far I have used the notion of dependency to distinguish between two classes of lexical categories—a dependent class (consisting of verbs, adjectives, and adverbs) and an independent class (consisting of nouns). This distinction is summarized in (6).

(6) *Category Types:*
Dependent (V, Adj, Adv): Categories expressing a function that applies to another element in the sentence.
Independent (N): The category that does not express a function applying to another element in the sentence.

We can further subdivide the set of traditional syntactic categories by distinguishing between two types of dependent elements as follows.

(7) *Dependent Category Types:*
Type 1: Categories that depend on an independent element.
Type 2: Categories that depend on a dependent element.

The first type of dependent category consists primarily of verbs and adjectives—elements that must combine with an (independent) nominal category. The second type consists of adverbial elements—words that must combine with another dependent element (i.e., with a verb, an adjective, or another adverb).

Introducing terminology borrowed from Jespersen (1965), we can use the dependency contrasts we have been considering to define the following three distinctions.

(8) a. *Primaries:* Independent elements (e.g., the nominal *Harry* in *Harry left*).
b. *Secondaries:* Elements that depend on a primary (e.g., the adjective *fresh* in *fresh bread* or the verb *left* in *Harry left*).
c. *Tertiaries:* Elements that depend on a dependent element (a nonprimary) (e.g., *wonderfully* in *wonderfully happy* or *He sings wonderfully*).

Of the various additional distinctions that one might wish to draw among conventional syntactic categories, the most central involves adjectives and verbs, both secondaries on the current analysis. A first observation to make about this contrast is that it is not found in all languages. According to Dixon (1982), for instance, Chinese, Hausa, and Chinook do not include an adjectival category and use intransitive verbs (in addition to nouns and particles in some cases) to predicate properties of individuals. Still another system is found in Korean, in which there is a very large class of stems that alternate between the verb and the adjective classes, although none is inherently adjectival (in contrast with English). The stem *coh* (good), for instance, can be encoded as either an adjective or a verb (AM = adjective marker; VM = verb marker).

(9) a. coh-un saram
    good AM man
   b. saram coh-a-yo.
    man good VM Decl
    "The man is good."

Facts like these suggest that not all languages distinguish subtypes of secondaries in the same way.

In English, however, it seems necessary to acknowledge the existence of distinct lexical categories for adjectives and verbs. In addition to an obvious morphological difference (only verbs can be marked for tense and aspect), the two categories can also be distinguished in terms of the type of elements on which they depend. In particular, it seems that verbs can combine only with categories that I will soon identify as NPs—nominals that either are referring expressions (e.g., *Harry, the man*) or are quantified (e.g., *all people, a girl, water, noises*). (I consider verbs that take clausal arguments in chap. 4.)

(10) a. Harry left.
    b. The boy left.
    c. *Boy left.

In contrast, adjectives can combine with either a simple noun (the "attributive" use exemplified in [11a]) or an NP (the "predicative" use illustrated in [11b]).

(11) a. Tired boys
    b. The boys are tired.

These contrasts point toward the following tentative definitions for the lexical categories we have been considering.

(12) a. *Noun:* A primary (i.e., the independent category).
    b. *Verb:* A secondary dependent on one or more NPs (and compatible with tense and aspect marking).
    c. *Adjective:* A secondary dependent on either an N or an NP (and not compatible with tense and aspect marking).
    d. *Adverb:* A tertiary (i.e., a category dependent on a dependent element).

Although further subdivisions are obviously desirable (to distinguish among subtypes of adjectives and adverbs, e.g.), the preceding categorial distinctions will suffice for our purposes, and I will not attempt further refinements here.

The categories that we have recognized form part of syntactic representations such as (13), in which the superscripts make explicit the dependency properties of the lexical categories (p = primary, s = secondary). (Where possible, I will simplify syntactic representations by eliminating superscripts not needed to illustrate a specific point.)

(13)

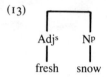

In representations such as (13), I will say that the adjective "depends" on the noun or, alternately, that the noun "supports" the adjective.

Two questions now arise. The first has to do with the type of operation that is responsible for combining lexical categories and the second with the nature of the phrases created by the amalgamation of two or more words. I will deal with the latter question first.

1.3.2 Phrasal Categories

We are working under the assumption that a combinatorial operation (to be discussed below) applies to pairs of categories to create a larger unit that can then become part of a still larger phrase and so on. There are indisputable parallels between categorial contrasts involving lexical items and those involving phrasal units. For instance, just as there is a contrast between dependent and independent lexical categories, so a comparable distinction manifests itself at the phrasal level. We can therefore distinguish between phrases like *fresh snow* (usually called an NP) and phrases like *run quickly* (usually called a VP) on the grounds that only the latter is a dependent category (denotes a predicate that must apply to another linguistic category).

Distinctions among subtypes of dependent categories are also manifested at the phrasal level. Hence it is appropriate to distinguish between phrases like *very fresh* (a so-called AdjP), which combine with nominal elements, and items like *very quickly* (a so-called AdvP), which must combine with a verbal or an adjectival element—the very contrast found at the lexical level.

(1) a. [very fresh] snow
    b. run [very quickly]

Similarly, we must distinguish between *very fresh*, which can combine with a noun (cf. [1a]), and *runs quickly* (a VP), which can combine only with an NP—just the distinction between adjectival and verbal elements required at the lexical level.

(2) a. *Boy [runs quickly].
    b. The boy [runs quickly].

Given these parallels, it seems plausible to think that the categorial status of phrases is determined by general principles from properties of their component words. We can automatically restrict the set of possible phrasal categories in language if we assume that the combinatorial operations that create these units seek to satisfy the requirement stated in (3).

(3) *The Dependency Requirement:*
    All combinatorial operations must satisfy a dependency.

The Dependency Requirement permits the existence of a category formed by combining an adjective and a noun (e.g., *old man*) since this will satisfy the adjective's dependency requirements. It also permits the combination of a verb and an adverb (e.g., *run quickly*), which would satisfy the adverb's dependency requirements. However, there should be no category consisting of an adverb and a noun (e.g., *quietly tiger*) since neither elements depends on the type of category to which the other belongs. This seems to be correct.[4]

The character of subsentential phrasal categories can be further specified with the help of the following principle.

(4) *The Phrasal Category Principle:*
    A phrase takes on the category of a component with an unsatisfied dependency.
    If it has no such component, it is a primary (nominal).

The intuition underlying (4) is that, when a combinatorial operation satisfies the dependency requirements of only one of the elements on which it acts, the resulting phrase takes on the categorial properties of the other element and is used accordingly. This predicts that the phrase *very old* will be adjectival since it contains an adjectival secondary (*old*) with an unsatisfied dependency on a nominal.

(5)   AdjP
    Adv Adj
    very old

The phrase should therefore be able to combine with a nominal, as it does in *very old bread*. Likewise, phrases such as *leave quickly* and *see Harry* will count as verbal elements according to (4) since each contains a verb with an unsatisfied dependency on a nominal.

(6) a.   VP

Vⁱ   Adv

leave quietly

b.   VP

Vᵗʳ   NP

see   Harry

In (6a) the intransitive verb *leave* exhibits an unsatisfied dependency on a nominal, guaranteeing that the resulting phrase will also be a verbal category. The same is true of (6b), in which only one of the transitive verb's dependencies on a nominal is satisfied by combining it with *Harry*. The phrases in both (6a) and (6b) should therefore be able to combine with a nominal element, as they do in *John left quickly* and *John saw Harry*.

Consider next the phrase *very quickly*, which should have the combinatorial properties of a manner adverb in the system I am proposing. This is because the dependency requirements of the degree adverb *very* are satisfied by combining it with *quickly*, while the latter element exhibits an unsatisfied dependency on a verbal element.

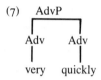

(7)   AdvP

Adv   Adv

very   quickly

This is confirmed by structures such as *leave very quickly* in which the putative AdvP combines with a verb. Finally, the phrase *fresh snow* will count as a nominal since neither of its components exhibits an unsatisfied dependency (*snow* is a primary, and the dependency requirements of *fresh* have been satisfied by combining it with the noun).

(8)   NP

Adj   N

fresh snow

As a primary, *fresh snow* should be able to support a verbal secondary, as it does in *Fresh snow fell*.

The structures in (5)–(8) differ from those commonly employed in categorial grammar in respecting a notational distinction between lexical and phrasal categories. I intend the phrasal category labels to have the interpretations in (9). Because these phrasal category labels are simply abbreviations for maximal categories of various types, I will sometimes omit them from syntactic representations or will place them in parentheses.

(9) NP: The maximal nominal category.
VP: The maximal verbal category.
AdjP: The maximal adjectival category.
AdvP: The maximal adverbial category.

At least one of the maximal categories listed in (9) is subject to special semantic constraints. As noted earlier, NPs are well formed only if they either consist of referring expressions (e.g., *John, the man*) or are "quantified" (e.g., *all people, a boy*). There are no well-formed NPs in English consisting simply of a singular count noun. Although this fact is not part of the definition of NP, I will assume it in what follows.

To complete the characterization of phrasal categories, we now need only a treatment of S. I will take S to be the category that is formed by combining two maximal phrasal categories (e.g., NP and VP) in accordance with the Dependency Requirement. We can now posit the following representation for the sentence *Fresh snow melts quickly.*

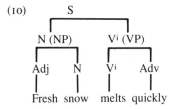

(10)

The structure in (10) accurately represents the most widely accepted categorial and organizational properties of the sentence in question, and I will assume that it is correct.

Phrase-creating Elements
Various minor lexical categories appear to participate in the formation of phrases in English. Foremost among these is the category "preposition," which applies to an NP to create a dependent phrase (called a PP) with the properties of either a secondary or a tertiary. This is illustrated in (11) and (12). (I use the superscripts s and t to designate a secondary and a tertiary, respectively.)

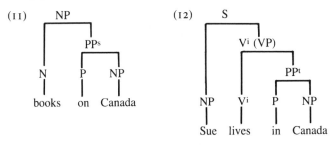

I will assume that prepositions belong to a special set of connectives that apply to NPs, converting them into secondaries in cases in which they combine with a nominal element (cf. [11]) and into tertiaries in cases in which they are attached to a verbal element (cf. [12]).[5]

A somewhat similar effect is achieved by the genitive suffix 's, which I assume applies to an NP primary, converting it into a secondary (a dependent phrase) that can then combine with another nominal element. This is illustrated in (13).

(13)

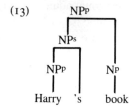

In traditional grammar, the NP bearing the 's ending in (13) is often said to be "adjectival"—the result of its conversion into a dependent element according to my proposal.

Another connective category consists of copula verbs, which I will take to apply to NP primaries and adjectival secondaries to create an intransitive verbal category. This is illustrated in (14).

(14)

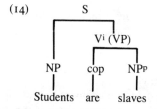

Still another minor category involved in the formation of phrases consists of so-called determiners (e.g., *the, a, each, this,* etc.). I will assume that these elements combine with a nominal primary to yield an NP with referential or quantificational properties. This is illustrated in (15).

(15)

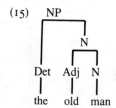

Summary of Categorial Definitions

I summarize below the lexical and phrasal categories whose existence I have posited in the preceding discussion.

N: A primary (the independent category).

V^i: A secondary dependent on one NP.

V^{tr}: A secondary dependent on two NPs.

Adj: A secondary dependent on an N or NP (and not compatible with tense and aspect marking).

Adv: A tertiary (an element that depends on a dependent category).

NP: The maximal nominal category.

VP: The maximal verbal category.

AdjP: The maximal adjectival category.

AdvP: The maximal adverbial category.

P: An element that converts an NP (primary) into a secondary or tertiary.

PP: A secondary or tertiary formed by combining a P with an NP.

Det: An element that combines with a nominal category to give an NP.

S: The phrase formed by combining two maximal phrasal categories (e.g., NP and VP).

This is the inventory of syntactic categories commonly used in linguistic analysis. However, these categories differ from the entities of the same name in other theories in the manner in which they are defined. Instead of assuming that syntactic categories are primes or that they are defined in terms of their distributional properties, I have taken the position that categorial distinctions in the syntax reflect differences in the dependency properties of individual words and that these properties are determined by the predicate types named by these words. Moreover, I have assumed that the categorial status of phrases can be predicted from the properties of their component elements, in accordance with the Phrasal Category Principle. I will now attempt to show how this system of categorial contrasts enters into the formation of more complex syntactic representations.

1.4 Syntactic Principles

As a first approximation, I will assume that the major grammatical device underlying sentence formation in English is the Adjacency Principle of (1).

(1) *The Adjacency Principle (AP):*
     Combine adjacent elements.

As we shall see as we proceed, the AP applies to strings of words drawn from the lexicon and assigns them structural representations in cases in which they correspond to grammatical sentences. In the simplest case, the

AP is used in conjunction with the Phrasal Category Principle to assign
structures like those in (2).

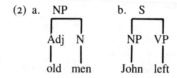

I assume that independent conventions stipulate those aspects of word
order not covered by the AP. Hence the grammar of English will have to
specify that determiners and adjectives precede the nominals on which they
depend, that PPs follow the element with which they combine, and so on.
It is quite possible that general principles underlie these ordering conventions (see, e.g., Hawkins 1979; and Flynn 1983), but I will not be concerned with this aspect of the linearization problem here.

I assume that the AP is applied iteratively until each component of a
putative sentence has been incorporated into syntactic structure and all
dependencies have been satisfied. If either of these requirements is not
met, the string cannot be a sentence of English. Consider in this respect the
following strings.

(3)   a. *Went.
      b. *Harry arrived the book.
      c. *The ran.

The string in (3a) is ungrammatical since the dependency of *went* on an NP
is unsatisfied (see n. 2), and (3b) is ill formed because there is no place for
the book in the syntactic representation (*arrive* being in intransitive verb).
The string in (3c), on the other hand, cannot even undergo a combinatorial
operation since neither element (the determiner or the verb) depends on the
other. (Recall that the Dependency Requirement stipulates that all combinatorial operations satisfy a dependency.)

The intuitive idea here is simply that the presence of each word in a
sentence must be grammatically justified in some manner. In transformational grammar this intuition is captured in part by requiring that all NPs
receive Case, an abstract feature assigned only to NPs filling certain structural positions (see Chomsky [1981] for details). "Predicate" categories
such as AdjPs and VPs, on the other hand, must satisfy quite a different
condition. According to Rothstein (1985), such elements are subject to a
rule of "predicate linking" that associates them with an argument to which
they bear a particular relation in S-structure. In the theory I am proposing
all categories have their presence justified in the same way: they must

combine with another element to satisfy a dependency in accordance with the Dependency Requirement.

Questions arise as to whether the AP should associate (4a) or (4b) with the string *very old men*.

(4) a.

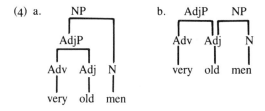

Notice that whereas *very* and *old* form a unit that then combines with the noun *men* in (4a), (4b) exhibits two independent combinatorial relations—one between *very* and *old* and the other between *old* and *men*. Although there is widespread agreement that (4a) accurately reflects the internal organization of the phrase we are considering, either representation seems consistent with the type of semantic information available to language learners. In particular, both configurations are consistent with an interpretation in which there is a set of men with a particular property (oldness) that is present to a strong degree. This suggests that ordinary semantic considerations will not suffice to choose between the representations we are considering and that a principle such as (5) must be formulated.

(5) *The Hierarchical Structuring Requirement (HSR):*
    Combinatorial operations create phrases to which subsequent combinatorial operations apply.

The HSR ensures that the phrase created by combining *very* and *old* will function as a unit with respect to subsequent applications of the AP, thereby guaranteeing that the grammar will generate the structure depicted in (4a), as desired.

The HSR allows us to see the AP as an iterative, generative device that takes as its input a string of words drawn from the lexicon and proceeds to combine adjacent elements (in accordance with their dependency requirements), creating a phrase that can then be combined with another element, and so on. In the case of (6), then, the AP combines *fresh* with the adjacent *snow* (yielding an NP according to the Phrasal Category Principle) and *quickly* with the adjacent *melt* (creating a VP). The resulting phrases are then combined to give S.

(6)

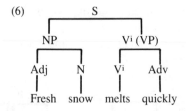

Note that each application of the AP satisfies the dependency requirements of one of the elements on which it operates (in accordance with the stipulation that all combinatorial operations satisfy a dependency). Notice too that our principles allow no other structure to be assigned to the sentence we are considering. Hence *melt* cannot combine just with *snow* since verbs depend on well-formed NPs, not Ns. Similarly, *quickly* cannot combine with *Fresh snow melts* since such adverbs depend on verbal or adjectival secondaries, not Ss. The grammar I am developing therefore assigns precisely one well-formed structure to the sentence in question, as desired.

Consider now a structure such as *John sees Mary*. The traditional view, which I also adopt, is that English word order is used in these sentences to distinguish between the two NPs in terms of their syntactic role. Thus the preverbal NP corresponds to what is traditionally called the "subject" and the postverbal NP to the "direct object." As things now stand, the AP could form either of the structures depicted below.

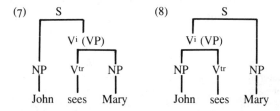

In both (7) and (8), a transitive verb combines with an NP to give a verbal category that now depends on only one NP (i.e., a V^i). However, they differ in terms of which NP combines with the transitive verb. The structure in (7) results from combining the verb *sees* with the NP *Mary* and the resulting unit with the NP *John*. The structure in (8), on the other hand, is the result of combining *sees* with *John* and the resulting phrase with *Mary*. As I will show in chapter 2, the interpretation of this sentence is consistent with either of these structures and therefore provides no clue that would enable the language learner to choose one or the other.

Two issues arise here. The first has to do with how we can ensure that the proper "argument" of *see* is encoded as subject and the second with whether this grammatical role can be equated with a particular combinatorial position. I will postpone discussion of the first issue until chapter 2, assuming in the meantime that there is a mechanism in the grammar to ensure that the agentive argument of an active verb is encoded as subject. With respect to the second question, I will be assuming that the subject relation can in fact be defined in terms of a combinatorial position in accordance with (9).

(9) *The Subject-Last Requirement (SLR):*

The subject combines with VP (the maximal verbal category).

Although condition (9) says nothing about which NP (e.g., agent or patient) should be realized as subject, it does indicate how an element bearing this relation is to be structurally encoded, stipulating that it is incorporated into the clause only after the VP has been formed (hence the name "Subject-Last Requirement").[6] This entails selection of the syntactic representation in (7) over that in (8). This is, of course, the traditional view and is supported by the usual range of constituency tests. Hence *sees Mary,* but not *John sees,* can be replaced by an "anaphoric device"—a usual sign of phrasehood.

(10) John sees Mary and Sue does too.
    (does = sees Mary)

The Grammar

The preceding remarks point toward the existence of a grammar with the internal organization depicted below. (Here and elsewhere I deliberately ignore the place of the morphology and the phonology. I discuss the lexicon in more detail in chap. 2.)

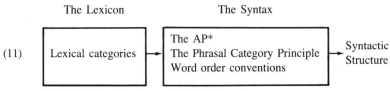

(11)

The Lexicon	The Syntax	
Lexical categories	The AP* The Phrasal Category Principle Word order conventions	Syntactic Structure

*Constrained by the Hierarchical Structuring and Subject-Last requirements.

I take the grammar in (11) to be part of the model of competence characterizing the English speaker's knowledge of the relation between form and meaning in terms that are neutral with respect to comprehension and production. Thus (11) should be taken to mean only that words are combined by the AP to create phrases with the categorial properties determined by the Phrasal Category Principle.

1.5 The Learnability Issue

As noted at the outset, a central thesis of my work is that innate linguistic principles do not play a role in grammatical development. This is not to say that the biological endowment has no influence on the course of language development or on the final form of the grammar. However, consistent with the thesis of general nativism, I will be arguing that the innate notions needed for the acquisition of the categories and principles I have proposed are not restricted to just the language faculty. As noted at the outset, this implies not that linguistic categories and principles (e.g., NP, VP, the AP, etc.) have direct counterparts in other cognitive domains but only that they are constructed with the help of notions and strategies that are not specific to the language faculty. This is to be distinguished from the more widely held view (at least in the transformational literature) that there are innate principles and categories that are specific to the language faculty (special nativism).

Before proceeding, it is necessary to acknowledge that claims about general nativism must be treated with a great deal of caution. Not only are there very few serious precedents for the type of proposals I am making, but this type of work also runs against extremely compelling and productive trends within special nativism. This notwithstanding, it seems to me that the thesis of general nativism is of enough inherent interest to be worth pursuing, and I will therefore attempt to do so.

1.5.1 Conditions on Learning

In pursuing the line of inquiry I have just sketched, I will adopt two assumptions that underlie virtually all work on language learnability. First, I assume that language acquisition is driven by a process of hypothesis formation and testing. While approaches to language learning differ over the types of hypotheses they attribute to children and over whether some hypotheses may be "given in advance" (i.e., innate), they all agree that any learning that does take place is based on this type of process. Indeed, as Fodor (1975) notes, no other proposal for how learning might occur has ever been advanced. Second, I assume (following Baker [1979]) that children do not receive systematic or direct information about the possible ungrammaticality of the sentences they hear and produce. In order to acquire a grammar, then, either children must formulate the correct hypothesis from the outset or they must advance erroneous hypotheses that can be corrected on the basis of observations about the speech they actually hear in their environment.

The first step toward establishing the learnability of a grammar involves determining the circumstances under which a stimulus in the linguistic environment can trigger learning (the formation of an hypothesis). It seems reasonable to suppose that at least three conditions must be met before development of any sort can take place.

A. The child must have access to the concepts in terms of which the principles and categories to be learned can be formulated.

B. The child must have access to experience rich enough to support formation and (if necessary) revision of the relevant principles and categories.

C. The child must have access to a learning procedure that will exploit the available concepts and experience to formulate the desired principles and categories.

In addition to these three conditions, it seems reasonable to assume that, in many cases of learning, a fourth condition is also met.

D. The child has access to previously acquired knowledge that can facilitate learning by narrowing the set of concepts in terms of which principles and categories should be formulated.

I will assume that conditions A–C establish the following requirements in the case of the categories and principles we have been considering.

A. The child needs access to the concepts of adjacency and dependency.

B. The child's experience has to provide information about dependency relations in an adequate sampling of utterances.

C. The relevant learning procedure involves the formation of generalizations by identifying a property found in specific structures and using it to define general categories and principles relevant to other structures.

Let us consider each of these points in turn, beginning with condition A.

Both adjacency and dependency should be available to children independent of language. Adjacency, for instance, must be part of the child's general conceptual inventory since it is required to deal with spatial and temporal relations outside of language. Its use in the formation of grammatical rules would therefore be consistent with the thesis of general nativism. Dependency, for its part, can be seen as an asymmetrical relation in which one element requires another for some condition to be satisfied. In the case of language, a word's dependency requirements are determined by the type of predicate it denotes. Outside of language, dependency will naturally manifest itself in other ways, but there is nothing about this relation that would restrict it to just the linguistic domain.

Initially at least, then, it seems plausible to think that the key notions of adjacency and dependency exist independent of language. While it is likely that these concepts are genetically determined in some way, there is no reason to believe that such innate knowledge would be faculty specific (i.e., manifest itself only in the language faculty). The postulated role of these notions in grammatical development is therefore consistent with the thesis of general nativism.

In order to discover categorial and combinatorial contrasts based on dependency and adjacency, children will obviously need information about the type of predicates encoded by different words. In order to take note of the contrast between an independent category such as *Harry* and a dependent one such as *arrived*, for instance, they need to know that only the latter word names a predicate that applies to a linguistically expressed argument. I will assume that this information is present in the mental representation of sentence meaning that I will call "semantic form."

Although one suspects that the organization and ontogeny of semantic form is biologically determined (at least in part), so little is known about the actual properties of this representation that it is difficult to determine the precise contribution of the genetic endowment. The crucial question, of course, has to do with whether this contribution will undermine the thesis of general nativism. This need not be the case. Nothing in the proposal I have just made presupposes the existence of objects in semantic form that would be equivalent to actual lexical or phrasal syntactic categories. All that is required is a contrast between predicates that apply to linguistically expressed arguments and those that do not. There will therefore be no need to posit the prior existence of innate semantic objects that would be isomorphic with syntactic phrases.

Recent work on the nature of semantic form has yielded proposals consistent with the claims I have just advanced. Jackendoff (1983), for example, has suggested that semantic form is identical to what he calls "conceptual structure"—the mental representation at which linguistic, sensory, and motor types of information are compatible. If this idea is correct, the genetically determined properties of semantic form will not be narrowly grammatical in character and therefore should be consistent with the thesis of general nativism.

Another pressing question has to do with whether children can match strings of words with the appropriate semantic forms. The viability of this matching is essential to my analysis since it provides the raw data that children must use to discover the role of dependency in the formation of syntactic representations. Unless children can see that *arrive*, for instance, contrasts with *Harry* in naming a predicate that applies to a linguistically expressed argument, they cannot acquire the contrasts I have posited. Two problems arise here, one having to do with how strings of sounds are segmented into morphemes and the other with how these formatives are matched with semantic concepts and contrasts. I will have nothing to say about the first issue, other than to refer readers to Peters (1983) for a discussion of some plausible segmentation strategies. As far as the second problem is concerned, it is now a fairly well established fact (see Pinker [1979] for discussion) that utterances composed of words familiar to children are often used by adults in situations that allow sentence meaning (by definition, semantic form) to be inferred from the nonlinguistic context without the help of syntactic knowledge. Slobin (1975, 20), for example, reports:

Judith Johnson and I have gone through transcripts of adult speech to children between the ages of two and five, in Turkish and English, looking for sentences which could be open to misinterpretation if the child lacked basic syntactic knowledge, such as the role of word order and inflections. We found almost no instances of an adult utterance which could possibly be misinterpreted. That is, the overwhelming majority of utterances were clearly interpretable in context, requiring only knowledge of word meaning and the normal relations between actors, actions and objects in the real world.

Without belittling the enormous problems associated with the acquisition of word meaning and an understanding of "normal relations" in the world, this conclusion is an important one since it suggests that children are able to match a significant set of utterances with the appropriate semantic forms. This in turn provides the data on which generalizations about grammatical principles and categories are based.

Finally, consider the learning procedure that I have tentatively proposed. Generalization is at once one of the most powerful and problematic mechanisms available for hypothesis formation. Used in an unconstrained manner, it will almost certainly fail to provide language learners with correct conclusions about the grammar they are trying to acquire. What, for instance, is to prevent a child from concluding from a sentence such as (1) that all nouns name people and that all verbs name actions?

(1) Harry left.

Similarly, what is to prevent a child from concluding from the same sentence that if *left* can combine with the word *Harry* it can combine with any word? This problem requires a twofold solution. First, restrictions must be placed on the type of notions available to children to formulate grammatical generalizations. If, for instance, notions such as "person" and "action" are not used to form hypotheses about the initial organization of syntactic categories, the first of the spurious generalizations mentioned above should not occur. Second, there must be some constraints on how children use the notions available to them to form generalizations. Do they, for instance, use these notions to formulate the broadest generalizations consistent with experience (the case with the second spurious generalization), or do they perhaps form the most restrictive hypothesis consistent with their observations? General answers to both these questions will begin to emerge in the course of the next several chapters. For the time being, however, I will be assuming that the notions relevant to the formation of syntactic categories are defined in terms of dependency rather than ontological classes such as "person" and "action" and that children use the categorial contrasts to which they have access to form conservative generalizations about combinatorial relations. From a sentence such as (1), then, they will conclude that *arrive* combines with a nominal, not that it can combine with anything. Both these assumptions will be refined and defended as we proceed.

1.5.2 The Acquisition of Lexical Categories

My next task must be to show that, when children use the information represented in syntactic structure and semantic form to formulate generalizations in terms of notions like dependency and adjacency, they will arrive at the categories and principles posited in earlier sections of this chapter. The basic idea is that children form general categories by noting contrasts among the dependency properties of individual words. (These contrasts will be manifested in semantic form, where predicates of different types are found.) After exposure to even a small sampling of simple syntactic structure/semantic form mappings, language learners should be able to note that some words express predicates that apply to other linguistic elements (e.g., *old* in [1a], *arrived* in [1b], and *really* in [1c] while other words do not (e.g., *John* in [1d]).

(1) a. old man
    b. Harry arrived
    c. really tired
    d. John left.

Once this initial contrast between dependent and independent categories has been identified, the next step will involve distinguishing between the two major classes of dependent elements—secondaries and tertiaries. This advance will have to occur in the same manner as the discovery of the contrast between dependent and independent categories. That is, children will have to note that some dependent elements name predicates that apply to arguments encoded as independent categories while others name predicates that apply to arguments encoded by another dependent category.

Once the distinction between lexical and phrasal categories emerges (see below), further distinctions involving secondaries must be noted. For one thing, it must be discovered that, while some of these elements (verbs) apply to arguments expressed only by NPs, others (adjectives) can apply to arguments expressed by either an N or an NP. It will also be necessary to distinguish transitive verbs from intransitives (in terms of the number of NPs on which they depend). These developmental advances are summarized in table 1.1.

Table 1.1: The Development of Lexical Categories

Step 1: The distinction between items that name a predicate applying to a linguistically expressed argument (dependent words) and those that do not (independent words).

Step 2: The distinction between categories that depend on an independent element (secondaries) and those that depend on a dependent element (tertiaries).

Step 3: The distinction between secondaries that depend on NP primaries (verbs) and those that can depend on simple nouns (adjectives).

Step 4: The distinction between verbs that depend on one NP (intransitives) and those that depend on two (transitives).

According to table 1.1, contrasts among lexical categories develop as the language learner classifies words in accordance with the type of predicate they express. Exploiting the notion of dependency, children move from an initial distinction between only two classes of words to successively more refined sets of contrasts until they have finally attained the categorial definitions repeated in (2).

(2) N: A primary (the independent category).
    V: A secondary dependent on one or more NPs.
    Adj: A secondary dependent on an N or an NP.
    Adv: A tertiary (an element that depends on a dependent category).

Notice that each of these categories is defined in terms of its dependency properties, information that can be drawn from the semantic forms corresponding to even simple utterances in children's linguistic environment. There is apparently nothing in this type of development that supports the need for innate syntactic categories.

This approach to the development of grammatical categories differs in important ways from two other well-known proposals, the distributional approach advanced by Maratsos (1982) and the "semantic bootstrapping" hypothesis outlined in recent work by Macnamara (1982) and Pinker (1984). In the distributional approach to the ontogeny of lexical categories, the classification of words takes place without the help of a priori syntactic classes. Instead children note the networks of co-occurring distributional, morphological, and semantic properties associated with different types of words. The category "noun," for example, might be formed by noting that certain words can occur preverbally, can take the *'s* ending or the plural suffix, can be preceded by a determiner, and so on. In this way, children gradually identify the contrasts underlying the categorial distinctions appropriate to their language.

While I recognize the importance of distributional properties and morphological markers for distinguishing among grammatical categories, I do not define categorial contrasts in terms of these phenomena. Rather categories are distinguished from each other in terms of dependency contrasts and then associated with different word order patterns and morphology. In the theory I have proposed, children identify the noun class by observing that words such as *Harry* and *desk* do not name predicates in semantic form that apply to linguistically expressed arguments. At a later point, they will be able to characterize the distribution of the "possessive" suffix (e.g.) by noting that it combines with this class of words. According to this view, then, distributional and morphological patterns are stated in terms of previously discovered syntactic categories; they do not in themselves lead to the creation of these categories. This allows the postulation of a universal inventory of syntactic categories independent of cross-linguistic variation in word order and morphology. Hence both French and English will have a "noun" class defined as the instantiation of the independent category even though the two languages differ in terms of their morphological and distributional patterns.

Now consider the semantic bootstrapping hypothesis. According to this view of category development, children are innately endowed with both a set of categorial distinctions (N, V, NP, etc.) and a set of correspondences between these categories and elementary semantic types. Nouns, for instance, are linked with concrete objects, verbs with actions, and so on. By noting the distributional and morphological properties of names for concrete objects and actions in the language they are acquiring, children then supposedly identify criteria (e.g., positioning, suffixes) that they can use to classify words with more abstract referents (e.g., *policy, optimism, wonder,* etc.).

Such assumptions are unnecessary in the system I have proposed. Because lexical categories are defined entities rather than primitives, the problem of matching individual words with the appropriate category does not arise in the same form. Once syntactic categories have been posited (in the manner outlined above), the assignment of individual words to the appropriate class takes place on the basis of their dependency properties. In order to learn that *Harry* belongs to the category N, for instance, children need only consider the semantic form associated with a sentence such as *Harry is here,* in which this word does not depend on another linguistic element. Similarly, in order to learn that *arrive* is a verb, it suffices to note that it names a predicate that takes a linguistically expressed NP argument in sentences such as *Harry arrived*. In this system, then, a word's predicate type ensures its assignment to the appropriate syntactic category, and there is no need for an innate set of prototypical word-category correspondences.

This is not to suggest that no bootstrapping occurs. As is well known, many words name predicates that can alternate in their type, sometimes applying to a linguistically expressed element and sometimes not. A typical example of this would involve a word such as *transfer,* which sometimes expresses an "action" predicate (*They transferred Harry to a new department*) and sometimes a "thing" predicate (*The transfer took place last week*). The former type of predicate belongs to the dependent class and is encoded as a verb, while the latter is independent and is realized as a noun. It seems reasonable to assume that children use the morphological and distributional patterns associated with unambiguous predicate-category mappings (e.g., nouns such as *Harry* and *desk*) to analyze unclear cases and to identify *transfer* as a noun in the second of our examples.[7] Where my proposal differs from the nativist version of bootstrapping is in the status of the basic correspondence between categories and predicate types. Whereas nativists see these as inborn, I take the view that they can be constructed in the manner outlined earlier.

Although I do not assume the innate categories and correspondences posited by the semantic bootstrapping hypothesis, I do recognize that children's first nouns may well name objects and that their first verbs may well refer to actions. Rather than attribute this to special innate linguistic knowledge, however, I would trace such connections to the fact that nouns naming concrete objects are prototypical instances of words that do not encode a predicate applying to a linguistically expressed argument and are therefore the most obvious instances of the independent category I have posited. Similarly, verbs referring to actions are probably the clearest examples of words expressing predicates that must apply to other elements (the "participants" in the action) and therefore are the first manifestation of the dependent category.

An important advantage of this is that it allows us to describe the development of lexical categories as a continuous process centered around the classification of words in terms of their dependency properties. This in turn offers a way to resolve a long-standing dispute over the relation between children's early hypotheses about grammatical categories and the categorial distinctions needed in the adult grammar. According to one view, children initially form categories in terms of a set of semantic notions such as "thing" and "action" that are unrelated to the abstract syntactic categories usually posited for the adult grammar. This raises the problem, never satisfactorily resolved, of when and how children make the transition between the two types of system. (This is sometimes called the "discontinuity problem.'') The alternate view, adopted by nativists, is that abstract syntactic categories are innately specified and either are present from birth or emerge at the appropriate time. According to the view I have presented, syntactic categories do not evolve from notions such as ''thing'' and ''action''; nor are they innate. Rather they are formulated from the outset in terms of the dependency-based contrasts we have been considering. The preponderance of words naming things in early noun classes and of words naming actions in early verb classes is taken to reflect the fact that these are prototypical instances of independent and dependent predicate types, not an attempt to establish lexical categories along notional lines.

1.5.3 The Acquisition of Phrasal Categories

Once the basic categorial contrasts among lexical items have been discovered, children can begin to identify the structural conditions under which these elements can be combined. Here it seems reasonable to assume that the large number of cases in which a word's dependency requirements are satisfied by combining it with an adjacent word (e.g., *old man, John left, leave quietly*) will support formation of the Adjacency Principle, interpreted so as to comply with the Dependency Requirement.

(1) *The Adjacency Principle (AP):*
   Combine adjacent elements.

(2) *The Dependency Requirement:*
   All combinatorial operations must satisfy a dependency.

Discovery of the AP opens two new avenues of development, one pertaining to the conditions governing this combinatorial operation (e.g., the Subject-Last Requirement) and the other to the categorial distinctions manifested in the phrases that it creates. The major mechanism for category assignment is the Phrasal Category Principle, repeated here.

(3) *The Phrasal Category Principle:*
   A phrase takes on the category of a component with an unsatisfied dependency.
   If there is no such element, it is a primary (nominal).

As in the case of lexical categories, we can assume that the relevant distinctions in predicate types (e.g., dependent vs. independent) can be represented in semantic form once the existence of phrasal units has been established by the AP. The key observation from the language learner's perspective will then be that the phrasal units formed by the AP exhibit the same dependency properties as a component element with an unsatisfied dependency. Thus children must note that when the verb *leave* and the adverb *quietly* are combined, the resulting phrase denotes a predicate that implies the same type of linguistically expressed argument as *leave* does (*leave* being the element with an unsatisfied dependency here). Similarly, in a case such as *really tired,* they must note that the phrase formed by combining *really* and *tired* has the dependency properties of an adjective (i.e., it expresses a property that can be predicated of the denotata of nominals). It must also be observed that a phrase such as *fresh snow,* which contains no element with an unsatisfied dependency, functions as an independent category in not implying a separate linguistically expressed argument. These generalizations constitute the essence of the Phrasal Category Principle since they ensure formation of phrasal categories corresponding to each of the lexical categories. (Recall that the maximal categories of each type correspond to NP, VP, AdjP and AdvP, respectively.)

(4) Nominal phrase: A nominal primary (the independent category).
    Verbal phrase: A verbal secondary dependent on one or more NPs.
    Adjectival phrase: A secondary that can depend on a simple N.
    Adverbial phrase: A tertiary (an element depending on a dependent category).

In order to add the phrasal category PP to this list, two observations must be made—one about the type of category to which prepositions apply (NPs) and the other about the categories with which the resultant phrase combines (a V^i in *Harry slept on the floor,* an N in *books on the floor*). Since a V^i can only combine with one NP (its subject), and since an N cannot combine directly with any categories of this type, it should be possible to infer that the preposition has as its syntactic role the conversion of an NP into a dependent phrase (a secondary or a tertiary) that can combine with either a V^i or an N, as the case may be. Since this syntactic role can be inferred in this way only if the combinatorial properties of V^is, Ns, and NPs are already known, I predict that prepositions should be a relatively late acquisition. As we shall see below, this is correct.

A crucial feature of the proposed scenario for the development of phrasal categories is that it requires no new notions. Categorial contrasts continue to be defined in terms of dependency, except that the required distinctions are now made among phrases formed by the AP rather than words. This allows us to maintain the view outlined above that the development of syntactic categories is a continuous process centered from the outset on dependency properties of linguistic elements. As before, the relevant data consist of the semantic forms corresponding to simple sentences from the child's linguistic environment.

Summary
According to the proposals just outlined, the formation of hypotheses about linguistic structure involves a process of generalization whereby the prop-

erties associated with particular items and relations are identified and then used to form general categories and principles. Thus the observation that words like *old* and *arrived* are dependent on other elements leads to the initial formation of a general class of words (secondaries) whose defining feature is this very property. Finer dependency-based contrasts are then noted in particular cases (e.g., *arrive* depends on one NP, *hit* on two) and generalized to form further categorial distinctions (here intransitive vs. transitive). In a similar fashion the presence of dependency relations between particular adjacent elements triggers formation of a general principle (the AP), which then applies in an extremely broad range of cases.

A problem with the use of generalization (or any other type of learning strategy) to explain development lies in determining how language learners discover the notions that allow formation of fruitful hypotheses. Even assuming that children's general innate endowment includes the concepts needed to formulate categorial distinctions and the AP, we are still left with the problem of explaining how they discover the relevance of adjacency and dependency to the data they are considering. One possibility is that linguistic development in the presyntactic period facilitates discovery of the relevant concepts. (This would fall under condition D, outlined above in sec. 1.5.1 above.) If, for example, children in the one-word stage come to think of sentences as linear strings of words, they might seek to analyze utterances in terms of spatial notions relevant to the linear arrangement of elements (e.g., adjacency and precedence). Moreover, if young children come to realize that the expressive power of language stems from the fact that the meanings of individual words can be combined to create complex messages, we would also expect their initial hypotheses about the organization of sentences to draw on information about the semantic objects involved (e.g., their predicate types). This in turn would presumably facilitate discovery of the dependency contrasts on which categorial distinctions and the AP are based. I reconsider this matter in more detail in chapter 7.

1.5.4 Acquisition of the HSR and the SLR

The particular interest of the Hierarchical Structuring Requirement and the Subject-Last Requirement for a theory of language learning lies in the fact that normal forms of experience, including the observable semantic contrasts, do not provide children with information that bears directly on the need for such devices.

(1) *The Hierarchical Structuring Requirement:*
    Combinatorial operations create phrases to which subsequent combinatorial operations apply.

(2) *The Subject-Last Requirement:*
   The subject combines with VP (the maximal verbal category).

As noted earlier, for example, there is apparently nothing in the interpretation of a sentence such as *Sue saw Harry* that would require a child to conclude that *saw* combines with *Harry* to create a phrase that then combines with *Sue*. Before concluding that this data deficiency supports the thesis of special nativism, however, it is productive to examine the possibility that the HSR and the SLR might be acquired with the help of principles that structure the human mind in a more general way. Consider, for example, the possibility that the child is endowed with a tendency to seek principles that apply across the board and that a linguistic device that applies in all cases will therefore be preferred to one that applies in only some instances. Given this, there is an interesting scenario that could lead to discovery of the mechanisms I have posited. Consider first the HSR.

   Let us assume that, as suggested above, children acquire the AP on the basis of extremely simple structures (perhaps even two-word utterances). If this happened, they would then note that hierarchical structuring is necessary if the verb is to combine with an adjacent element in constructions such as (3).

(3) Harry likes old cars.

If there is no hierarchical structuring, the element to the right of the verb would be the adjective *old,* as illustrated in (4). Since neither element exhibits a dependency on the other, the two cannot be combined, and there can be no well-formed syntactic representation.

(4)
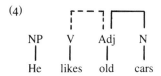

NP   V   Adj   N
| | | |
He likes old   cars

The outcome would be very different if the elements combined by the AP form units to which subsequent combinatorial operations apply. Under such circumstances, the element with which the verb combines in (4) would be the phrase *old cars,* an instance of the independent (nominal) category since neither of its components exhibits an unsatisfied dependency. The verb could then combine with such a phrase, giving the representation in (5). Assuming a tendency to apply principles as generally as possible, the child should conclude form cases like this that, since the HSR is required in some instances, it applies in all cases. This is precisely the result we are seeking.

(5)

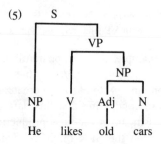

A comparable scenario might lead to discovery of the Subject-Last Requirement (SLR), which ensures that the subject combines with the maximal verbal category VP. Assuming early acquisition of the AP and the HSR, consider the problems that structures such as (6) would create for the language learner.

(6) John runs fast.

Notice that (6) can be assigned a well-formed structure only if the AP applies in accordance with the SLR. Were the preverbal NP (the subject) to combine with the verb *leave* before the adverb, the result would be the ill-formed structure depicted in (7).

(7)

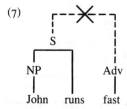

Because *fast* depends on a verbal category, it cannot combine with the S in (7), and the sentence therefore cannot be assigned a well-formed structure. The way for children to avoid this problem is to form the syntactic representation in accordance with the SLR by first creating a VP consisting of *runs* and *fast* and then combining it with the preverbal NP. On our earlier assumption that children seek to apply principles in a maximally general way, they should then treat other NPs with similar positional and morphological properties in the same way, applying the SLR uniformly to the formation of all syntactic representations.

A crucial assumption underlying the preceding proposal is that children know that elements such as *fast* are verb modifiers rather than, say, sentence adverbs. The developmental evidence supports this assumption since children produce two-word structures such as *go there* and *go fast* in which the adverb must be interpreted as a verb modifier.[8]

(8)

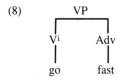

This is all that is required for sentences such as (6) to trigger formation of the maximal verbal category (VP) before the subject-marked NP is incorporated into syntactic structure.

It might be suggested at this point that children could draw a quite different conclusion from the facts just noted, namely, that adverbs have been wrongly characterized and that they can in fact combine with either V or S. I will assume that this does not happen because children seek a unique characterization of a category's combinatorial properties. That is, all other things being equal, they will prefer an analysis of (6) that allows them to maintain the unique characterization of adverbs developed in the two-word stage. Since this characterization takes these elements to be dependent on verbal categories, the syntactic representation in (7) will be rejected, as desired.

Finally, it is important to note that my proposal does not presuppose that children have some a priori notion of "subject." Rather it is simply the case that children establish a correlation between certain formal properties (e.g., preverbal position, a specific case marking, etc.) and a structural relation (i.e., combination with VP). This combinatorial feature is the defining property of what we take to be the grammatical role of subject. I will elaborate on this point in the next chapter.

1.5.5 Accounting for the Developmental Sequence

Before concluding this chapter, it is worthwhile to consider the developmental data relevant to the phenomena we have been discussing. While acquisitional data generally cannot be used to distinguish between development through learning and development through maturation (since both may involve gradual change accompanied by errors), it often can provide insights into the system of rules and representations attained by the child (i.e., the product of development). This is especially true if we assume that, in cases in which a component of the adult grammar has been correctly identified, there will be some fairly direct evidence for its emergence during the language acquisition process. (I will defend an even stronger version of this assumption in chap. 7.)

To begin, let us consider the one-word stage. Because the formation of multiword utterances is guided by the Dependency Requirement (which ensures that each combinatorial operation satisfies the dependency requirements of one of the elements involved), there must be a period during which a preliminary classification of words on the basis of their dependency properties takes place. Such a period could manifest itself in either of two ways. It could, for instance, be characterized by the use of words (i.e., nouns) that do not name functions that apply to other linguistic categories. The end of such a period would be marked by the appearance of dependent categories and the resultant use of two-word utterances in which the dependency requirements of one element are satisfied by combining it with another category. Alternately, the period during which initial categorial contrasts develop might be characterized by the use of both independent and dependent categories, but without dependencies being overtly satisfied. The end of this stage would also be marked by the appearance of two-word utterances in which the combinatorial relation satisfies the dependency requirements of one of the words.

Because it is virtually impossible to be certain about the semantic forms associated with children's one-word utterances, it is difficult to make any strong claims about which of the two options I have just sketched is correct. The circumstantial evidence suggests that both types of system occur, perhaps in succession. In the first part of the one-word stage, children's utterances consist primarily of noun-type words and expressions of indeterminate categorial status (e.g., *hi, more, allgone, here*). It seems plausible to assume that such words are not taken to name predicates that must apply to other linguistic categories. The first six of Greenfield and Smith's (1976) substages for the one-word period involve such utterances. (See table 1.2.) In later parts of the one-word period, however, children use utterances such as *up* and *down* to describe actions in ways that suggest that they should have linguistically expressed arguments. Shortly after this, two-word utterances in which these dependencies are overtly satisfied do appear. However, the fact that these two events are not simultaneous suggests that there may be a period when children use dependent words without overtly satisfying their dependencies.

Table 1.2

Semantic function	Age (months)	Instance
Performative	7	*hi*, while waving
Performative object	8	*dada*, looking at father
Volition	11	*nana*, response to mother's *no*
Dative	11	*dada*, offering bottle to father
Object	13	*ball*, having just thrown bail
Agent	13	*daddy*, hearing father approach

Turning now to the structure types that predominate in the two-word stage, we find the following patterns.

(1) *Pattern:*   *Example:*

    Possessor-possessed   Daddy['s] car
    Agent-action   Daddy go
    Action-patient   hug Mommy
    Modifier-head   big chair
    Object-location   car there

A common reaction to these patterns (e.g., Brown 1973) has been to conclude that children are formulating rules for sentence formation in terms of semantic notions such as "agent," "possessor," and the like rather than syntactic categories. The point that is typically raised in support of this view is that a characterization of children's linguistic abilities should not posit categories (such as syntactic classes) for which there is no direct evidence. A serious problem with this position is that it implies a major discontinuity between early language, in which word classes are semantically defined, and later stages of development, in which there are genuine syntactic categories. (For more on this, see Pinker [1984, 138ff.].) As noted in our earlier consideration of lexical categories, this problem can be avoided by assuming that even children's early utterances exhibit dependency-based categorial distinctions. Since the formulation of the dependency contrasts underlying syntactic categories requires only a very small sampling of different predicate types, the narrow semantic range of two-word patterns does not undermine this claim and can be attributed to facts about conceptual development rather than the absence of syntactic categories. An account of these limitations will therefore come from a theory of conceptual development, not grammatical theory.

While the theory of syntactic development has little or nothing to say about why children express the possessor relation (e.g.) from such an early stage, it does have something to say about the form of these and other utterances. Particularly significant here is the fact that all these utterance types consist of categories (typically a primary and a secondary) that can combine with each other in the type of grammar I have proposed. Moreover, the agent-object utterance type (e.g., *Mommy [sees] Daddy*), which consists of two independent elements whose amalgamation would not satisfy a dependency, occurs infrequently (Macrae 1979, 164).[9] This is just what we would expect if the two-word stage marked acquisition of the Adjacency Principle and the resulting combination of syntactic categories in accordance with the Dependency Requirement to form phrases with the properties specified by the Phrasal Category Principle.

The development of phrasal categories during the two-word stage paves the way for the emergence of utterances consisting of three words or more (in which a phrase is formed and then combined with another element). Some examples of such utterances from Brown's (1973) subject, Adam, are given in (2).

(2) me get John.
    towtruck come here.
    Dale get you pepper
    pick Dale up

Since the Phrasal Category Principle and the AP work in the same manner for four- and five-word utterances as for other constructions longer than two words, there is no reason to expect children to pass through a three-word stage. This helps explain the well-known fact that children typically go from the two-word stage to a multiword stage with no intervening three-word period and provides an alternative to the view that limitations on processing capacity prevent production of longer utterances in the early stages of language acquisition. As Bloom (1970) has pointed out, this latter view is problematic and is not supported by what is known about children's processing capabilities in general.

Specific Grammatical Categories

Interesting predictions can also be made about the development of specific grammatical categories. A first prediction is based on the fact that tertiaries (e.g., adverbials) are defined as categories that depend on secondaries (verbs and adjectives) and the latter category types as elements that depend on primaries (nominals). Since the definition of tertiaries presupposes the existence of secondaries and that of secondaries the existence of primaries, these categories should develop in the order primary > secondary > tertiary. Evidence in support of this prediction is provided by Gentner (1982), who uses data from half a dozen languages to argue for the very developmental sequence I have just proposed. (Gentner attributes this sequence to innate properties of the perceptual system rather than to grammatical considerations; as far as I know, her proposal has no independent support.)

   Gentner's results notwithstanding, claims about the development of syntactic categories must be made with a great deal of caution since it is hard to know at precisely what point children start to construct genuine categories instead of simply treating each word as a unique case. It is easy to find apparent use of tertiaries (e.g., locatives) in even one-word speech, but it is not clear that children take all such words to be instances of a single category defined in terms of dependency. Such considerations must obviously be taken into account as work in this area proceeds.

Further predictions might be made about the manner in which prelimi-nary categorial distinctions (e.g., primary vs. secondary) evolve into finer contrasts involving verbs and adjectives, for example. Although the on-togeny of linguistic categories is still poorly understood (but see Maratsos 1982; and McCawley 1983), it is known that two-word syntactic patterns manifest themselves before the appearance of tense, aspect, and the other grammatical contrasts that help distinguish verbs from adjectives. This points to the possible existence of an acquisitional stage in which children distinguish between primaries and secondaries but not between subtypes of secondaries (i.e., adjectives and verbs). This prediction is also consistent with the known developmental data. Although children's early multiword utterances contain apparent instances of dependent categories combining with a nominal (cf. [3]), there are no morphological or syntactic grounds for distinguishing between adjectives and verbs at this point. (These utter-ances are from Gia, one of Bloom's [1970] subjects.)

(3) a. Mommy busy.
    b. Mommy push.
    c. Microphone hot.
    d. Baloon throw.

As these examples show, the morphological signs of the verb-adjective distinction (e.g., tense and aspect marking) are absent at this time. Of course, this does not mean that the category of secondaries is entirely ho-mogeneous in this stage. Since the dependent elements that will later be manifested as adjectives primarily denote properties and those that will later be verbs generally denote actions, there are grounds for various se-mantic distinctions.

Still another prediction made by the proposed grammar pertains to the emergence of prepositions and copula verbs. As elements that combine with an independent category (i.e., a nominal) to create a dependent phrase, these words should not be acquired until the contrasts underlying more basic categorial distinctions have been mastered. For instance, until children know that phrases such as *the door* are independent nominals and that words such as *stand* depend only on a subject NP, they will not under-stand the syntactic role of the preposition in sentences such as *Harry stood near the door,* in which *near* converts the NP *the door* into a tertiary that can combine with the intransitive verb. (See (4).) Similarly, until children know that phrases such as *a student* are instances of the independent cate-gory, they will not understand the need for a copula in sentences such as *Harry is a student,* in which *is* converts *a student* into a dependent phrase that can combine with the NP *Harry.* (See (5).)

(4)

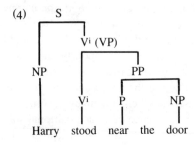

Harry stood near the door

(5)

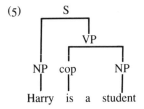

Harry is a student

Pinker (1984, 101) reviews developmental data that support the view that prepositions and copulas are acquired after the other categorial contrasts we have been considering.

Table 1.3 summarizes the developmental sequence I have posited. As noted earlier, this developmental sequence is unified by the notion of dependency, which is used first to make rudimentary distinctions between two classes of words (dependent and independent) and then to formulate the more refined categorial contrasts (involving N, V, NP, VP, and so on) typical of the adult grammar.

Table 1.3: Early Grammatical Development

Stage	Advances
The one-word stage	Dependency-based contrasts among lexical items
The two-word stage	The Adjacency Principle
	The Phrasal Category Principle
Multi-word stage	Contrast between Vs and Adjs
	Appearance of adjectival and verbal inflections
	Appearance of prepositions and copulas

Still other predictions about the developmental sequence follow from my proposals about the acquisition of the Hierarchical Structuring Requirement and the Subject-Last Requirement. Since I have claimed that these mechanisms are learned rather than innate, there could well be a period (however brief) during which they are not present. Circumstantial evidence that the HSR had not been acquired would come from the demonstration that no grammatical rules presuppose the existence of phrasal categories and that none of the strings produced by children require the formation of phrases. This predicts that there will be no sentences of the form *see brown dog,* in which *brown* must combine with *dog* to form an NP if the AP is to combine *see* with an adjacent nominal category (see the discussion in sec. 1.5.4 above). If there is such a period during the production of multiword utterances, it has not been noted to my knowledge. However, Matthei [1979] and Hill [1983] have used semantic evidence to argue that syntactic representations initially lack a hierarchical structure.

The question of when the SLR is acquired may be somewhat easier to resolve. A crucial class of evidence will come from observations about the point at which children begin to formulate rules that make reference to grammatical relations (e.g., subject-verb agreement in English). According to the proposals that I will make in the next chapter, grammatical roles such as subject and direct object are defined in terms of syntactic representations formed in accordance with the SLR. I therefore predict that no rules referring to grammatical relations can be formulated before acquisition of the SLR. Since acquisition of this device is crucially dependent on mastery of NP V Adv strings such as *Sue runs fast* (see above), I also predict that children will use such structures before formulating rules that make reference to grammatical relations. This prediction is consistent with what is known about the acquisition of rules such as subject-verb agreement in English which is acquired relatively late (after age three and a half, according to Brown [1973]).

There are also important developmental areas in which the theory I have proposed has the advantage of making no predictions. A good example of this involves the strategies children initially use in trying to segment strings of sounds into words. It is well known that there is considerable variation in how individual language learners go about this. While some children apparently adopt what has been called a "referential/nominal/bottom up" approach characterized by a large vocabulary of individual words (especially nouns), other children opt for an "expressive/pronominal/top down" strategy that favors rote-learned phrases and a high percentage of pronouns (for a review, see Bloom, Lightbown, and Hood [1975] and Nelson [1975]). Nothing in the theory I have proposed would rule out either of these strategies. There is no reason why a child's first primaries must be nouns rather than pronouns and no reason why a child must succeed in isolating word-size units from the outset. Ultimately, of course, children must develop productive rules for sentence formation, but this does not prevent them from initially memorizing a set of formulaic utterances that can be used as unanalyzed wholes prior to the discovery of smaller units. The only prediction I make here is that, as word-size units are identified, they will be classified in accordance with the proposals made above.

1.6 Conclusion

The major thesis of this chapter has been that the grammar consists of principles and categories that are built on notions that we can reasonably expect to be part of the child's general conceptual inventory; that the acquisition of these principles and categories presupposes only forms of experience that we can reasonably expect to occur in any normal linguistic environment; and that the relevant learning procedure involves the formation of generalizations. This seems to constitute a reasonable first step in the elaboration of a research program that seeks to integrate claims about linguistic competence into the broader study of language acquisition and its relation to the structures and categories of general cognition. Although problems remain, the preceding discussion has provided support for the earlier claim that an adjustment in basic assumptions about the character of linguistic rules and representations can bring about quite radical modifications in our understanding of the language faculty and of language acquisition.

The proposals made in this chapter have also provided an outline of the more general view of linguistic competence that I am trying to develop. A fundamental claim in this regard has to do with the character of the concepts employed by sentence grammar. While I differ from many opponents of special nativism in accepting the existence of sentence grammar as a distinct cognitive system, I am taking the position that the rules and categories required for language are formulated in terms of notions that are not specific to the language faculty (e.g., adjacency and dependency). Thus I do not claim that categories such as N and VP are manifested outside of language, only that the notions on which they are built are not particular to the language faculty. This view will be maintained in the analyses of grammatical relations, extraction, and anaphora that follow.

While the position that I have just outlined appears to have certain advantages in terms of satisfying the learnability conditions associated with general nativism, it raises problems of a different sort. In particular, it must be asked how we are to account for the existence of universal linguistic properties in the absence of a specific genetic endowment for language. There is, of course, no contradiction between the claims I have made about the nature of the grammar and the existence of linguistic universals: syntactic categories defined in terms of dependency can just as easily be universal as syntactic categories that are primes. The problem that I must face has to do with why no languages build syntactic categories around a notion other than dependency. This is a very legitimate question and one that must be considered by proponents of general nativism. While this concern is subordinated here to the issue of learnability, I will reconsider it and make some specific proposals in chapter 7.

The key to a viable treatment of language acquisition within the framework of general nativism lies in the development of a theory of grammar and learning with a deductive structure and predictive power equivalent to that of current work within special nativism. Needless to say, such a goal cannot be achieved through analysis of one or two phenomena, and it is therefore necessary to exercise considerable caution with respect to the proposals outlined in this chapter. At the same time, however, it is also important to recognize that tentative analyses and cautious proposals are a necessary first step for the type of inquiry that I have undertaken. I will therefore continue in this fashion through the next five chapters, developing proposals for a varied set of individual phenomena. I will then use chapter 7 to attempt a synthesis of these proposals, discussing in more detail the theory of language and learning to which they point.

GRAMMATICAL
RELATIONS AND
THEMATIC ROLES

2.1 Introduction

The preceding chapter was primarily concerned with the categorial composition of syntactic representations. Two major points were developed. First, it was argued that lexical categories such as N, V, and Adj can be defined in terms of contrasts involving the dependency properties of the predicates that they name. Second, it was proposed that the formation of phrasal categories (NP, VP, etc.) takes place in accordance with general principles that determine the categorial status of phrases from the properties of their component parts (the Phrasal Category Principle) and regulate their organization into sentences (the Subject-Last Requirement). The present chapter will be concerned with two other sets of traditional syntactic notions—grammatical relations such as subject and direct object and thematic roles such as actor and patient. Consistent with the overall theme of this book, an attempt will be made to characterize these notions in terms consistent with the thesis of general nativism.

Current approaches to syntax are divided over the status of grammatical relations, with two major positions being discernible. On the one hand, there are theories (such as Relational Grammar and Lexical Functional Grammar) that make extensive use of GRs in the statement of syntactic rules but consider them to be primes (entities that cannot be defined in terms of more basic notions). On the other hand, there are theories (especially transformational grammar [TG]) that do not formulate syntactic rules in relational terms but consider GRs to be definable by reference to more basic configurational notions. In this book I will advocate still another position, namely, that GRs are definable and that syntactic rules can make direct reference to them. The major goal of this chapter will be to characterize GRs and related notions in a manner consistent with the thesis of general nativism.

As I noted in the last chapter, a theory of GRs must deal with at least two separate issues, one having to do with whether grammatical relations can be represented in terms of structural positions and the other with how NPs bearing various thematic roles (e.g., actor, theme, etc.) are associated with subjects and objects (however these are represented). I will deal with these issues in several steps. To begin, I will consider the question of whether GRs can be characterized structurally and will argue that the subject–direct object distinction can be captured in terms of configurational asymmetries. I will then examine the relation between a verb and the element(s) to which it assigns a thematic role and will defend the view that this relation cannot be equated with GRs such as subject and direct object.

In section 2.4, I consider the type of information that is present in the lexicon and the relation between thematic roles and GRs. I propose a simple device to capture this relation and then consider its role in the statement of rules such as passivization and "dative movement."

2.2 Grammatical Relations

2.2.1 Subjects and Objects

In what follows, I will assume that it is appropriate to recognize at least a three-way relational contrast involving subjects, direct objects, and nonarguments (i.e., phrases that are neither subject nor object). In a sentence such as (1), I will take *Mary* to be subject, *the book* to be direct object, and *the floor* to be a nonargument (of the verb).

(1) Mary saw a book on the floor.

In (2), on the other hand, I will assume that only the NP *a book* is an argument (the subject).

(2) A book was seen by Mary.

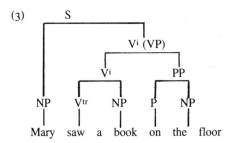

Assuming that (1) has the structure depicted in (3), we can distinguish between syntactic arguments and nonarguments along the lines proposed in (4).

(4) NPs satisfying a verbal dependency are syntactic arguments.

According to this definition, *a book* and *Mary* are syntactic arguments since they satisfy a verbal dependency. In contrast, the PP *on the floor,* which is a tertiary according to the proposals made in chapter 1, is not an argument by my criterion. This is because it does not satisfy a verbal dependency but rather combines with a V^i to give another category of the same type. The only dependency that is satisfied by this combinatorial relation is that of an adverbial modifier (the PP) on a verbal category. I will take such elements to be (adverbial) "modifiers" or "adjuncts," consistent with the definition outlined in (5).

(5) Phrases depending on a verbal category are syntactic modifiers (adjuncts).

Another way to state (4) would be to say that arguments are phrases that combine with a verbal category to give a category of a new type (a category with a different set of combinatorial properties). In our example, then, *a book* is an argument since it combines with a V^{tr} to give a V^i (a verb that depends on a single NP). The PP *on the floor,* in contrast, does not have argument status since it combines with the V^i to give another category with the same combinatorial properties (i.e., a verb that still depends on a single NP). Finally, *Mary* is also an argument since it combines with a V^i (the maximal verbal category) to give an S.

Turning now to the difference between subject and direct object arguments, an interesting characterization of this contrast can be based on the Subject-Last Requirement (SLR), the well-formedness condition that identifies as subject the NP that combines with the maximal verbal category.

(6) *The Subject-Last Requirement:*
    The subject combines with VP.

As noted in the previous chapter, the SLR does not presuppose the prior existence of the notion "subject." Rather, it is built on the observation that an NP with certain (language-particular) features such as positioning or case must combine with a VP in intransitive sentences such as *Harry runs fast.* This combinatorial property is then generalized to all NPs with those positional and/or morphological features and the term "subject" is applied to the NPs in that class. Assuming that subjects are marked by occurrence in preverbal position in English declarative sentences, the SLR will ensure the formation of structures such as (7), in which *Mary* combines with the verbal element after *John* does.

(7)

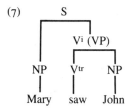

Given this structure, it is possible to propose the following distinction between subject and direct object arguments. (I consider the problem of defining indirect objects in sec. 2.5 below.)

(8) *The direct object:* The first argument to be incorporated into the clause.
The subject: The last argument to be incorporated into the clause.

The definitions in (8) identify *John* as direct object and *Mary* as subject in (7).

It is important to reiterate at this point that nothing in either the SLR or the definitions in (8) presupposes the existence of a priori subject and direct object categories. Rather it is the case that the grammar forms sentences in ways that distinguish at least two combinatorial positions for syntactic arguments (NPs that satisfy a verbal dependency), namely, "sister" of V^{tr} and "sister" of VP. Although I am referring to the former position as "subject" and the latter as "direct object," these notions do not exist independent of or prior to the combinatorial operations that form sentences.

The proposed relational definitions have a number of broader consequences, including the prediction of facts that must be stated as separate generalizations in theories such as Relational Grammar that take GRs to be primes. Two such generalizations are the Final 1 (Subject) Law and the Stratal Uniqueness Law (Perlmutter and Postal 1983), paraphrased below.

(9) *The Final 1 Law:*
All clauses must have a subject in surface structure.

(10) *The Stratal Uniqueness Law:*
There can be no more than one subject and one direct object at any level of syntactic representation.

Given the relational definitions proposed here, these laws follow as simple theorems. Since clauses (Ss) are formed by combining a VP with an NP and since, by definition, this NP is the subject (last argument), it follows that all clauses must have a subject. Moreover, since only one argument can be first and only one can be last, it also follows that there will be no more than one subject and one direct object in any syntactic representation.

Below I will consider the relevance of the proposed definitions to "relation-changing" rules such as passivization.

Another advantage of the approach to GRs that I have adopted is that it is applicable to all languages. Since all languages have the basic categories I have posited for English (i.e., N, V, Adv, VP, etc.), they must also all have the Subject-Last Requirement. It is no more possible to assign a well-formed structure to the Malagasy sentence in (11) than to its English counterpart if the maximal verbal category (VP) is not formed before the subject-marked NP is incorporated into syntactic structure, as stipulated by the SLR.

(11)

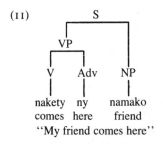

nakety   ny   namako
comes   here   friend
"My friend comes here"

An especially interesting consequence of the universality of the SLR is that it forces formation of discontinuous constituents in languages in which the verb and its complement are not contiguous. Thus Tagalog (a VSO language) and Korean (a "free word order" language in which OSV patterns are common) will have representations resembling (14) and (15) for the sentences in (12) and (13), respectively. (For expository convenience, I use a line drawn beneath the string of words to connect the components of a discontinuous constituent.)

(12) Binili ni John ang libro
     bought Nom-John Ac-book
     "John bought a book."

(13) Sue-rul John-i piphanha-yess-ta.
     Sue-Ac John-Nom left
     "John criticized Sue."

(14)

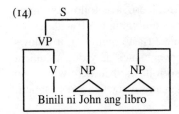

(15)

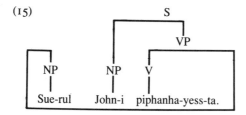

In O'Grady (1985a) I present independent evidence that discontinuous constituents are present in these cases. I review some of this evidence in chapter 5.

The existence of discontinuous phrases is not problematic for a categorial grammar so long as there is no universal requirement that only adjacent phrases can be combined. The fact that Tagalog and Korean allow discontinuous constituents suggests that the Adjacency Principle cannot be universal and that a less restrictive combinatorial operation is at work in these languages. In chapter 3 I will suggest that the Adjacency Principle is also too strong for English and that a simpler and more general mechanism can be posited.

2.2.2 Other Approaches

The proposed characterization of the subject–direct object contrast resembles a variety of other theories in accepting the following two claims.

(1) *The Configurationality Claim:*
   Grammatical relations can be defined in terms of configurational properties of syntactic structure.

(2) *The Asymmetry Claim:*
   Within the structures relevant to the definition of GRs, direct objects combine with V and subjects with VP.

The Configurationality and Asymmetry claims are accepted in transformational grammar, where the subject is defined as the NP immediately dominated by S (i.e., [NP,S]) and the direct object as the NP immediately dominated by VP (i.e., [NP,VP]) in a structure such as (3). (For elaboration, see Chomsky [1981].)

(3)

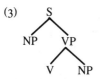

The Configurationality and Asymmetry claims are realized in a slightly different way in Montague Grammar, where relational contrasts are defined in terms of the combinatorial rules used to form phrasal constituents. For instance, Dowty (1982) has suggested that the direct object be defined as the NP that is combined with a transitive verb by the rule that forms a VP while the subject corresponds to the NP that is combined with the VP by the rule that forms an S. These rules are paraphrased in (4). (F1 and F2 specify language-particular ordering and agreement operations that need not concern us here. The elements within the inner angled brackets are the phrases to which the combinatorial rules apply; the category label to their right names the resulting phrase.)

(4) *The Subject-Predicate Rule:*
   $\langle F_1, \langle VP, NP \rangle S \rangle$
   The Verb-Direct Object Rule:
   $\langle F2, \langle V, NP \rangle VP \rangle$

Below I will consider the versions of the Configurationality and Asymmetry claims developed by Marantz (1984).

The major difference between my approach to GRs and the other theories that adopt the Configurationality and Asymmetry claims involves the learnability of the proposed definitions. As noted in chapter 1, the Subject-Last Requirement, on which my characterization of GRs is built, is learnable thanks to the existence of sentences such as (5).

(5) Mary runs quickly.

Recall that, unless the NP that is traditionally called "subject" combines with the maximal verbal category in (5), this sentence cannot be assigned a well-formed structure. This is illustrated in (6), where *quickly*—an adverbial element dependent on a verbal category—cannot combine with the phrase *Mary runs*.

(6)

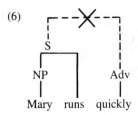

Mary   runs   quickly

In (6) the NP that occurs preverbally and triggers number agreement must combine with the maximal verbal category (VP) *runs quickly* if the syntactic representation is to be well formed. As mentioned in chapter 1, I assume that children note this correlation between an NP's positional and morphological properties on the one hand and its combinatorial position on the other. By extending this correlation to all NPs with these positional and/or morphological properties, children will always form syntactic representations in which the NP that we wish to identify as subject combines with VP, the maximal verbal category.[1]

The evidence motivating other configurational approaches to GRs is of a quite different sort. Within TG, for example, the structural properties of the syntactic representation would presumably have to be justified by reference to c-command asymmetries, as Williams (1984) and Saito (1985) have proposed. A plausible example of this involves anaphoric dependencies, which are usually assumed to be subject to some variant of Reinhart's (1981) c-command principle. (Recall that x c-commands y if the first branching node above x dominates y.)

(7) A pronoun cannot c-command its antecedent.

Assuming that the verb and its direct object combine to form a VP, (7) will account for the contrast between (8) and (9).

(8) *[$_S$ He$_i$ [$_{VP}$ saw John's$_i$ friend]]

(9) [$_S$ John's$_i$ friend [$_{VP}$ saw him$_i$]]

In (8), the first branching node above *he* (S) also dominates the intended antecedent *John's,* leading to a violation of (7). In (9), on the other hand, the first branching node above the pronoun (VP) does not dominate the intended antecedent, and the anaphoric dependency is therefore permissible.

To the extent that the configurational properties of the syntactic representation are motivated by data about blocked anaphora and other types of unacceptable structures, they will presumably not be directly accessible to language learners, who have no information about the possible ungrammaticality of utterances. It is therefore necessary to assume that the relevant configurational properties are innately specified, a conclusion endorsed by Williams (1984, 651), who asks rhetorically: "What madness, other than UG itself, could drive children to posit a VP in such a discouraging stimulus environment?" Such a conclusion is unproblematic for TG, of course, since this theory is already deeply committed to special nativism.

A rather different type of evidence appears relevant to the version of the Configurationality Claim adopted in Montague Grammar. As Dowty (1982) notes, we can obtain a reasonable characterization of the truth conditions of a sentence such as *Harry likes baseball* if we assume that there is a phrase *plays baseball* denoting "the set of things that play baseball." The sentence would then be true if and only if Harry belongs to that set. While this would seem to provide a simple and accessible semantic motivation for the existence of VPs, such is not the case. This is because children could just as easily account for the truth conditions of the sentence under consideration by assuming that the subject and verb form a phrase denoting the set of things that Harry plays. The sentence would then be true if and only if baseball belongs to that set. From the child's perspective, then, there would be nothing in the sentence's truth conditions to support one structural configuration over the other.

A more promising semantic motivation for the Configurationality and Asymmetry claims is proposed by Marantz (1984). Working with sentences that have not undergone relation-changing rules (such as passivization), Marantz notes that subject NPs appear to receive their thematic role from the entire VP rather than just the verb, the element that assigns a thematic role to the direct object. Consider in this regard the following sentences.

(10) a. Harry threw a baseball.
   b. Harry threw support behind the candidate.
   c. Harry threw a boxing match.
   d. Harry threw a party.
   e. Harry threw a fit.

(11) a. Sue took a book from the child.
   b. Sue took a bus to New York.
   c. Sue took a nap.
   d. Sue took an aspirin for a cold.
   e. Sue took a letter in shorthand.

Marantz claims that the thematic role of the subject in these sentences is determined by the entire VP, not just the verb (which is held constant in each group of sentences). Thus, according to Marantz, the subject in (11a) is agentive, the subject in (11b) theme, and the subject in (11c) experiencer despite the fact that the verb is the same in all cases. Significantly, there is little evidence that the thematic role of the direct object is determined by anything other than the verb itself. As the following sentences show, the thematic role of the direct object (patient) remains constant despite changes in the choice of the subject phrase.[2]

(12) a. Harry hit the boy.
   b. A ball hit the boy.
   c. The bus hit the boy.

Marantz also argues that the structure of idiomatic expressions provides support for the claim that the verb and its object combine to form a predicate. The key observation here is that, while there are many verb-object idioms (cf. [13]), subject-verb idioms seem to be nonexistent.

(13) kick the bucket
    lay an egg

take a dive
hit the skids

Even granting the correctness of Marantz's observations, questions arise as to the relevance of his data to the language acquisition problem. It seems improbable that idioms, which are inherently idiosyncratic and generally acquired late, would shape the child's understanding of GRs. The facts pertaining to thematic role assignment are more promising in this respect, but they seem incapable of triggering the Subject-Last Requirement on their own. The child might, for instance, simply take the facts exemplified in (10)–(12) to indicate that there is widespread polysemy in the verb system and that postverbal phrases serve a disambiguating function. On this view, then, the direct object *baseball* would signal one sense of *throw* in (10) (i.e., "project through the air") while the direct object *boxing match* would signal another (i.e., "lose deliberately"), and so on. In each case, the verb would assign a thematic role to the subject phrase once it was properly disambiguated by the complement NP, but it would not actually have to combine with this latter element first. There would therefore be no need for the child to conclude that there is a semantic predicate corresponding to the syntactic VP, unless there was an a priori innate requirement to this effect.

We are left, then, with the conclusion that the only relational definitions that do not presuppose innate specification of the desired structural configuration are based on the Subject-Last Requirement, a learnable component of the categorial grammar I have proposed.

The predominance of verbs with actor arguments in early child language makes it difficult to determine when children come to equate the subject relation with a particular syntactic configuration (i.e., combination with VP). In the view of many (e.g., Maratsos and Chalkley 1980), knowledge of this sort should not be attributed to children until it can be demonstrated that a purely semantic account of subjecthood is no longer feasible. This point is uncontroversially marked by the acquisition of passive constructions since these sentence types have patient subjects. So long as children's "subjects" all belong to the same thematic role class, however, it is appropriate to question (so the argument goes) whether they possess a notion of syntactic subject.

I cannot agree with this point of view. According to the proposal I have made, the configurational property associated with the subject relation (combination with VP) is independent of semantic considerations. Rather it owes its existence to the fact that sentences such as *Sue runs fast* can be formed only if the preverbal NP combines with the maximal verbal category in accordance with the Subject-Last Requirement (see the earlier discussion). According to my theory, then, exposure to these sentences—not mastery of the passive—is the crucial trigger for the development of relational notions. Two considerations support this proposal.

First, for children to acquire passive structures they must presumably be able to observe that sentences such as *The book was lost* have patient subjects. But this observation is possible only if they already have access to the notions "subject" and "patient." These conditions are met by my proposal since the notion "patient" is part of children's general conceptual inventory and the notion "subject" corresponds to a combinatorial relation discoverable on the basis of nonpassive sentences.

A second advantage of my account has to do with languages in which there is no passive construction. (According to Harris [1984], Udi is such a language.) If exposure to passive sentences provided the crucial trigger for acquisition of the subject relation, we would expect such languages to have no grammatical relations—a counterintuitive result. On my account, the subject relation is universally present thanks to the generality of the Subject-Last Requirement and is in no way linked to the existence of a passive construction.

2.3 Thematic Roles

2.3.1 Thematic Dependency

In this section, I will be concerned with the nature of the relation between an NP and the element to which it looks for its thematic role. I will be taking the position that thematic roles have no a priori or independent existence but rather are entailed by the lexical semantics of individual predicates. Thus a verb such as *hit,* for instance, has a meaning that entails the existence of a "hitter" and a "hittee," while *run* entails a "runner," and so on.

Although each predicate will determine a unique thematic role (or roles), I assume that most of these roles can be grouped into classes. For the purposes of preliminary discussion, I will posit four such classes. The first is made up of what I will call "actor" roles, which are assigned to the more active entity in a particular action or event. I intend this class to include not only volitional agents (cf. [1a]) but also the roles associated with the italicized NPs in the other sentences below. (In this I follow Foley and Van Valin [1984].)

(1) a. *The man* cut the grass.
    b. *The hammer* drove the nail into the wood.
    c. *The student* received his grades in the mail.
    d. *The dog* heard a noise.

    e. *The man* knew the answer.

    f. *The wind* destroyed the house.

The italicized NPs in these sentences all have in common the fact that their referent plays the more active role in the action or event named by the verbal predicate.

A second class of thematic roles that I will posit consists of "patient"- and "theme"-type roles. Following Jackendoff (1972), I assign this type of role to an NP whose referent undergoes movement or change.[3] The italicized NPs in the following sentences have a role belonging to the theme or patient class.

(2) a. Harry rolled *the ball* down the hill.

    b. Max sold *the book* to Sue.

    c. The magician turned *the coach* into a pumpkin.

Notice that, while the movement associated with the theme role is concrete in (2a), it is more abstract in (b) and (c), involving changes in possession and identity rather than physical position.

I will also assume that it is appropriate to distinguish a recipient role for nonactor NPs whose referents take possession of the theme. An obvious example of an NP bearing the recipient role is found in sentences such as *I gave Harry the book*. Finally, I will assume that there is a class of locative roles exemplified by the NPs occurring after the preposition in sentences such as (3).

(3) a. I saw a book on *the floor*.

    b. I left the car near *the school*.

    c. He found the cat under *the table*.

Other classes of thematic roles can be distinguished, of course, but no further contrasts are required for our present purposes. I will therefore not pursue the classification issue further here, although I do discuss it at greater length in O'Grady (1985b).

Let us now consider the nature of the relation between a lexical item and the phrases to which it assigns a thematic role. For the sake of convenience, I will refer to this relation as "thematic dependency" and will call the elements that receive their thematic role from a particular lexical item its "thematic dependents." There is an important distinction between thematic dependency and the type of dependency relation considered in the preceding chapter. The latter relation, which I will now call "combinatorial dependency," occurs where one element must combine with another because of its predicate type. While verbs often exhibit a combinatorial dependency on the elements to which they assign a thematic role (their subject and direct object), the two types of dependency must be kept distinct since many combinatorial dependencies do not even involve elements that assign a thematic role. Thus the adverb *really,* for instance, exhibits a combinatorial dependency on an adjective, although neither assigns a thematic role to the other.

A more difficult question has to do with whether we can equate an element's thematic dependents with its arguments. Recall that, according to the proposal made earlier, arguments (subjects and objects) are neither primes nor semantically defined categories. Rather they correspond to NPs partaking in certain combinatorial relations, the direct object being the phrase that combines with a V^{tr} to give a V^i and the subject being the phrase that combines with the maximal verbal category to give an S. While there are many cases in which these phrases are also thematic dependents of the verb, I will take the position that the two notions are distinct. A number of constructions provide support for this position, including the sentence in (4).

(4) The book was destroyed by Sue.

Here *Sue* has the "destroyer" role and must therefore be a thematic dependent of the verb. Yet it is obviously not a syntactic argument (subject or direct object) according to the definitions given earlier since it combines with the preposition *by* and not the verb. Moreover, since passive verbs are widely assumed to be intransitive (see below), they take only one argument—the subject phrase. This suggests that a lexical item can have thematic dependents that are not arguments and points to the need to distinguish between the two notions.

Another sentence type supporting the same conclusion is exemplified in (5).

(5) Sue gave the book to John.

In (5), *John* cannot be an argument of the verb since it combines with the preposition *to,* which creates a dependent PP (a tertiary). Nonetheless, *Joh* appears to bear a recipient-type role determined by the lexical semantics of *give.* If this is so, then the NP in question is a thematic dependent of the verb, although it is not one of its arguments in the technical sense.

A possible objection to the first part of this conclusion might be based on the common assumption (e.g., Jackendoff 1972; Marantz 1984) that the NP we are considering bears a generalized "goal" role assigned by the preposition *to* rather than a recipient role determined by the verb. According to this alternate view, then, *John* would have the same type of thematic role in (5) as the NP *his mother* in (6).

(6) The child ran to his mother.

Since *run* does not entail a goal (i.e., one can run in one place), it seems reasonable to suppose that the goal-type role associated with *his mother* comes from the preposition *to*. The question is whether the same type of role is also found in (5). A major difference between the two patterns has to do with the possibility of substitution by the "locative anaphor" *there*. While this is allowed in the second pattern, it is not permitted in the first.

(7) *Sue gave a book to John and I gave one there too.

(8) The child ran to his mother and Harry ran there too.

This suggests that a distinction must be made between the recipient role assigned by *give*-type verbs and the goal role assigned by *to*. In the former class of structures, the preposition has evidently taken on a purely syntactic function, converting an NP into a dependent category (a PP) without attributing to it a thematic role.

　　Another class of sentences exhibiting the same point is exemplified in (9).

(9) a. Sue talked to John.
　　b. Sue yelled at John.
　　c. Sue counted on John.
　　d. Sue thought about John.
　　e. Sue pleaded with John.

I will take the position that the NP *John* in (9) receives its thematic role from the verb rather than the preposition, functioning as addressee in (a), (b), and (e), as the person relied on in (c), and as the focus of Sue's thoughts in (d).[4] A variety of considerations support this conclusion. First, there are important contrasts between the NPs in (9), whose thematic roles are linked to the lexical semantics of the verb, and those in (10), which bear more obvious spatial roles.

(10) a. Sue walked to the store.
　　 b. Sue lives at the beach.
　　 c. Sue stood on the chair.
　　 d. Sue ran about the yard.
　　 e. Sue left with John.

Notice that, whereas the PPs in (10a)–(10d) can be replaced by the "pro-PP" *there,* those in (9a)–(9d) cannot.

(11) a. Sue walked *to the store* and Harry walked *there* too.
　　 b. *Sue talked *to John* and Harry talked *there* too.

(12) a. Sue lives *at the beach* and Harry lives *there* too.
　　 b. *Sue yelled *at John* and Harry yelled *there* too.

(13) a. Sue stood *on the chair* and John stood *there* too.
  b. *Sue counted *on John* and Harry counted *there* too.

(14) a. Sue ran *about the yard* and John ran *there* too.
  b. *Sue thought *about John* and Harry thought *there* too.

Similarly, whereas (10e) has a paraphrase involving *together*, (9e) does not.

(15) a. Sue and John left together.
  b. *Sue and John pleaded together.
    (* as a paraphrase of [9e])

These contrasts point to the need to distinguish between locative-type roles, which are assigned by prepositions, and theme- and addressee-type roles, which are associated with the lexical semantics of the verb despite the presence of a preposition. Since NPs bearing the latter type of role in (9) are not arguments of the verb, we are once again led to the conclusion that a verb's thematic dependents cannot be equated with its arguments.

A final group of structures that provide support for the distinction between arguments and thematic dependents is exemplified in (16) and (17).

(16) a. Harry destroyed the house.
  b. Harry's destruction of the house

(17) a. Harry fears snakes.
  b. Harry is fearful of snakes.
  c. Harry's fear of snakes

While the lexical items in each of these groups exhibit different combinatorial properties (e.g., the verbs combine directly with an NP, but the nouns do not), there are also obvious parallels that must be accounted for. This can be done in the theory I am proposing by assuming that related lexical items assign identical sets of thematic roles. Thus both *destroy* and *destruction,* for instance, would assign a "destroyer" (actor) role and a "destroyee" (theme) role. The two lexical items would differ in terms of their syntactic category—one being a verb and the other a noun. According to the theory proposed in the preceding chapter, only verbs exhibit combinatorial dependencies on NPs. Thus whereas the verb *destroy* can occur in syntactic representations such as (18), where it has two arguments, the noun *destruction* cannot. Rather as an instance of the independent category the noun *destruction* can combine only with phrases that depend on it— genitives and PPs, including those formed with the help of semantically "empty" prepositions such as *of*. (Compare (19) and (20).)

(18)

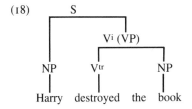

(19) *Harry destruction the book
(20) Harry's destruction of the book.

A similar set of contrasts underlies the distinction between nominal and verbal forms of *fear*. The adjective *fearful*, onthe other hand, represents an intermediate case since it depends on a single nominal (the element realized in [17b] as subject). The other phrase to which it assigns a thematic role can therefore not be encoded as a primary if it is to combine with the adjective. As (21) shows, the semantically "empty" preposition *of* is used to create a dependent phrase that can combine with *fearful* to create a larger adjectival expression.

(21)

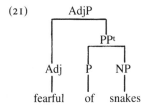

Summarizing, then, I attribute the similarity involving *destruction* and *destroy* on the one hand and *fear* and *fearful* on the other to the fact that they assign identical thematic roles. The difference between the lexical items stems from the fact that they belong to different syntactic categories and therefore exhibit correspondingly different combinatorial properties.

2.3.2 The Learnability Problem

The major thrust of the preceding discussion has been that it is necessary to posit a dependency relation in addition to the one defined in the previous chapter. In particular, it seems necessary to identify a relation in which an NP looks to another element for the determination of its thematic role. I have called this a thematic dependency, distinguishing it from the dependency relation discussed in chapter 1 wherein one element expresses a function that requires it to combine with another category (a combinatorial dependency).

The preceding discussion suggests that the two types of dependency relation are complementary rather than overlapping. Thus whereas a verb expresses the type of function that creates a combinatorial dependency on one or more NP arguments, these latter entities look to the verb for the assignment of their thematic roles. However, it would be wrong to think that the two types of dependency are somehow mirror images of each other. Recall, for example, that while all prepositions exhibit a combinatorial dependency on an NP, only some NPs receive their thematic role from the preposition with which they combine, as we have seen. Moreover, manner adverbials (e.g., *quickly* in [1]) exhibit a combinatorial dependency on a verbal element without either category receiving a thematic role from the other.

(1) Harry reads quickly.

Turning now to the learnability problem, it seem appropriate to assume, with Jackendoff (1977), that thematic contrasts relevant to my proposal are part of the child's general (nonlinguistic) knowledge. Since the dependency relation once again involves one element looking to another to meet a requirement (here the expression of a thematic role), it should also be part of the child's general conceptual inventory (see the discussion in chap. 1). The major challenge for the language learner will involve identifying the elements that assign thematic roles to particular NPs. Although I cannot undertake an exhaustive discussion of this matter here, this advance will presumably take place as children match the thematic roles borne by NPs with the semantics of individual lexical items. Thus if a sentence such as (2) were used in a context in which it was clear that the tree was the thing that was destroyed, assignment of the patient role would be linked to the verb *destroy*.

(2) Harry destroyed the tree.

Similarly, exposure to a sentence such as (3) in contexts in which it is clear that *the table* names a location will establish a link between this thematic role and the element designating a locative relation—the preposition *on*.

(3) Harry sat on the table.

A crucial step in the development of thematic roles will involve discovering that certain prepositions (e.g., *on, to,* and *of*) sometimes do not assign a thematic role to the NP with which they combine. In (4), for example, the italicized NPs have thematic roles associated with the semantics of a preceding verb or noun, not the type of spatial roles often associated with the preposition with which they combine.

(4) a. Harry was counting on *Sue.*
    b. I gave a book to *Sue.*
    c. The destruction of *the library.*

The crucial observation here will be that the particular thematic roles associated with the NPs in (4) co-occur with the verbs and nouns rather than the prepositions. Thus the recipient role in (4b), for instance, does not occur in sentences such as *He ran to the door* even though the preposition *to* is present. However, the recipient role is found in other sentences containing *give,* including those without the preposition (e.g., *I gave Sue the book*).

It would be interesting to know whether children find it easier to identify the thematic role assigner when it corresponds to the element that combines with the NP (e.g., the verb in [2] and the preposition in [3]). My suspicion is that this is so and that children will find it easier to use and understand prepositions designating a concrete spatial relation than those serving the purely syntactic function of converting an NP into a dependent category. If this is right, children can be expected to employ the type of VP exemplified in (2) and (3) before the phrases found in (4). Frequency of occurrence constitutes an unfortunate confounding factor in some of these cases, however. Since patterns such as *I thought about it* are likely to be more frequent in maternal speech than *I considered it,* the lexical item *think (about)* may well be mastered first. However, I think that it is still possible to predict that the first VPs in child language will not be of the *think about* type. It also seems reasonable to expect that nominal structures such as *the destruction of the city* (in which the NP *the city* receives its thematic role from the noun rather than the preposition) will emerge after the corresponding verbal construction *destroy the city,* in which the NP is assigned its thematic role by the verb with which it combines.

2.4 The Lexicon

2.4.1 Types of Lexical Information

The next major issue that we must consider involves the type of information about individual lexical items that should be represented in the lexicon. Word-based information is crucial to the operation of combinatorial rules in a categorial grammar since the dependency properties of individual words determine both their distribution and the categorial status of the phrases in which they occur (cf. the Phrasal Category Principle in chap. 1). I will assume that three types of information can be represented in the lexicon.

A. Information about the number and type of elements on which a word depends.

B. Information about the thematic roles that a word can assign.

C. Information about the number and type of any obligatory modifiers.

As a preliminary illustration of these three types of information, let us consider the lexical entries for the verbs *run* and *criticize*.

(1) a. *run* (V): NP_a
    b. *criticize* (V): NP_a NP_t

In (1), the contrast in the dependency requirements of intransitive *run* and transitive *criticize* is expressed by listing the NPs on which the verb depends. Subscripts are used to classify a verb's arguments in terms of the type of thematic roles it receives, with "a" indicating the actor class and "t" the theme class. In cases in which a lexical item's thematic dependents are not arguments, I will enclose them in curly braces. The verb *give*, for instance, would have the lexical entry in (2) to account for its use in structures such as *John gave the book to Sue*, in which the NP bearing the recipient role is a nonargument ("r" = recipient).

(2) *give* (V): NP_a NP_t {to NP_r}

Since nouns do not depend on other elements (i.e., do not have syntactic arguments), their thematic dependents will always be nonarguments. The lexical entry for a noun such as *criticism* would therefore resemble (3), setting aside "double PP structures."

(3) *criticism* (N): {NP_a's}   {of NP_t}

In a number of central cases, this system of lexical representation together with the combinatorial principles discussed in chapter 1 will ensure that each NP receives one and only one thematic role (an intuition that is captured by a special principle, the Theta Criterion, in TG). In the case of an intransitive verb such as *run*, for instance, the lexical entry stipulates that the NP on which it depends bears a particular thematic role (i.e., actor; see [1a] above). Since no more than one NP can combine with *run* (by the Dependency Requirement of sec. 1.3.2), there is no danger of the sentence containing an NP with no thematic role. The same result is ensured in the case of transitive verbs (e.g., *criticize* om [1b]), except that two NPs rather than one are permitted. Matters are also straightforward in the case of prepositions that assign a thematic role (e.g., *near*). Since prepositions can combine with one and only one NP, there will be one phrase of this type per preposition, and that phrase will have a thematic role (e.g., locative).

The major problem for this proposal comes from prepositions such as *of* as well as some instances of *to, on, about,* and *by,* which do not assign a thematic role to the NP with which they combine. Here we must find a way to ensure that the NPs in question receive a thematic role from the element with which the PP combines (a verb, a noun, or an adjective). This will presumably involve matching such PPs with the corresponding element in the lexical entry of the category with which it combines (e.g., the *to* phrase in the lexical entry for *give* in [2] above). Although there are various ways to implement this, I will not attempt to resolve this matter here.

In addition to information about a lexical item's syntactic arguments and thematic dependents, the lexicon will presumably also have to include information about categories of a different sort. A good example of this involves the verb *put,* which not only requires a direct object NP but also a locative adverbial phrase.

(4) a. *Harry put.
    b. *Harry put the book.
    c. Harry put the book on the table.

Let us assume that *put* has a lexical entry resembling (5), in which curly braces are again used to indicate a nonargument phrase.

(5) *put* (V): NP_a NP_t {PP}

According to (5), *put* is a transitive verb dependent on two NPs and requiring a locative PP modifier (a type of tertiary). In this, it would be distinct from a verb such as *drop,* which takes an optional locative phrase and would therefore have a lexical entry resembling (6).

(6) *drop*(V): NP_a NP_t ({PP})

An alternate characterization of the facts exemplified in (4) would involve the assumption that *put* belongs to a special category of verbs that depends on a PP in addition to two NPs. In other words, we would think of *put* as a function from two NPs and a PP to an S. An unfortunate consequence of this proposal is that it substantially undermines the system of categorial distinctions outlined in chapter 1. Thus the verb *put* could no longer count as a secondary since this category type is characterized by a dependency on nominal primaries and PPs are obviously not nominals. Moreover, since the PP required by *put* would satisfy a verbal dependency on the alternate analysis we are considering, it would differ from other PPs with exactly the same composition in not being a tertiary since members of this category depend on (rather than support) verbal secondaries. Since such innovations would seriously weaken the use of dependency contrasts to define natural classes broad enough to include all verbs or all adverbials, I will reject them, at least for the present.

Summarizing, then, I take a word's lexical entry to provide a record of its combinatorial properties and, where appropriate, the thematic roles that it assigns. As noted earlier, both types of information are manifested in sentences in ways that should make them accessible to the language learner (see the discussion of the ontogeny of syntactic categories in chap. 1 and of thematic dependency in this chap.). While there are many issues relating to the structure and development of the lexicon that I am unable to deal with here, the proposals that I have made seem promising enough to warrant consideration of some additional lexical phenomena and their relation to sentence formation, a matter to which I now turn.

2.4.2 Mapping

An adequate theory of the relation between a verb's dependency requirements, as expressed in a lexical entry such as (1), and syntactic structure will obviously have to ensure that the actor argument (a-argument) is expressed as subject.

(1) *criticize* (V): NP_a NP_t

If the verb *criticize* has the a-argument *Bakunin* and the theme argument (t-argument) *government*, the corresponding sentence must be *Bakunin criticized government*, not *Government criticized Bakunin*. Let us attempt to capture this fact by means of the following device.

(2) *The Mapping Filter:*
NP_t
NP_a

The Mapping Filter provides a representation of the "combinatorial order" to be employed when there is more than one argument phrase. Reading from the top down, (2) stipulates that a theme argument is encoded as first argument (direct object) and an actor argument as last argument (subject).

It seems reasonable to suppose that the Mapping Filter is a product of generalization by language learners. The crucial triggering stimulus will come from sentences such as *The boy threw the ball,* in which a verb occurs with two arguments, one bearing the a-role and the other the t-role. Since the agentive argument has the positional and morphological properties associated with the last argument position in English, this is a clear instantiation of the correspondence stipulated in the Mapping Filter and provides the experience needed to form the relevant generalization.

In order for these generalizations to be formed, of course, children must have access to the notions subject (last argument) and direct object (first argument) as well as a rudimentary set of thematic roles (these being the concepts in terms of which the Mapping Filter is stated). This should not be problematic. As noted earlier, it seems reasonable to assume, with Jackendoff (1977), that thematic role distinctions are the product of conceptual development. Moreover, since the GRs of subject and direct object are defined with reference to the combinatorial relations imposed by the Subject-Last Requirement, they should be available to the child as soon as the latter mechanism is mastered. Since, as I noted earlier, the triggering stimulus for the SLR comes from NP V Adv strings such as *John runs fast,* the required advance should take place at a relatively early point. The learnability conditions outlined in chapter 1 are thus met in the case of the Mapping Filter: children have access to the concepts in terms of which this device is formulated, and they are exposed to the types of experience (sentences such as *Harry threw the ball*) that support formation of the desired generalization.

Results from a number of studies support the view that the Mapping Filter is in fact acquired at an early point in the language acquisition process. It is well known, for instance, that the first NPs to be encoded as subject in children's speech are agentive in character (i.e., a-arguments) (for discussion, see Pinker [1984]). Experimental results compatible with this finding have been reported by Marantz (1982), who attempted to teach English-speaking children aged three to five to use novel verbs to describe various events. While some of the novel verbal forms followed the usual pattern for English (as specified by the Mapping Filter), others did not. Thus some of the novel verbs were used in sentences such as *The book is puming Larry,* meaning "Larry is lifting a book up and down on his knee"—an interpretation that seems to require taking the subject to be a theme and the direct object an actor (contrary to the Mapping Filter). Marantz found that the three- and four-year-olds had significantly more difficulty learning this type of verb, a fact that points to the early acquisition of the Mapping Filter.[5]

2.4.3 Precombinatorial Rules

To this point, we have considered only one type of grammatical rule—the operations that combine elements to form syntactic representations with a certain internal organization and category composition. However, there is reason to believe that a second type of grammatical rule operates prior to combinatorial rules and has the effect of changing a lexical item's dependency requirements. (I will call this a "lexical rule.") In principle two types of lexical changes should be possible: a dependency could be added, or a dependency could be canceled. One of the most widely studied changes of the latter type involves passivization, a process that allows a normally transitive verb such as *criticize* to appear in a structure such as (1), where it has only one argument.

(1) Government was criticized by Bakunin.

In (1) only the NP bearing the t-role functions as argument since only it combines with a verbal category (the VP). The other NP receiving its thematic role from the verb (the agentive phrase *Bakunin*) combines with the preposition and is therefore not an argument according to our earlier definition.

In the most straightforward cases,[6] passivization can be described as a precombinatorial (lexical) rule that cancels the verb's dependency on its a-argument. This is stated in (2).

(2) *Passivization:*
     Drop the a-argument.

Passivization will apply to a verb with the dependency requirements listed in (3) to yield those listed in (4).

(3) V: NP_a NP_t

(4) V: NP_t ({by NP_a})

The major difference between (3) and (4) is that the thematic dependent of the verb bearing the actor role no longer has the status of an argument. Rather, following Passivization, the verb depends on a single NP (the theme argument). Since no change is made to the verb's lexical meaning, it still implies an actor role. However, the NP bearing this role is now realized as an adjunct (nonargument). As illustrated in (5), the connective *by* is used to convert this NP into a tertiary.

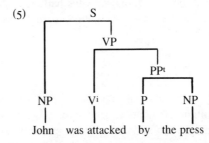

(5)

Perlmutter and Postal (1977) have proposed that passive structures universally exhibit the following two properties.

(6) a. The subject of the passive sentence is the direct object in the corresponding active sentence.

b. The subject of the active sentence is neither subject nor direct object in the corresponding passive sentence.

According to the account of Passivization that I have proposed, both these properties follow automatically from the nature of syntactic categories and the subject relation. Consider first property (a).

Property (a) follows from the fact that dropping the a-argument leaves only one NP on which the verb depends (the t-argument). Since clauses are formed by combining a verbal category (VP) with an NP on which it depends, and since there is now only one such NP, it follows that the t-argument will be encoded as subject. Property (b) also follows from the change to the verb's dependency properties brought about by Passivization. Since a passivized verb depends only on the t-argument, all other phrases that combine with it will have to be adjuncts—elements that combine with an intransitive verb to give another category of the same type. According to the theory of combinatorial relations developed in chapter 1, these other NPs must be tertiaries—phrases (like the English *by* phrase) that exhibit a combinatorial dependency on a verbal category.

A major difference between my proposal and other approaches to passivization is that I do not take the grammatical subject of the passive construction to be direct object at any "underlying" or "initial" level of representation. Since grammatical relations are defined in terms of combinatorial relations, it makes no sense to talk about subjects or direct objects in the lexical entry—the representation to which Passivization applies. The Passivization rule brings about a simple change in the verb's dependency requirements, dropping its a-argument. This in turn has consequences for the structure of a sentence in which the verb occurs since the Mapping Filter allows a t-argument to be encoded last (i.e., as subject) only in the absence of an a-argument.

There are of course many other facts about Passivization that a theory of grammar must be able to explain. In Dutch, for example, intransitive verbs can have impersonal passives of the form illustrated in (7).

(7) Er wordt hier door de jonge lui veel gedanst.
   It is here by the young people a lot danced
   "It is danced here a lot by the young people."

Such sentences are presumably formed by applying the rule "Drop the a-argument" to an intransitive verb with a lexical entry such as (12).

(8) V: NP_a

Because Passivization eliminates the only argument NP, it is necessary to insert the dummy phrase *er* to provide a category with which the VP can combine to form an S.

By using the same Passivization rule ("Drop the a-argument") for intransitive and transitive verbs, we correctly predict that there will be no impersonal passive where the intransitive verb expresses a process rather than an action and therefore has a t-argument rather than an a-argument. (Such verbs are called "unaccusatives" in Relational Grammar; see Perlmutter and Postal [1984]).

(9) *Er werd door vele kinderen in de rook gestikt.
    it was by many children in the smoke suffocated
    "It was suffocated by many children in the smoke."

We also predict that even transitive verbs that do not have a-arguments will have no passive forms. The ungrammaticality of the following sentences from Perlmutter and Postal (1984) suggests that this prediction is correct.

(10) *That book will be bought by five dollars.
    (cf.: Five dollars will buy that book.)

(11) *The end of World War II was seen by 1945.
    (cf.: 1945 saw the end of World War II.)

There are obviously many other facts about passivization that could be considered here. However, I will not attempt a more thorough discussion of these phenomena at this point, although I do undertake such a project in a monograph currently nearing completion. I will conclude my discussion of passivization by considering some aspects of the learnability problem.

The Passivization rule I have proposed is presumably learned following exposure to sentences such as (12) in a context in which the intended meaning is clear.

(12) John was attacked.

In (12), a verb that is elsewhere dependent on two NPs and takes its a-argument as subject (by the Mapping Filter) combines only with a subject-marked t-argument. This points to the conclusion that the verb's dependency on its a-argument has been canceled, resulting in the creation of an intransitive verb that depends on a single NP—the t-argument. At this point, the child presumably concludes that *be attacked* has the lexical entry in (13).

(13) *be attacked* (V): NP_t

The status of the NP in the *by* phrase would then be determined on the basis of sentences such as *John was attacked by the press* (cf. [5] above). Here the NP in the *by* phrase receives its thematic role from the verb (i.e., is interpreted as the one who attacks) but cannot be a syntactic argument since it combines with *by* and since sentences such as (12) establish that the verb is intransitive. This should lead to an adjustment in (13), to yield a lexical entry in which there is an optional nonargument agent.

(14) *be attacked* (V): NP_t ({by NP_a})

Because this analysis of the NP in the *by* phrase is partially contingent on the prior realization that the passivized verb is intransitive (as shown by [12]), we predict that children will acquire agentless passives before the agentive passive exemplified by (5). This is correct (Hayhurst 1967).

A particularly subtle contrast that children must master in the course of acquiring passive structures is exemplified in (15).

(15) a. The ship was sunk (by the enemy).
     b. The ship sank (*by the enemy).

Notice that, unlike the passive, the intransitive verb in (15b) cannot occur with a nonargument bearing the a-role. This suggests that it has a lexical entry resembling (16).

(16) *sink* (V): NP_t

This lexical entry is just like that for the passive in the first stage of development (see [13] above), but differs from the mature version in not including an actor dependent.

(17) *be sunk* (V): NP_t ({by NP_a})

The two types of lexical entry will be differentiated at the point at which children take note of sentences in which the passive occurs with an agentive nonargument governed by the preposition *by*. Since no such structures containing the nonpassive intransitive occur, there is no reason to think that children will revise the type of lexical entry associated with *sink* (i.e., [16] above).[7] (I return to the assumptions underlying this claim in chap. 3.)

2.5 The Indirect Object Relation

Thus far I have been working under the assumption that there are only two types of syntactic arguments—subject and direct object. However, at least some languages (including English) allow structures such as (1) in which a third NP seems to combine with a verbal category.

(1) Harry sent Sue the book.

Structures like this are to be distinguished from (2), in which the third NP receiving its thematic role from the verb combines with a preposition to form a PP (a tertiary) and therefore does not count as an argument of the verb according to our earlier assumptions.

(2) Harry sent the book to Sue.

In (1) it is common to identify *Sue* as "indirect object" in recognition of the fact that this type of argument is found only when there is also a direct object. Thus sentence (3), with just one postverbal NP, has only an interpretation in which *Sue* is taken to be direct object (the one who is sent).

(3) Harry sent Sue.

In the light of these facts, let us assume that *send* has the lexical entry in (4) (ignoring the possible optionality of the PP).

(4) *send* (V): NP_a NP_t NP_r
         (V): NP_a NP_t {to NP_r}

According to (4), *send* can assign three thematic roles, one of which (the recipient role) can be associated with either an argument (as in [1]) or a nonargument PP (as in [2]). A comparable lexical entry will be used for verbs such as *buy*, which can occur with a benefactive NP (NP_b) realized as either an argument (as in [5a]) or an adjunct (as in [5b]).

(5a) John bought Sue a book.
(5b) John bought a book for Sue.

(6) *buy* (V): NP_a NP_t NP_b
        (V): NP_a NP_t {for NP_b}

Given that we have already defined the direct object as first argument and the subject as last argument, there would seem to be only one definition available for indirect objects, namely (7).

(7) Indirect objects are middle arguments.

In cases in which the NP bearing the recipient role is realized as an argument, the expanded Mapping Filter in (8) will take effect.

(8) *The Mapping Filter (expanded):*
     NP_t
     $NP_{r,b}$
     NP_a

According to (8), sentences such as (1) will be assigned the structure in (9).

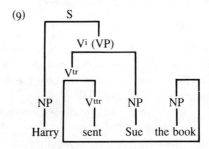

In (9) the verb combines first with the t-argument (its direct object), then with the r-argument (the indirect object), and finally with the a-argument (the subject). (I use the label "V^{ttr}" for verbs that depend on three NPs.)

The existence of structures such as (9) will obviously require revisions to the Adjacency Principle to account for the fact that the verb *send* combines with a nonadjacent element (*the book*). However, this is not necessarily undesirable since I will argue on other grounds in the next chapter that the AP is too strong in its current form and should be weakened. Moreover, the positing of a discontinuous structure for the "double object" construction may help explain why this sentence type is acquired later than the prepositional construction exemplified by (2) above (Roeper et al. 1981). It would not be implausible to think that this discontinuous constituent causes processing difficulties (of the sort suggested by Slobin [1972] and Kuno [1973]) that might hinder the acquisition of this type of structure.

Another advantage of characterizing indirect objects as middle arguments is that we can automatically account for the fact, noted above, that these elements can only occur when there is also a direct object (first argument). Thus the sentences in (10) are ungrammatical on interpretations in which *Sue* is taken to be a recipient or benefactive—roles associated with the indirect object relation.

(10) a. They sent Sue.
     b. They bought Sue.

The status of indirect objects as middle arguments is also crucial for understanding the following well-known contrast.

(11) a. John sent Sue the book.
     b. Sue was sent the book.
     c. *The book was sent Sue.

According to the proposal made above, "passivization" consists of a precombinatorial operation that drops the verb's a-argument. In the case of simple transitive verbs, the only remaining argument (the t-argument) is encoded as subject. In the case of (11), however, dropping the a-argument would leave two arguments (the NPs bearing the t- and r-roles). Since the r-argument is the latter one in the Mapping Filter (repeated here), it must be encoded as subject.

(8) *The Mapping Filter (expanded):*
    NP_t
    $NP_{r,b}$
    NP_a

This is what happens in (11b). In the ungrammatical (11c), on the other hand, the NP bearing the t-role is encoded as subject in violation of the combinatorial order stipulated in the Mapping Filter. Of course, in cases in which the NP bearing the r-role is nonargument (because it combines with the preposition *to* rather than the verb), the theme NP is the only argument phrase remaining after Passivization and therefore can (indeed must) be realized as subject.

(12) a. The book was sent to John.
        NP_t NP_r
     b. *John was sent the book to.
        NP_r NP_t

Still another piece of evidence in favor of the configuration depicted in (9) comes from idioms and parallels one of Marantz's arguments for a VP constituent. In particular, it seems that there are cases in which the verb and its direct object form an idiomatic expression of which the indirect object is not a part. This is exemplified in (13).

(13) Sue showed John the door.

Sentence (13) can have the meaning "Sue expelled John from the room," an interpretation in which the verb and its direct object make up an idiomatic expression corresponding to the discontinuous syntactic phrase I have posited.

This leaves us with the problem of deciding precisely how we should capture the relation between the two sets of dependency requirements associated with verbs such as *send,* restated here as (14).

(14) *send* (V): NP_a NP_t NP_r
           (V): NP_a NP_t {to NP_r}

One possibility is that we simply assume that lexical items are assigned dual sets of dependency requirements on a case-by-case basis. Thus *send,* but not *transmit,* will have the type of dual entry illustrated in (14). This would account for the inadmissibility of the double object construction in cases such as (15b).

(15) a. John transmitted the message to Mary.
     b. *John transmitted Mary the message.

Alternately, we might assume that there is a lexical rule of the sort outlined in (16).

(16) *Ditransitivization:*
     Add an r- or b-argument.

The precombinatorial rule in (16) will apply to certain transitive verbs to create a dependency on an NP bearing a recipient or benefactive role. Since transitive verbs already have a first and last argument, the new NP will have to function as middle argument—in accordance with the expanded Mapping Filter, restated as (17).

(17) *The Mapping Filter (expanded):*
$$NP_t$$
$$NP_{r,b}$$
$$NP_a$$

At least two considerations favor the lexical rule over other approaches. First, as Pinker (1984) and others have noted, there seems to be some productivity in the formation of new ditransitive verbs, as the forms in (18) illustrate.

(18) a. Could you xerox me this article?
    b. I'll telex you the answer.

Second, as Mazurkewich and White (1984) and others have observed, children appear to make errors in the formation of ditransitive verbs—a fact that suggests that they are applying a rule such as the one I have proposed. Some of these errors involving benefactives (compiled in Pinker [1984, 312]) are given in (19).

(19) a. Mummy, open Hadwen the door.
    b. I'll brush him his hair.
    c. How come you're putting me that type of juice?

Apparent overgeneralizations of this sort not only point to the existence of a lexical rule but also raise important questions about how children ultimately come to restrict its application in the appropriate ways. This matter is discussed at considerable length by Pinker (1984), and I have nothing to add to his proposals at this time. I will therefore follow him in assuming that children ultimately note that ditransitive verbs have certain phonological and semantic properties (in particular, their r-argument must correspond to the "prospective possessor" of the theme). Having arrived at this generalization, they then restrict ditransitivization in the required ways and expunge any lexical entries that are inconsistent with the new rule.

Much more could be said about the properties of Ditransitivization in English and other languages. For one thing, there is good reason to think that many languages make no provision for verbs that depend on three separate NPs. In Korean, for instance, the NP that corresponds to the English indirect object is marked by the postposition *-eykey*.

(20) Nay-ka John-eykey chayk-ul poyecwu-ess-ta.
     I-N   John-Dat   book-Ac showed
     "I showed John the book."

Significantly, however, NPs bearing exactly the same marker are found in constructions in which there is not even a transitive verb.

(21) Nay-ka John-eykey malha-yess-ta.
     I-Nom   John-Dat   talked
     "I talked to John."

(22) John-i Bob-eykey piphan-tangha-yess-ta.
     John-Nom Bob-Dat criticize Passive
     "John was criticized by Bob."

Recall that, according to our earlier proposal, the passive verb in (22) should depend only on a t-argument. The dative marked NP in (22) can therefore not count as an argument even though it will continue to receive its thematic role from the verb, just like its English counterpart (see the earlier discussion).

A unified characterization of -eykey NPs could therefore obviously not treat them as middle arguments of verbs. A more promising hypothesis would be that there is no indirect object argument in Korean and that -eykey consistently marks a nonargument thematic dependent of the verb. Hence the dative marked NP in (20–22) would receive its thematic role ("recipient" in [20], "addressee" in [21], and "actor" in [22]) from the verb but would count as a tertiary (nonargument), as illustrated in (23).

(23)

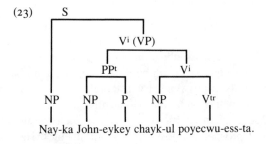

Nay-ka John-eykey chayk-ul poyecwu-ess-ta.

2.6 Concluding Remarks

This chapter has been primarily concerned with the nature of grammatical relations and lexical entries. I have suggested that the lexicon represents information about the syntactic arguments, modifiers, and thematic dependents associated with individual lexical items. Subject to changes in the verb's dependency requirements by a precombinatorial operation such as Passivization, these phrases are then encoded in the syntactic representation in accordance with the Mapping Filter and the usual combinatorial and categorial mechanisms, including the Subject-Last Requirement.

Just as it is necessary to specify the nature of the mapping relation between the categories listed in the verb's lexical entry and the syntactic representations in which they occur, so it is necessary to specify the relation between syntactic structure and the compositional semantics. As noted earlier, proponents of categorial grammar commonly assume that the syntactic structure is a projection of the compositional semantics, with syntactic phrases matched in a one-to-one fashion with semantic entities.[8] Hence a typical SVO structure would derive its configurational properties from a semantic representation in which there is a predicate isomorphic with the verb and its object. Similarly in a phrase such as *very old men* there would be a predicate in the compositional semantics corresponding to the syntactic AdjP *very old*.

I have no argument with the view that children posit a relation (perhaps approaching isomorphism) between syntactic structure and the compositional semantics. What I would question, however, is the direction of the projection relation. While there seems to be nothing in children's experience that would allow them to discover directly the configurational properties of the semantic representation, we have already seen that the phrasal structure of the syntactic representation is specified by learnable devices— the Adjacency Principle constrained by the Hierarchical Structuring Requirement and the Subject-Last Requirement. It might therefore be fruitful to consider the possibility that the mapping relation between the syntactic and semantic representations resembles (1).

(1) *The Syntactic Projection Principle:*
    The compositional semantics is a "projection" of the syntactic structure.

According to (1), language learners will posit semantic entities to match the syntactic phrases that result from their discovery of the HSR and the SLR. The obvious advantage of this is that it not only posits a projection relation between syntactic structure and the semantic representation but also exploits learnable syntactic devices to account for the organization of both these levels. This in turn allows a further minimization of the innate contribution to the parts of the language faculty concerned with the representation of meaning.

There are many other problems and possibilities worth considering here. Recent work on lexical rules (Wasow 1977; Bresnan 1982; Selkirk 1982; and others) has uncovered a broad range of precombinatorial phenomena that will ultimately have to be subsumed into any adequate theory of language and learning. (A categorial approach to some of these phenomena is outlined in Lieber [1983].) However, since my main concern in this book is with the combinatorial operations responsible for sentence formation, I will not attempt to add to these proposals here. In a manuscript currently nearing completion, I extend my analysis of relational phenomena to include not only passivization and ditransitivization in a broad range of languages but also unaccusative and unergative intransitive verbs, ergativity, causativization, possessor ascension, raising, and impersonal constructions.

3

EXTRACTION FROM PHRASES

3.1 Introduction

The preceding two chapters have been primarily concerned with the categories and relations making up syntactic representations. I return now to the problem of how these syntactic representations are formed, concentrating on structures in which a *wh* word has been "extracted" from the phrase to which it belongs and placed at the beginning of the sentence. Within transformational grammar (TG) the formation of these sentences involves the operation of movement rules constrained by general principles such as the Subjacency Condition. Because these constraints are assumed to form part of Universal Grammar, their study is directly relevant to the question of whether the human language faculty must include innate syntactic principles.

The main objective of this chapter will be to show that the phenomena used to justify constraints on movement rules within TG can be characterized by principles that do not support the thesis of special nativism. Because space does not permit an exhaustive examination of extraction, I will concentrate my remarks in this chapter on the formation of monoclausal *wh* questions in English and other languages. I will discuss multiclausal structures in chapter 4. In both chapters I will focus my attention on the range of facts for which the Subjacency Condition of transformational grammar was originally formulated. I will therefore deliberately ignore phenomena involving the formation of questions containing two or more *wh* phrases, parasitic gaps (e.g., Chomsky 1982), and other patterns not directly relevant to subjacency-type effects.

3.2 Extraction in TG

Within transformational grammar, the formation of *wh* structures involves the movement of a phrase from a sentence-internal location into COMP (the position immediately dominated by S'). The relevant rule is often stated as (1).

(1) *Wh Movement:*
    Move *wh* into COMP.

Wh movement will convert a structure resembling (2a) into (2b). (Recall that *t* [trace] marks the position from which an element is moved.)

(2) a. [$_{S'}$ [$_S$ did Mary see who]]
    b. [$_{S'}$ Who [$_S$ did Mary see *t*]]

As noted in chapter 1, *wh* movement is constrained by the Subjacency Condition (SC), restated here as (3).

(3) *The Subjacency Condition:*
    A rule cannot move a phrase from position *y* to position *x*
    . . .*x* . . .[$_\alpha$ . . .[$_\beta$ . . .*y* . . .] . . .] . . .*x* . . .
    where α and β are bounding nodes (NP or S).

The SC correctly blocks movement in structures such as (4), where the *wh* phrase would have to be extracted from both NP and S.

(4) *[$_{S'}$ Who [$_S$ did John destroy [$_{NP}$ a book about *t*]]]

The adequacy of the SC is challenged by the existence of grammatical sentences such as (5) and (6) in which the *wh* word has apparently been extracted from a phrase dominated by both NP and S.

(5) [$_{S'}$ Who [$_S$ did you read [$_{NP}$ a book about *t*]]]

(6) [$_{S'}$ Who [$_S$ did you see [$_{NP}$ a picture of *t*]]]

In recent work (e.g., Chomsky 1981), an attempt has been made to subsume the contrast between (4) and (5)–(6) under the Empty Category Principle (ECP), an innate component of Universal Grammar stated in (7).

(7) *The Empty Category Principle:*
    An empty category (trace) must be properly governed.

Simplifying slightly, we can say that a trace is governed if there is a lexical category "L" (i.e., a verb, a preposition, a noun, or a tense marker) that meets the following two conditions.

A. L c-commands the trace. (We can assume that A c-commands B if the first branching node above A dominates B.)

B. The trace is not dominated by any maximal phrasal category (e.g., S', NP, etc.) that does not also dominate L.

According to the version of TG I will consider here, proper government is a special type of government in which L is a verb. (This is one of the ideas considered by Chomsky [1981].)

As (8) shows, the trace in an ungrammatical sentence such as (4) is not properly governed.

(8)

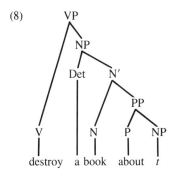

In (8), the trace is governed by the preposition but not by the verb since there are two phrasal categories (the larger NP and PP) dominating the trace that do not dominate the verb.

This brings us to the problem of sentences such as (5) above, which would appear to have the structure in (8) even though they are perfectly acceptable. Following earlier work by Hornstein and Weinberg (1981), Chomsky (1981) suggests that an ECP violation is avoided in this case by "reanalyzing" the V . . . P sequence to form the complex verb *read a book about* marked as V* in (9).

(9)

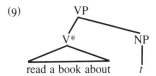

In (9), the complex verb properly governs the trace, avoiding a violation of the Empty Category Principle.

Questions of descriptive adequacy aside, the proposed analysis provides an excellent illustration of why transformational grammar has come to rely so heavily on special nativism. Since it is unlikely that anything in children's experience would lead them to formulate a principle in terms of proper government, and since this notion apparently has no counterpart outside of language, it is natural to conclude that the ECP—if correct—is innate. It remains to be seen whether an analysis of comparable empirical promise can be formulated without recourse to inborn linguistic notions and principles.

3.3 Wh Questions in Categorial Grammar

In the remainder of this chapter, I will be concerned with an approach to the description and acquisition of *wh* questions in terms of the categorial

grammar outlined in the preceding chapters. The first step is to determine
the structure that should be assigned to basic *wh* questions such as (1).

(1) Who did John see?

Assuming the correctness of the Subject-Last Requirement (SLR), restated
here as (2), this sentence will have to be assigned the structure depicted in
(3). (I assume that the auxiliary verb forms a discontinuous constituent
with the VP. However, in order to simplify the syntactic representation, I
will not attempt to indicate this.)

(2) *The Subject-Last Requirement:*
    The subject combines with VP.

(3)

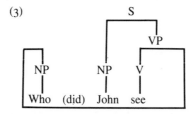

In (3), the direct object *who* combines with the nonadjacent verb *see* to
create a VP that then combines with the subject NP *John*.[1]

  Although (3) contains a discontinuous constituent and is formed in violation of the Adjacency Principle (since *who* and *see* are not adjacent), the
existence of sentences like (4) and (5) suggests that such configurations
must be permitted.

(4) Where did John put the book?

(5) When did Harry arrive?

On the usual assumption that *when* and *where* are adverbial elements (i.e.,
tertiaries), (4) and (5) can be assigned a well-formed structure only if the
SLR is respected. This is illustrated in (6) and (7).

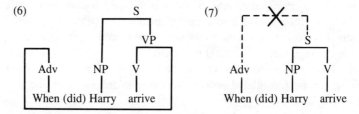

As (6) and (7) show, the adverb *when* can be incorporated into syntactic
structure only if it combines with the verb *arrive*. This results in the discontinuous VP depicted in (6).

The formation of discontinuous constituents such as the ones found in (3) and (6) ensures the independence of a word's combinatorial properties and its position in the linear string. If, for instance, a verb is transitive in the theory I have proposed, its dependency properties require it to combine with a direct object NP (a first argument). By permitting discontinuous constituents, we allow this requirement to be satisfied regardless of the word order pattern in which the verb occurs.[2] A similar intuition is captured in current versions of transformational grammar by means of the Projection Principle (Chomsky 1981), which has the effect of ensuring that a transitive verb, for example, will have a direct object NP in every structure in which it occurs. However, instead of allowing a combinatorial relation between a verb and a nonadjacent constituent, transformational grammar satisfies its Projection Principle by allowing empty categories (traces) to appear in NP positions (see [2] in the preceding section).

Only part of the motivation for discontinuous constituents comes from their role in satisfying the combinatorial requirements of individual words. As we shall see as we proceed, discontinuous constituents are also central to the account of constraints on extraction and binding that I will be proposing. Before considering these matters, however, it is first necessary to revise the statement of the combinatorial operation underlying sentence formation.

The existence of discontinuous constituents suggests that the Adjacency Principle is too strong and that it should perhaps be weakened to (8).

(8) *The Combinatorial Principle (CP):*
    Combine elements.

Although this principle appears far too weak, its adequacy is greatly enhanced by mechanisms such as the Subject-Last Requirement, which ensures that the constituents making up the VP combine with each other before the subject phrase is incorporated into syntactic structure. Moreover, if the Mapping Filter is correct, the direct object will combine with the verb before the indirect object, thereby further limiting the set of options allowed by the Combinatorial Principle. A good deal of this and the next chapter will be concerned with other independently motivated constraints on the combinatorial relations permitted by the grammar. The end result will be a system in which principles of different sorts interact to constrain the formation of syntactic representations in the desired way.

Despite the elimination of an adjacency requirement on combinatorial relations, there is little doubt that the unmarked case still involves the combination of adjacent elements. In fact, one might suppose that an adjacency requirement on dependency is automatically adopted by language learners and abandoned only on the basis of appropriate experience. Thus no child would ever assume that a sentence such as *Big animals have small brains* could mean "Small animals have big brains," with *big* depending on the nonadjacent *brains* and *small* on *animals*. Rather adjacency would be taken to be a property of adjective-noun dependencies, and NPs would be assumed to be continuous until evidence to the contrary was uncovered.

Although the particular pattern just considered does not occur in English, some languages appear not to exploit adjacency to the same degree. Frequently mentioned examples of such languages include Latin, Walpiri, and Dyirbal, from which Pullum (1982) cites the following example. (Of course, this is only one of the many word orders that could be used for this sentence.)

(9) bayi yaRangu jugumbiRu buran wangal   banggun bangul bulganu.
      Abs. man   woman   saw boomerang Erg. Gen. big
      "The woman saw the big man's boomerang."

Although it is often assumed that free word order languages are "nonconfigurational" to varying degrees and that they lack some or all of the phrasal categories found in English, various problems would arise if the Hierarchical Structuring Requirement (HSR) were suspended in these cases. For one thing, the theory of grammatical relations proposed in the preceding chapter presupposes the formation of syntactic representations that include a phrase consisting of the verb and its complement(s). Moreover, as I will note in chapter 5, constraints on anaphora seem to presuppose the existence of VP constituents even in "free word order" languages. In light of these considerations, I will therefore assume that the HSR holds even in languages with relatively free word order. In cases such as (9), this will result in the creation of a series of discontinuous constituents with concomitant increases in the complexity of the sentence.

In order to capture the obvious differences between Dyirbal on the one hand and English on the other, I will assume that the Combinatorial Principle in the latter language is interpreted with the help of the Adjacency Preference outlined in (10).

(10) *The Adjacency Preference:*
      Combine adjacent elements, where permitted.

Let us take (10) to mean that both the language learner and the language user will attempt to combine adjacent elements within the parameters laid down by the Subject-Last Requirement, the Mapping Filter, and so on. Thus with the exception of structures such as *What did John see?* where the SLR forces abandonment of the Adjacency Preference (since *see* must combine with *what*), the Combinatorial Principle will be used to amalgamate adjacent elements in the manner outlined in chapter 1.

The paradigm case of discontinuous constituents in English involves the appearance of a phrase in presubject position, as in (11)–(14).

(11) *Which man* did Bob criticize?

(12) I wonder [*which man* Bob criticized].

(13) This is the man [*who* Bob criticized].

(14) *This man,* Bob criticized.

I will assume (subject to later refinement) that phrases that are not adjacent to the element with which they combine must occur in S-initial position. On the analysis I am proposing, then, there is no movement transformation and no underlying level of representation for *wh* questions: the *wh* phrase simply appears S-initially and combines with a nonadjacent element in accordance with the usual principles (the SLR and the Dependency Requirement). This notwithstanding, I will occasionally use the term "extraction" for expository convenience and will sometimes make use of traces and gaps to help indicate the phrase to which a displaced constituent belongs.

Let us now turn our attention to the problem of determining the nature of the constraints on discontinuous constituents.

3.4 Extraction from NPs

The literature on *wh* structures in transformational grammar has been primarily concerned with two related issues: the relative markedness of different types of extraction and the nature of the required constraints. The least marked type of extraction seems to involve elements that are either arguments or modifiers of the verb, as illustrated in (1).

(1) a. Who left?
    b. Who did Harry see ____?
    c. With whom did Harry leave ____?

Not only are structures like these well formed in English, but they are also extremely common in other languages.

A somewhat more restrictive situation is found in cases in which the displaced phrase is part of an adverbial PP.

(2) a. Who did Harry sit [$_{PP}$ near ____]?
    b. What was Harry hit [$_{PP}$ with ____]?

Although these structures occur quite freely in English,[3] they are found in only a handful of other languages, as we shall see shortly. An even more restricted type of *wh* structure is exemplified in (3), in which the displaced phrase is part of an adjectival PP (a PP depending on a nominal).

(3) a. Who did Harry see [$_{NP}$ a picture of ____]?
    b. Who did Bob read [$_{NP}$ a book by ____]?

Not only are sentences like these very rare outside English and closely related languages such as Swedish and Danish, their occurrence is quite restricted even in these languages, as the apparent unacceptability of (3c, d) shows.

(3) c. *What did Harry destroy a book about ____?
    d. *Who did Harry read Bob's book about ____?

I will begin my discussion of the facts exemplified in (1)–(3) by considering the markedness issue.

Markedness
A plausible starting point for our discussion of the relative markedness of *wh* constructions is with the effect that the Subject-Last Requirement has on their formation. Consider in this regard the following three constructions, presented in increasing order of markedness.

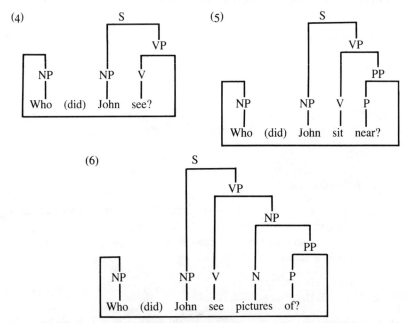

The representations depicted in (4)–(6) contain a number of phrases exhibiting discontinuities in the sense of the following definition.

A phrase is *discontinuous* if one or more of the elements it contains are separated from it.

The notion of "containment" used here corresponds roughly to ordinary "dominance" (not "immediate dominance") in TG. Thus the VP in (5) "contains" the verb *sit*, the preposition *near*, and the NP *who*, while the PP contains only the latter two elements.

Reconsider now the markedness contrasts exemplified by (4)–(6). In the least marked structure (i.e., [4]), only the VP is discontinuous. In the more marked (5), in contrast, both the VP and the PP are discontinuous since the "fronted" *wh* element is a component of both these phrases. Finally, in the most marked structure (i.e., [6]), there are three discontinuous constituents—VP, NP, and PP—since the *wh* word is a component of all three phrases. This suggests that the unmarked case for natural language might well correspond to the state of affairs outlined in (7).

(7) *The Continuity Requirement:*
    All phrases must be continuous.

This seems to capture the relevant markedness contrasts: the least marked of the structures we are considering is the one that departs the least from (7) (with only a discontinuous VP), while the most marked exhibits the greatest degree of noncompliance (with three discontinuous phrases).

The Continuity Requirement is almost certainly independently motivated in that it seems reasonable to suppose that the mechanisms responsible for processing language operate more easily on continuous strings than on noncontiguous elements. In fact, virtually all models of processing associate some cost (in terms of push-down storage, e.g.) with phrases that cannot be attached to an adjacent element. Support for this conclusion comes from a variety of sources, including a study by Wanner and Maratsos (1978) that showed that displaced *wh* words occasion an increase in memory load during the processing of relative clause structures. Moreover, Slobin (1972) has suggested that language learners consistently avoid what he calls "interrupted" (discontinuous) linguistic units. (Slobin calls this Operating Principle D.)

Let us suppose, then, that the Continuity Requirement constitutes a sort of "computational ideal" for natural language but that specific languages can depart from it to varying degrees. A possible example of a language that exhibits strict compliance with (7) would be Chinese, which does not have *wh* movement at all, as (8) shows.[4]

(8) a. Ni kanjian-le shei?
        you saw   who?
    b. *Shei ni [VP kanjian-le ____]?
        who you   saw?

In contrast with Chinese, Korean seems to allow extraction from a VP but not from any other category. (*Wh* movement in Korean is optional, however.)

(9) *Discontinuous VP:*
Nwukwu-rul John-i [$_{VP}$ —— poass-ni]?
who   Ac   N   saw
Who did John see?

(10) a. *Discontinuous PP and VP:*
*Nwukwu John-i [$_{VP}$ [$_{PP}$ —— kunche-ey] ancass-ni]?
Who   N   near Loc   sit
Who did John sit near.?

   b. *Discontinuous VP:*
[Nwukwu kunche-ey] John-i [$_{VP}$ —— ancass-ni]?
who   near   Loc   N   sit?
Near whom did John sit?

(11) a. *Discontinuous NP, PP, and VP:*
*Nwukwu John-i [$_{VP}$ [$_{NP}$ [$_{PP}$ —— eykwahan] chayk-ul] ilkass-ni]?
who   N   about   book Ac   read?
Who did John read a book about?

   b. *Discontinuous NP and VP:*
*[Nwukwu eykwahan] John-i [$_{VP}$ [$_{NP}$ —— chayk-ul] ilkass-ni]?
who   about   John N   book Ac   read
About whom did John read a book?

These facts suggest that Korean may be subject to the following version of the Continuity Requirement.

(12) *The Continuity Requirement (Korean):*
Only a VP may be discontinuous.

A slightly more liberal system seems to manifest itself in Dutch, which allows a phrase to be "extracted" from a VP or a PP that is not itself part of a larger NP (as noted by Koster [1978]). Consider:

(13) *Discontinuous VP:*
Wie hebt je [$_{VP}$ —— gezien]?
who have you   seen?

(14) *Discontinuous PP and VP:*
Waar heeft hij [$_{VP}$ [$_{PP}$ —— mee] gewerkt]?
what has   he   with   worked
What has he worked with?

(15) *Discontinuous PP, NP, and VP:*
*Wie hebt je [$_{VP}$ [$_{NP}$ een foto [$_{PP}$ van ——]] gezien]?
who have you   seen   a picture   of
Who did you see a picture of?

We can account for these facts by assuming that Dutch is subject to the version of the Continuity Requirement outlined in (16).

(16) *The Continuity Requirement (Dutch):*
     Only a VP or PP may be discontinuous.

Notice that (16) rules out discontinuous NPs such as those found in (15). (As the syntactic representation in [6] above shows, extraction from a PP lying within a nominal category creates a discontinuous NP.)

   In contrast with Dutch, French seems to allow extraction from a VP or an NP but not from a PP. Consider:

(17) *Discontinuous VP:*
     Qui avez-vous [$_{VP}$ vu ____]?
     Who have you   seen?

(18) *Discontinuous VP:*
     De qui avez-vous [$_{VP}$ parlé ____]?
     Of whom have you   spoken?

(19) *Discontinuous PP and VP:*
     *Qui avez-vous [$_{VP}$ parlé [$_{PP}$ de ____]]?
     Who have you   spoken   about?

(20) *Discontinuous NP and VP:*
     De qui avez-vous [$_{VP}$ vu [$_{NP}$ une photo ____]]?
     Of whom have you   seen   a picture?

(21) *Discontinuous NP, PP, and VP:*
     *Qui avez-vous [$_{VP}$ vu [$_{NP}$ une photo [$_{PP}$ de ____]]]?
     Who have you   seen   a picture   of?

A somewhat similar state of affairs seems to manifest itself in Polish, which allows some genitives (e.g., [22]) to be separated from the element with which they combine but does not tolerate preposition stranding—that is, discontinuous PPs (cf. Borsley 1983).

(22) Czyjego [$_{VP}$ widziałeś [$_{NP}$ brata ____]]?
     Whose (you) saw   brother?

We might suppose, then, that French (and perhaps Polish) is constrained by a Continuity Requirement resembling (23).

(23) *The Continuity Requirement (French and Polish):*
     Only a VP or NP may be discontinuous.

This leaves English as the most liberal of the languages we have been considering, with VPs, NPs, and PPs all allowed to be discontinuous, as our earlier examples show (cf. [4]–[6]).

On this basis of the preceding considerations, let us assume that natural language observes the following continuity hierarchy for phrase types.[5]

(24) *The Phrase Type Hierarchy:*
    a. No discontinuous constituents.
    b. Only VPs may be discontinuous.
    c. Only VPs and PPs may be discontinuous, or only VPs and NPs may be discontinuous.
    d. VPs, NPs, and PPs may be discontinuous.

The existence of such a markedness scale raises the important question of whether and how this type of fact can be accommodated in a theory that does not posit an innate Universal Grammar. While this matter will be considered in more detail in chapter 7, the required line of inquiry should be obvious. Somehow it must be shown that the relative markedness of one structure with respect to another can follow from principles that are either not inborn or not specific to the language faculty.

In the case of the particular phenomenon we are considering, the key observation would seem to be that the internal structure of (24) exhibits a certain natural logic in that each of the marked states of affairs implies the existence of the less marked alternatives, but not vice versa. Thus the existence of systems in which VPs, NPs, and PPs can be discontinuous (i.e., [24d]) obviously implies the existence of systems (e.g., [24c]) in which a subset of these categories can be discontinuous. More interestingly, the existence of discontinuous NPs or PPs requires the discontinuity of VPs as well since the former phrase types occur within the latter category. Thus extraction from a PP will create a discontinuity not only in this phrase but also in the VP that contains it (see the syntactic representation in [5] above). This motivates the relative markedness of (24c) with respect to (24b). I will reconsider this matter at greater length below in my discussion of the learnability issue.

Semantic Restrictions on Extraction in English

Although English is not subject to the narrow continuity requirements that are found in many other languages, constraints of other sorts must be at work since, as noted at the outset, not all PPs can be discontinuous. This is illustrated in the following sentences.

(25) a. Who did he read a book about ____?
    b. Which car does she like the gears in ____?
    c. Which office did you receive a request from ____?

(26) a. ?*Who did he destroy a book about ____?
    b. *Which car does she like the girl in ____?
    c. *Whose handwriting did you receive a request in ____?

These contrasts have been examined in a number of studies (e.g., Bolinger 1972; Cattel 1979; Erteschik-Shir 1981; Erteschik-Shir and Lappin 1979). There is a consensus that semantic and pragmatic factors underlie these distinctions, although there is disagreement over how these should be characterized. Since such factors are apparently independent of the syntactic issues I have been considering, I will not attempt to deal with them further here.

Still another type of semantic constraint that interacts with syntactic principles to limit the occurrence of discontinuous constituents is manifested in (27).

(27) a. What did you buy [$_{NP}$ a book on t]?
  b. *What did you buy [$_{NP}$ John's book on t]

Within the version of transformational grammar outlined in Chomsky (1977a), structures like (27b) are taken to violate the Specified Subject Condition, stated here as (28).

(28) *The Specified Subject Condition (SSC):*
  No rule can involve movement from position x to position y in
  . . . x . . . [$_\alpha$ . . . y . . .]
  where α has a subject distinct from y.

In (27), the direct object NP is taken to have a "subject" (the genitive) distinct from the moved phrase, in violation of the SSC.

Although it might appear that the ungrammaticality of (27b) could be accounted for in purely syntactic terms (as the SSC seems to imply), the ungrammaticality of sentences such as (29)–(32) suggests that the relevant variable may be the definiteness of the NP of which the *wh* word is a part rather than the presence of a genitive "subject."

(29) a. He examined that particular picture of the president.
  b. *Who did he examine [$_{NP}$ that particular picture of ____]?

(30) a. He wrote a certain controversial memo about a colleague.
  b. *Which colleague did he write [$_{NP}$ a certain controversial memo about ____]?

(31) a. He read the famous old article on the vowel shift.
  b. *What did he read [$_{NP}$ the famous old article on ____]?

(32) a. He read the report on the economy.
  b. ??What did he read [$_{NP}$ the report on ____]?

It seems reasonable to suggest in cases like these that the grammar of English includes a constraint resembling (33).

(33) *The Definiteness Prohibition:*
  A definite NP may not be discontinuous.

In addition to ruling out the (b) versions of (29)–(32), the Definiteness Prohibition also accounts for the ungrammaticality of (34b), in which a genitive NP is separated from the noun with which it must combine.

(34) a. I saw Harry's picture.
     b. *Whose did you see [$_{NP}$ ——— picture]?

The Definiteness Prohibition is presumably motivated in some way by semantic considerations. Precisely what these considerations are, however, is something of a mystery. If the proposals made by Erteschik-Shir and Lappin (1979) are correct, the relevant factors may well be pragmatic or discourse based. Since this problem falls outside the major focus of this book, I will simply set it aside and turn my attention to the learnability problem associated with the syntactic mechanisms I have proposed.

3.5 Learnability Considerations

The principal claim of this chapter has been that certain constraints on extraction can be characterized in terms of continuity requirements on the syntactic representations formed by the mechanisms outlined in earlier chapters. Thus far, however, our discussion has been more concerned with descriptive problems than with the deeper issue of how a child might master a language with the properties we have attributed to English. I will now turn my attention to this important question, laying the groundwork for the more extensive dicussion found in chapter 7. Since this book is primarily concerned with the ontogeny of syntactic devices rather than pragmatic or semantic principles, I will restrict my remarks to problems relating to the former topic.

The first problem that must be dealt with pertains to the learnability of the devices involved in the formation of *wh* structures themselves. As noted in section 3.2, these devices include a very general Combinatorial Principle, constrained by the Subject-Last Requirement (SLR).

(1) *The Combinatorial Principle:*
    Combine elements.

(2) *The Subject-Last Requirement:*
    The subject combines with VP.

It seems plausible to suppose that the SLR, whose learnability was established in chapter 1, and structures such as (3) and (4) provide the key to relaxing any adjacency requirement on combinatorial relations.

(3) What did Harry take?

(4) Where did Sue go?

Once children have acquired the SLR, exposure to sentences such as (3) and (4), in which the *wh* phrase is separated from the verb with which it must combine, will be crucial. Because of such constructions, the adjacency requirement on combinatorial relations will have to be dropped, presumably in favor of the simpler Combinatorial Principle proposed here and the accompanying Adjacency Preference.

(5) *The Adjacency Preference:*
   Combine adjacent elements, where permitted.

A more challenging learnability problem relates to the conditions under which a phrase can be separated from the element with which it combines. The precise challenge here is to determine how the usual three conditions on learning (restated in [6]) can be met in the case of the continuity requirements we have been considering.

(6) a. Availability of the required concepts.
   b. Availability of the required experience.
   c. Availability of a learning strategy.

Assuming that the relevant learning strategy involves generalization and that children's linguistic experience includes ample instances of *wh* structures, our main task will be to show that children have access to the concepts required to categorize the patterns to which they are exposed. Fortunately, this seems feasible since the relevant contrasts involve the continuity of different phrase types. This is advantageous for three reasons. First, because continuity is obviously not an inherently linguistic notion, it will be available to children independent of language. Second, since continuity is determined by whether the elements making up a phrase are adjacent to each other, it corresponds to a fundamental organizational property of syntactic structure that we can reasonably expect to be salient to children acquiring language. Finally, because the basic organizational properties of syntactic structure (including phrasal categories) are mastered early in the language acquisition process (see chap. 1), children should have access to the notions needed to formulate the proposed continuity requirements at the time at which they begin to acquire *wh* structures (well after the production of multiword utterances, according to Clark and Clark [1977]).[6]

Given the view just outlined, constraints on extraction (the appropriate Continuity Requirement) will emerge as children make use of their basic categorial knowledge to characterize the set of discontinuous structures occurring in their linguistic environment. In the case of Korean, this will result in the generalization that discontinuous phrases are always VPs. Children learning Dutch, on the other hand, will arrive at the generalization that discontinuous phrases are either VPs or PPs. In contrast, children learning English will be exposed to sentences in which NPs, PPs, and VPs are discontinuous and will therefore not develop the same restrictive generalizations that are justified in languages like Korean and Dutch.

An important question about the ontogeny of *wh* structures has to do with how children avoid overgeneralizations that would lead to the acceptance of structures that are forbidden in the language they are learning. Thus we must ask how children learning Korean, for example, avoid the equivalent of English (7) and (8).

(7) What has he worked with?

(8) Who did you read a book about?

Similarly, we must also ask how children learning Dutch manage to restrict their production of discontinuous constituents to VPs and PPs, thereby allowing structures equivalent to English (7) but ruling out the equivalent of (8).

The problem is an important one since it is generally believed that children do not have access to information about the possible ungrammaticality of the sentences they produce and hear. Because an overgeneralization of the type we are considering would therefore be very difficult for the language learner to correct, it seems necessary to suppose that such mistakes must somehow be avoided altogether. This supposition receives some support from the findings reported by Cho (1981), whose study of three Korean children (aged two years, two months, to three years, five months) in a naturalistic setting revealed the use of discontinuous VPs but no other discontinuous category.

As we proceed, we will find many comparable cases, all of which support the following hypothesis about the manner in which children formulate grammatical rules.

(9) *The Conservatism Thesis:*
   Children draw on the available grammatical concepts to formulate the most conservative hypothesis consistent with experience.

According to (9), children learning a language like Korean would note that discontinuous phrases are always VPs and would formulate their Continuity Requirement accordingly. The principle would then remain unchanged throughout the language acquisition process if we assume that learning is also subject to the following condition.

(10) *The Trigger Requirement:*
   No change is made in the grammar without a triggering stimulus in experience.

Since there is presumably nothing in Korean children's experience to undermine the generalization that discontinuous constituents must be VPs, the conservative version of the Continuity Requirement would be retained. In the case of a child acquiring Dutch or English on the other hand, this principle would have to be revised in the face of exposure to sentences in which other types of phrases are discontinuous. The Conservatism Thesis predicts that such adjustments will be conservative in character, so that Dutch children would come to allow discontinuous PPs—but not NPs—in response to sentences such as (11).

(11) Waar hebt hij [$_{VP}$ [$_{PP}$ —— mee] gewerkt]?
　　　what has　he　　　with　worked
　　　What has he worked with?

The Conservatism Thesis embodies a very strong claim about the manner in which children form grammatical rules. In the cases we have just considered, for instance, it makes specific predictions about the type of rules that children acquiring Korean and Dutch will not formulate. As we proceed, we will have occasion to examine a number of other grammatical phenomena whose ontogeny supports the claim of the Conservatism Thesis. Consideration of these cases will provide deeper insights into the manner in which children formulate hypotheses and will set the stage for the discussion in chapter 7 of a variety of problems and predictions associated with this proposal. Moreover, as I will note at that time, the Conservatism Thesis captures an intuition that must be adopted in other theories of language acquisition as well, including those that presuppose a transformational grammar.

The Developmental Sequence

Before concluding our discussion of acquisition, it is worthwhile to consider the relevance of the developmental data for the claims that have been made in this chapter about the syntax of extraction. The analysis I have proposed seems to make at least two significant predictions about the ontogeny of discontinuous constituents. First, since I have claimed that the syntax of extraction must be characterized in terms of continuity requirements on different phrase types, it should be the case that systematic use of *wh* questions is preceded by mastery of the relevant categorial contrasts. As noted above, this prediction seems to be correct since even the child's early two- and three-word utterances imply a rudimentary grasp of the syntactic categories and combinatorial principles we are assuming (see chap. 1).

A second set of predictions that my analysis makes has to do with the order in which different types of discontinuous constituents should emerge in children's grammars. In particular, we can predict that any differences in the onset time of these structures will reflect the phrase type hierarchy. Thus the order of emergence of discontinuous constituents should reflect (12), with discontinuity manifesting itself first in VPs followed by PPs and then NPs.

(12) a. *Discontinuous VP:*
      What did he see ____?
   b. *Discontinuous VP and PP:*
      What did he sit on ____?
   c. *Discontinuous VP, PP, and NP:*
      What did he see a picture of ____?

The motivation for the predicted developmental sequence lies in the fact that the later stages each involve the discontinuous phrase(s) present in the earlier stages plus one more. Hence structure (c) in (12) includes a discontinuous VP, PP, and NP—one more discontinuity than in (b) and two more than in (a). Moreover, because a discontinuous PP or NP entails the existence of a discontinuous VP (since the former categories lie within the latter phrase type), we predict that structure (b) will emerge after (a).

The limited information that is available about the developmental sequence for these structures supports this prediction. Thus the first discontinuous structures observed in the speech of children acquiring English involve VPs (with a displaced *where* phrase or a direct object *what,* according to Clark and Clark [1977, 352]). My predictions are also confirmed by the results obtained in Hildebrand's (1984) study of the development of *wh* questions in children aged four to ten. Hildebrand made use of an imitation task involving three tokens of each of the following sentence types. (The elements in parentheses indicate the discontinuous phrases in each sentence.)

(13) a. What did the little girl [$_{VP}$ hit ____ with the block today]?
        (VP)
   b. What did the little boy [$_{VP}$ play [$_{PP}$ with ____] behind his mother]?
        (VP, PP)
   c. What did the boy [$_{VP}$ read [$_{NP}$ a story [$_{PP}$ about ____]] this morning]?
        (VP, PP, NP)

There was also a sentence production task involving the following three sentence types. (Once again there were three tokens of each type.)

(14) a. The little boy on the road is pulling a car.
   b. The boy on the floor is drawing with a crayon.
   c. The little boy is watching a movie about a girl.

Production was elicited by first exposing the children to a sentence of one of the above types and then having them recast it in cleft form, with the final NP in the focus position. Thus sentences (14b) above would be recast as (15).

(15) This is the crayon that the boy on the floor is drawing with.

Recasting sentences of the first type presumably creates a discontinuous VP, while the second type leads to a discontinuous VP and PP and the third type to a discontinuous VP, PP, and NP. The children were given a pretest to ensure that they understood the cleft construction and were given ample practice before beginning the actual experiment.

The results of Hildebrand's two experiments are given in tables 3.1 and 3.2. As tables 3.1 and 3.2 show, children did best on the structures that involved only a discontinuous VP and next best on constructions involving a discontinuous VP and PP. Their performance was poorest on the constructions containing a discontinuous VP, PP, and NP. Moreover, the younger children did better on the structures with the fewest discontinuities, just as the Phrase Type Hierarchy would predict. The main effects of age and sentence type were significant ($p < .001$).

Table 3.1: Results from the Imitation Task (% Correct)

Discontinuous Phrases	Age Groups			
	4	6	8	10
VP (13a)	83	94	97	100
VP and PP (13b)	46	80	86	97
VP, PP, and NP (13c)	31	78	89	89

Table 3.2: Results from the Production Task (% Correct)

Discontinuous Phrases	Age Groups			
	4	6	8	10
VP (14a)	77	72	86	97
VP and PP (14b)	33	80	75	86
VP, PP, and NP (14c)	0	14	41	69

The types of errors made by the children on the two tasks also support the proposed phrase type hierarchy. Thus the most common error involved the elimination of one or more discontinuities by reformulating the structure of the sentence. On the imitation task, for instance, a sentence such as (16a) was often repeated as (b), with the discontinuous PP eliminated.

(16) a. What did the big woman shoot at ＿＿ three weeks ago?
     b. What did the big woman shoot ＿＿ three weeks ago?

Hildebrand's results appear to conflict with the findings reported by French (1984). Working with thirty-three children aged two years, eleven months, to five years, six months, French attempted to study the acquisition of preposition stranding with the help of an imitation task involving the two structure types exemplified in (17) and a comprehension task (involving picture selection) making use of the contrast in (18).

(17) a. What is the cat hiding behind ＿＿?
     b. Behind what is the cat hiding ＿＿?

(18) a. Show me the box which the boy hides in ＿＿.
     b. Show me the box in which the boy hides ＿＿.

The performance of the three- and four-year-olds on the comprehension test showed a slight preference for the structure with a continuous PP (cf. [18b]). However, all groups exhibited a strong preference for preposition stranding (the more marked structure) on the imitation task. The actual scores are presented in table 3.3.

Table 3.3: Results from French's Imitation Task (% Correct)

Sentence Type	Age 3	Age 4	Age 5
Nonstranded	11	18.3	56.4
Stranded	25.7	44.2	93.2

A potentially serious flaw in French's experiment arises from her decision to compare structures containing a stranded preposition with those in which the entire PP is "fronted" (i.e., [17a] vs. [17b]). This contrasts with Hildebrand's practice of comparing stranded preposition structures with sentences in which the displacement does not affect the PP at all (e.g., [13a] with [13b]). There are at least two reasons why such a comparison is preferable. First, when it comes to questioning a PP, the stranded structures (French's [17b] and [18b]) are far more frequent and natural than their nonstranded counterparts (cf. [17a] and [18a]). This might well influence children's performance in favor of the stranded structures. Second, the stranded structures in French's experiment place the preposition at the end of the sentence (the maximally salient position for children). Since noting the preposition is the key to performing successfully on French's imitation task, the stranded structures would once again be favored by the children even if they have mastered neither construction. In fact since the children's scores are strikingly low even on the imitation of relatively short sentences, it seems reasonable to suggest that their performance reflects something other than grammatical development per se (e.g., memory).

Neither of the problems associated with French's study arose in Hildebrand's utterances, in which stranded prepositions never occurred sentence finally and comparisons were made between structures that were roughly equal in terms of naturalness and frequency. Significantly, the results obtained in this study were those predicted by the Phrase Type Hierarchy. This provides additional support for the proposals about *wh* question formation I have made in this chapter. I will return to the deeper issues involved in the relation between developmental data and grammatical theory in chapter 7.

3.6 Conclusion

The major conclusion of this chapter has been that the formation of monoclausal *wh* questions can be characterized in terms of learnable principles that make reference to fundamental organizational properties of syntactic structure (the continuity of different phrase types). This analysis contrasts sharply with recent versions of TG that attempt to account for the range of facts discussed here by means of innate principles such as the Subjacency Condition and the Empty Category Principle. I will try to extend and refine this alternate approach to extraction in the next chapter.

4

EXTRACTION FROM
CLAUSES

4.1 Introduction

In this chapter I will attempt to extend my analysis of extraction to cases in which a *wh* phrase is separated from the remainder of the clause to which it belongs. As with my analysis of extraction from subsentential phrases, I will suggest that the relevant principles refer to general organizational properties of syntactic structure (particularly continuity) rather than bounding nodes or government. Consistent with the major theme of this book, I will also try to show that the principles I propose are learnable without the help of innate syntactic principles. I acknowledge in advance that my treatment of extraction from clauses is incomplete and that some of what I propose is very tentative. Nonetheless, as I try to show in this chapter, there do seem to be promising avenues of inquiry in this area for the type of theory I am proposing.

4.2 Extraction from Embedded Clauses

4.2.1 Subjacency

Unlike many languages, English allows a *wh* word to be "moved" to sentence-initial position from an embedded clause. Consider, for example, sentences (1) and (2).

(1) Who [$_S$ did John believe [$_S$ Mary liked ____]]
(2) What [$_S$ did Harry think [$_S$ Tom said [$_S$ Mary wanted ____]]]

The grammar I have been developing will assign the structure depicted in (3) to a sentence such as (1). (I assume that *believe* takes a sentential direct object.)

(3)

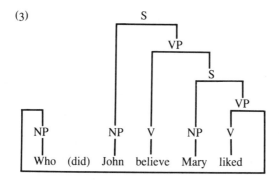

In (3) the transitive verb *like* combines with the S-initial *wh* phrase (its direct object), in accordance with the usual combinatorial principles. This results in the formation of a discontinuous embedded S, suggesting that we must add this category to the set of phrases that can be discontinuous in English.

A somewhat different approach to these structures is adopted within transformational grammar (TG), where it is assumed that extraction from an embedded clause involves movement of the *wh* phrase into COMP position in its S′ from where it is subsequently moved to COMP in the next highest S′ and so on. The positioning of the traces in (4) reflects this "successive cyclic movement."

(4) [$_{S'}$ Who [$_S$ did John think [$_{S'}$ *t* [$_S$ Mary liked *t*]]]]

Notice that, if the *wh* phrase moved from the position marked by the rightmost trace to the beginning of the sentence in one step, there would be a violation of the Subjacency Condition since two bounding (S) nodes would have to be crossed.

Explanations for the marked character of structures such as (4) typically focus on the assumed movement of the *wh* phrase through intermediate COMP positions. Chomsky (1981), for instance, suggests that a trace in COMP will normally violate the Empty Category Principle, restated here.

(5) *The Empty Category Principle:*
    Empty categories (traces) must be properly governed.

As noted in the preceding chapter, proper government is only possible if the following two conditions are met: (*a*) the trace is c-commanded by a verb, and (*b*) any maximal phrasal category (NP, VP, S′, etc.) dominating the trace also dominates the verb. The second of these conditions appears not to be met in (4), where the trace in COMP is dominated by an S′ node that does not dominate the verb *think*. Among the ideas considered by Chomsky is the suggestion that languages that allow (4) have a marked reanalysis rule that converts the offending S′ into S (a nonmaximal phrasal category), thereby allowing proper government of the trace by the adjacent verb.

As is frequently the case in work on transformational grammar, this analysis supports the case for special nativism. Nothing in experience would lead children to realize that bounding nodes, proper government, and reanalysis of S′ as S are crucial to the syntax of *wh* questions. If the proposed analysis is correct, the key notions and constraints will therefore obviously have to be innate. The only hope of avoiding this conclusion would be to propose principles of comparable descriptive promise that do not exploit the type of abstract linguistic notions employed by TG. I will now attempt to do this.

4.2.2 Extraction from Dependent Clauses

The first major descriptive problem that must be considered has to do with the fact that clauses in certain syntactically defined positions do not permit extraction. The sentences in (1) and (2) provide examples of this.

(1) a. Harry believed Mary saw Bob.
    b. Who did Harry believe Mary saw ____?
(2) a. Harry believed the claim that Mary saw Bob.
    b. *Who did Harry believe the claim that Mary saw ____?

Notice that (2b) is ungrammatical even though it is a virtual paraphrase of the well-formed (1b). Various approaches to this contrast have been adopted over the years within TG. One of the first and best-known proposals was made by Ross (1967), who attributed the ungrammaticality of (2b) to the Complex Noun Phrase Constraint (CNPC).

(3) *The Complex Noun Phrase Constraint (CNPC):*
    No element contained in an S dominated by an NP may be moved out of that NP.

Since the embedded S in (2) is dominated by an NP, the CNPC correctly blocks extraction.

In more recent work, the CNPC has been subsumed under the Subjacency Condition since extraction from the relevant type of embedded clause requires movement over an NP and an S boundary, as (4) illustrates.

(4) $[_{S'}$ Who $[_S$ did Harry believe $[_{NP}$ the fact $[_{S'}$ *t* that $[_S$ Mary saw *t*$]]]]]$

In some current work, it has been suggested that (4) also violates the Empty Category Principle since the trace within COMP in the lower S′ is not properly governed. (Since it is embedded within an NP as well as an S′, even S'-to-S conversion will not allow proper government by the matrix verb.)

The idea that I will pursue is that the two subordinate clauses we are considering differ in the way illustrated in (5) and (6). (I assume that the conjunction *that* can convert a clausal primary into a dependent phrase; I use the superscript p for a primary or independent category and s for a secondary.)

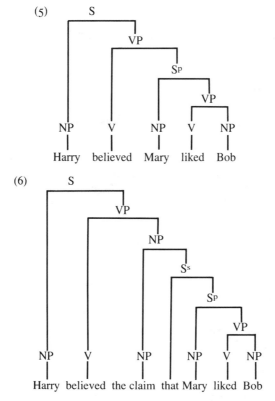

Notice that I take the subordinate clause to be an independent phrase (a primary) in (5) but a secondary dependent on the adjacent nominal in (6). This seems reasonable. The subordinate clause in (5) contains no elements with an unsatisfied dependency and should therefore count as a primary. Moreover, since this clause satisfies the matrix verb's dependency on a direct object argument, it should have the same dependency properties as an NP in this position would (i.e., it should be a primary). The embedded clause in (6), on the other hand, combines with an independent element (a noun) and should therefore be a secondary according to the theory developed in chapter I. While we might consider the possibility that this subordinate clause is a primary and that the noun *claim* is a dependent element that expresses a function from a clause to an NP, this idea is quite problematic. Not only does it subvert the definition of nouns as independent categories, but it also seems incompatible with sentences such as *I believed that claim too,* in which *claim* is clearly a primary.

Let us therefore proceed with the assumption that the clausal complement of an N is a secondary (a function from a nominal to a larger nominal, as in [6]) and attempt to exploit this fact to account for the extraction phenomenon noted above. The key notion underlying the analysis that I will develop involves a distinction between independent and dependent clauses, defined as follows.

(7) a. An *independent* clause does not depend on another element (i.e., it is a primary).

     b. A *dependent* clause depends on another element (i.e., it is a secondary or tertiary).

According to these definitions, the subordinate clause is independent in (1), where it is a primary, but dependent in (2), where it is a secondary depending on the noun *claim* (cf. [6]). Assuming the correctness of this distinction, the difference in "extraction" possibilities can now by captured by the principle outlined in (8).

(8) *The Independent Clause Requirement (ICR):*
     Only independent clauses can be discontinuous.

Principle (8) correctly rules out (2b), in which the displaced *wh* phrase is part of a dependent clause, but permits (1b), in which it is a component of an independent clause. Moreover, the ICR also correctly permits (9) since monoclausal Ss will always be continuous regardless of how their component elements are ordered.

(9) [$_S$ Who did Mary see ____]

In (9), the VP is discontinuous, but the clause is not since none of its component parts have been separated from it.

Comparable contrasts seem to occur in many of the languages of Europe, including French.

(10) a. Que croit-il ____?
        What believes he
     b. Que croit-il   [$_S$ que Jean a vu ____]?
        What believes he that John saw
     c. *Que croit-il (en) [$_{NP}$ le fait [$_S$ que Jean a vu ____]]?
        What believes he (in) the fact that John saw

The crucial contrast in (10) is between (b) and (c). Both sentences contain discontinuous embedded clauses, but only in the latter case is the lower S dependent (on the noun *fait*). This creates a violation of the ICR and results in an unacceptable sentence.

An obvious obstacle to the analysis I am developing comes from English sentences such as (11) and (12).

(11) a. John made the claim that Bob won the prize.
b. ?What did John make the claim [that Bob won ____]?

(12) a. John had a feeling that Bob won the prize.
b. ?What did John have a feeling [that Bob won ____]?

Notice that the (b) versions of (11) and (12) are more or less acceptable even though there is an apparent violation of the ICR since the discontinuous clause containing the *wh* phrase seems to depend on the adjacent noun (*claim* or *feeling*) and would therefore count as a secondary. Significantly, however, these sentences differ from genuine island structures in being built around expressions like *make the claim* and *have a feeling*, which have traditionally been seen as phrasal variants of the verbs *claim* and *feel*. This suggests that we might assume that (11a), for example, has a structure resembling (13), in which the subordinate clause combines with a complex verbal category.

(13)

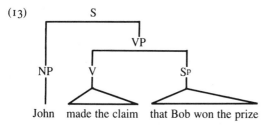

If this proposal is correct, there would be no violation of the ICR in (11b) or (12b) since the discontinuous embedded clause would in fact be independent.

If (13) is the correct structure for the sentence type we are considering, there should be some independent evidence to support the view that *make the claim* has been reanalyzed as a verb. One such piece of evidence comes from "gapping," a process that deletes the verb in the second conjunct of sentences such as (14).

(14) John read a book and Sue ____ a magazine.

Significantly, gapping can delete the string *make the claim* in sentences such as (15), suggesting that it too is a verb.

(15) John made the claim that Bob was late and Sue _____ that he was on time.

However, gapping of strings such as *believe the claim* and *hear the rumor*, which are not reanalyzed as verbs according to my proposal, gives very marginal results.

(16) a. ?*John believed the claim that Bob was late and Sue _____ that he was on time.
   b. ?*John heard the rumor that Bob was late and Sue _____ that he was on time.

The proposal we are considering also raises various difficult problems relating to the nature of complex verbs, the type of evidence that would allow children to establish their existence, and so on. Parallel problems exist for TG, of course, since it too typically assumes the existence of a complex V in sentences such as (11) and (12). Rather than attempting to explore this particular problem further, however, I will set it aside in favor of an attempt to motivate the ICR with respect to other structures.

One such sentence type involves relative clauses, as the sentences in (17) and (18) illustrate.

(17) a. They saw the book [$_S$ which Harry bought].
   b. *Who did they see the book [which _____ bought]?

(18) a. They welcomed all the people [$_S$ who John had sent an invitation to].
   b. *What did they welcome all the people [$_S$ who John had sent _____ to]?

I will assume that relative clauses are secondaries, dependent on the noun that they "modify." This coincides with the usual view that relative clauses express functions that apply to a nominal to give a nominal denoting a more restricted set of individuals. Given this assumption, the ungrammaticality of (17b) and (18b) will follow from the Independent Clause Requirement. This is because the sentence-initial *wh* phrase is separated from the dependent clause of which it is a part, creating a discontinuous phrase in violation of the ICR.

Another set of structures whose analysis bears on the correctness of the ICR is exemplified in (19)–(22).

(19) a. John ran away [when Harry attacked the policeman].
   b. *Who did John run away [when Harry attacked _____]?

(20) a. John found the gun [where Mary had dropped her purse].
   b. *What did John find the gun [where Mary had dropped _____]?

(21) a. John protested [because Bob criticized the president].
   b. *Who did John protest [because Bob criticized _____]?

(22) a. John went home [after Bob kissed Mary].

    b. *Who did John go home [after Bob kissed ____]?

The bracketed phrases in (19)–(22), which have all traditionally been categorized as adverbial clauses, will be assigned structures like (23) by the grammar. I assume here that elements such as *when, because,* and *after* are connectives that convert clausal primaries into tertiaries (as indicated by the superscript *t*) just as prepositions such as *near* change nominal primaries into tertiaries.

(23)

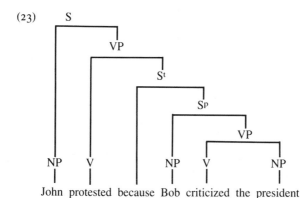

Given this analysis, adverbial clauses will fall into the dependent category, and extraction from them should be blocked by the ICR. This prediction seems correct, as the ungrammaticality of the (b) versions of (19)–(22) shows.[1]

A comparable analysis seems appropriate for the structures exemplified in (24)–(26).

(24) a. The play was so boring [that John read a book].

    b. *What was the play so boring [that John read ____]?

(25) a. The assignment was harder [than the teacher had told the class that it would be].

    b. *Which class was the assignment harder [than the teacher had told ____ that it would be]?

(26) a. Harry ran too fast [for Bob to hit him with the ball].

    b. ?*What did Harry run too fast [for Bob to hit him with ____]?

The ungrammaticality of the (b) versions of (24)–(26) would follow from the ICR if we assumed that the clauses containing the *wh* phrase are dependent. This would not be an unreasonable assumption since these clauses clearly function as modifiers—of an adjective (*boring* and *harder*) in the first two cases and an adverb (*fast*) in the third. Since only a tertiary can combine with either of these categories, the grammar would have to generate the structure depicted in (27) for sentence (24a). (I take *that* to function as a tertiary-creating connective in this case.)

(27)

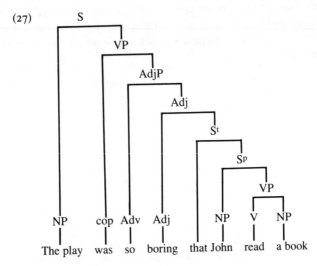

Since the subordinate clause in this type of construction is a tertiary (a type of dependent phrase), the ICR will prohibit the discontinuities found in (24)–(26).[2]

It is important to distinguish the structure type exemplified by (24)–(26) from the construction in (28).

(28) John was certain that Bob saw Mary.

Unlike the subordinate clauses in (24)–(26), the embedded S in (28) does not seem to function as a modifier (i.e., it does not specify how certain John was). Rather, the embedded clause seems to have much the same status as the complement S in (29), which functions as direct object of the matrix predicate.

(29) John knew that Bob saw Mary.

Let us therefore assume that both *know* and *certain* depend on a (subject) NP and a (complement) S, as indicated in (30).

(30) *certain* (Adj): NP S

On this analysis, the subordinate clause in (28) would support the adjectival secondary *certain* and would therefore be a primary.

(31)

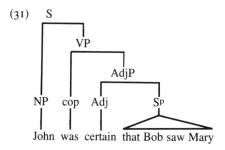

John was certain that Bob saw Mary

Since the complement clause here is a primary, "extraction" should be possible without violating the ICR. The grammaticality of the sentence in (32) suggests that this prediction is correct.

(32) Who was John certain [$_S$ that Bob saw ___]?

A final extension of the ICR that I will consider here involves sentences such as (33)–(35), first noted by Siegel (1983).

(33) a. Sue left with her hands dirty.
     b. *What did Sue leave [with ___ dirty]?

(34) a. She worked with the kitchen a mess.
     b. *What did she work [with ___ a mess]?

(35) a. She was knitting with a hockey game on TV.
     b. *Which game was she knitting [with ___ on TV]?

A plausible analysis for these sentences involves the assumption that they have the structure depicted in (36).

(36)

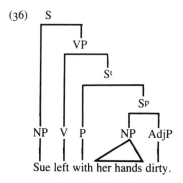

Sue left with her hands dirty.

In (36), the phrase *her hands dirty* functions as a clause. This assumption is consistent with our earlier definition of S as the phrase formed by combining two maximal categories (here NP and AdjP) and has been independently proposed within recent work in TG (e.g., Beukema and Hoekstra 1984).

Since this putative S contains no unsatisfied dependencies, it must be converted into a tertiary by the connective *with* if it is to combine with the verb and be incorporated into the VP. (Notice that *with her hands dirty* does have an adverb-type reading, close to that of a *"while* clause.") Because the resulting clausal phrase is dependent, it must also be continuous—a fact that rules out the *wh* questions in (33)–(35), as desired.

Not all languages are subject to a continuity requirement as severe as the ICR. According to Engdahl (1980), Swedish (and perhaps Norwegian) allows extraction from dependent clauses, as (37)–(38) show. Sentence (37) illustrates extraction from a relative clause and (38) extraction from a noun complement.

(37) Vilken flicka$_i$ verkar det inte finnas [$_{NP}$ nagon [$_S$ som
     which girl   seems there not to be   anyone   who
     minns [$_S$ vem$_j$ det var [$_S$ som t_j skulle hämta t_i]]]]
     remembers who it was   that   should pick up
     "Which girl does there not seem to be anyone who remembers who it was that picked up?"

(38) Den här artikeln$_i$ finns det fakiskt [$_{NP}$ en möjlighet
     this   article   is there in fact   a possibility
     [$_S$ att Dagens Nyheter tar in t_i]]?
     that Daily ,News accepts.
     "This article, there is in fact a possibility that the Daily News will accept."

The facts about extraction from other types of dependent clauses, in particular adverbial clauses, have apparently not been discussed in the literature. However, the judgments from native speakers whom I have consulted suggest that sentences such as (39) and (40) are unacceptable in Swedish.

(39) *Denne ar mannen som Bengt var   generad [efter som Inge kritiserade ___].
      this is   man   that Bengt was embarrassed after that Inge criticized
      "This is the man who Bengt was embarrassed after Inge criticized."

(40) *Den var en mask som Bengt blev hapen [nar Inge at ___].
      it was a worm that Bengt was startled when Inge ate.

If representative, these facts suggest that it will be necessary to distinguish between dependent clauses that are secondaries (e.g., [37] and [38]) and those that are tertiaries (e.g., [39] and [40]). Although I cannot explore this matter further here, a reasonable preliminary hypothesis would be that a discontinuity is somewhat less marked in a clausal secondary than a tertiary.

In sharp contrast with Swedish, there also appear to be languages that exploit continuity requirements that are more restrictive than the Independent Clause Requirement. Korean, for example, not only disallows discontinuous dependent clauses but also treats as unnatural sentences such as (42) in which the displaced *wh* phrase (*nwukwu*) is part of an independent clause. (See Lee [1983] for some discussion.)

(41) Nwukwu-rul John-i ____ poass-ni?
     who   Ac John N   saw Inter.
    "Who did John see?"

(42) ?*Nwukwu-rul Bob-i[$_S$ John-i ____ poassta-ko] mit-ni?
     who   Ac Bob N John N   saw believe Inter.
    "Who did Bob believe John saw?"

The more natural way of expressing (42) is to shift the entire object clause to the beginning of the sentence, with *nwukwu* at the beginning of that clause.

(43) [$_S$ nwukwu-rul John-i poassta-ko] Bob-i   mit-ni?
     who   -Ac John-N saw   Bob-N believe Inter.
    "Who did Bob believe John saw?"

Notice that there is no reason to think that the embedded clause is discontinuous in (43). Harris (1981) reports that Georgian also does not allow extraction from embedded clauses.

The preceding facts suggest that languages such as Korean and Georgian are subject to the principle outlined in (44), which could well constitute the unmarked case for human language (a possibility to which I will return shortly).

(44) *The Continuous Clause Requirement:*
    All clauses must be continuous.

The Continuous Clause Requirement correctly predicts the grammaticality of (43) as well as the unacceptability of (42) since the embedded clause is realized as a continuous string in the former case but not the latter one. I will assume that this is a correct first approximation and attempt to determine how it and the other options we have been considering might be acquired by speakers of the relevant languages. First, however, a brief summary is in order.

Summary
The facts we have been considering support formation of the following markedness hierarchy for extraction from clauses.

(45) *The Clause Type Hierarchy:*
    a. All clauses must be continuous.
    b. Only independent clauses may be discontinuous.
    c. Independent clauses and some dependent clauses may be discontinuous.

Case (a), which is exemplified by Korean, is the least marked state of affairs, while case (c), which manifests itself in Swedish, constitutes the most marked option. In contrast, English, French, and many other Indo-European languages opt for the intermediate alternative, allowing only independent clauses to be discontinuous.

The internal organization of the Clause Type Hierarchy is presumably not arbitrary. The unmarked status of option (a), for example, could well be due to the fact that the clause is a basic unit of processing, presumably because it constitutes a self-contained semantic unit (e.g., Fodor, Bever, and Garrett 1974). Sentences are easier to process, it could plausibly be argued, if their component clauses consist of continuous strings rather than randomly interspersed constituents. The relatively unmarked status of option (b) with respect to (c), on the other hand, might stem from a fundamental difference between independent and dependent clauses. Because dependent clauses already depend on one external element (relative clauses on a nominal and adverbial clauses on a verbal element), extraction moves them one step further from the posited ideal of a continuous self-contained unit with no external dependencies. This consideration could well inhibit extraction in a way that it would not in the case of independent clauses, which have no external dependencies.

The Clause Type Hierarchy coexists with the Phrase Type Hierarchy outlined in chapter 3 and repeated here.

(46) *The Phrase Type Hierarchy:*
   a. No discontinuous constituents.
   b. Only VPs may be discontinuous.
   c. Only VPs or PPs may be discontinuous, or only VPs or NPs may be discontinuous.
   d. VPs, PPs, and NPs may be discontinuous.

It is not clear what relation, if any, exists between the two hierarchies, although one would not expect a language to be conservative with respect to one and liberal with respect to the other. The facts studied in this chapter and the preceding one point to the following clustering of properties.

(47) a. Only VPs can be discontinuous; all clauses must be continuous (e.g., Korean).
   b. VPs and NPs can be discontinuous, as can independent clauses (e.g., French).
   c. VPs, PPs, and NPs can be discontinuous, as can independent clauses (e.g., English)
   d. VPs, PPs, and NPs can be discontinuous, as can independent clauses and at least some dependent clauses (e.g., Swedish).

This summary reveals no cases in which a language chooses the most conservative continuity requirement for clauses and the most liberal for other phrases or vice versa. However, there are cases in which the intermediate option on one hierarchy is adopted along with either the most marked or the least marked alternative on the other, while Swedish seems to allow the most liberal options on both hierarchies.

4.2.3 Learnability Considerations

Turning now to the problem of determining how children might come to identify the particular clause type requirements imposed by the language they are learning, it seems plausible to suggest that the usual conditions on learning, repeated here, can be met.

(1) a. Availability of the required concepts.
   b. Availability of the relevant experience.
   c. Availability of an appropriate learning strategy.

Condition (a) will be met if children have access to the concepts required to formulate the continuity requirements on clauses I have proposed. Since the relevant concepts ("clause," "independent," and "dependent") are all the product of very early grammatical development (see chap. 1), this condition is met. The second condition can also be satisfied in a straight-forward way since it requires only that children be exposed to sentences with discontinuous embedded clauses typical of the language they are learning. Thus children learning English will have to hear utterances such as *Who did John say Bob saw?* from time to time. This seems plausible. As usual, I will assume that the relevant learning strategy involves generaliza-tion, subject to the limitations mentioned below.

Given this, it should be possible for children acquiring English, for example, to note that all the discontinuous clauses to which they are ex-posed are independent (i.e., primaries). The real problem for acquisition theory lies not so much in showing that the Independent Clause Require-ment is a feasible generalization as in explaining why children seek to develop such constraints in the first place. Thus we must ask why a child acquiring English or Korean does not simply assume that any type of clause can be discontinuous, thereby incorrectly arriving at a grammar that would allow sentences such as (2) (as Swedish does).

(2) Who did you see a man who liked ____?

This problem is an important one since overgeneralizations of this type would presumably be very difficult to correct. (Recall that children do not have access to information about the possible ungrammaticality of utter-ances they hear and produce.)

The key to avoiding overgeneralization in these cases lies in the Conser-vatism Thesis, restated here.

(3) *The Conservatism Thesis:*
   Children draw on the available grammatical concepts to formulate the most conservative hypothesis consistent with experience.

According to (3), children will use the available grammatical concepts (including S, dependent, and independent) to form the most restrictive generalization consistent with the discontinuous clauses to which they are exposed. In the case of English, this would lead children to conclude that only independent clauses are discontinuous.

The formation of constraints on discontinuous clauses may be further enhanced by processing considerations. Because the clause constitutes a natural unit of processing (see above), it seems plausible to assume that sentences in which clausal units are mapped onto continuous strings would be favored by language learners. Departures from this, one might argue, would have to be motivated by experience and would be characterized in a conservative way with the help of the grammatical concepts available to the child (category types, dependency, etc.).

On this view, then, processing considerations would lead children to adopt the Continuous Clause Requirement as their initial hypothesis. This principle would then be retained unless and until it was proven inadequate by experience, in accordance with the Trigger Requirement (repeated here).

(4) *The Trigger Requirement:*
   No change is made in the grammar without a triggering stimulus in experience.

In the case of languages like Korean and Georgian, there is presumably nothing in the child's experience to contradict the Continuous Clause Requirement, and it would therefore be retained. In English, on the other hand, exposure to sentences such as *Who did John say Bob saw?* forces abandonment of the Continuous Clause Requirement and the eventual formulation of the weaker Independent Clause Requirement. This principle seems viable for English but would have to be abandoned in Swedish, in which even some dependent clauses can be discontinuous, as we have seen.

If the preceding proposal is correct, we would expect to find a developmental sequence that parallels the Clause Type Hierarchy in languages (like English and Swedish) in which more than just continuous clauses are allowed. Although I know of no data bearing on this question, we might begin by testing children's interpretation of sentences such as (5).

(5) Last night John said that Mary met Harry.

Sentence (5) is ambiguous, with *last night* interpretable as a component of either the matrix or the subordinate clause. Since the latter interpretation, but not the former one, entails a discontinuous clause, we would predict that it would develop later in children. Even in the absence of studies on this problem, this prediction seems to be a reasonable one.

A somewhat subtler test is provided by sentences such as (6).

(6) Who did you tell Sue had gone home?

This sentence is also ambiguous, with *who* serving as the object of the matrix verb *tell* and *Sue* as the subject of the embedded clause in one interpretation and with the opposite set of correspondences in the second interpretation. The theory I have proposed predicts that the former interpretation should develop first since it requires no discontinuous clauses. The latter interpretation, in contrast, associates *who* with the nonadjacent embedded clause, thereby creating a discontinuity in that syntactic unit.

4.3 Related Issues

The Subject Condition

It is a well-known fact that discontinuous subject phrases are invariably ungrammatical regardless of whether they consist of NPs, infinitival phrases, or tensed clauses. This is illustrated in (1)–(4).

(1) a. Pictures of Dracula frightened John.
    b. *Who did [$_{NP}$ pictures of ____] frighten John?

(2) a. A book by Nixon sold a lot of copies.
    b. *Who did [$_{NP}$ a book by ____] sell a lot of copies?

(3) a. To see Mary would embarrass Bob.
    b. *Who would [$_S$ PRO to see ____] embarrass Bob?

(4) a. That Harry finished the book surprised Sue.
    b. *What did [$_S$ that Harry finished ____] surprise Sue?

The ungrammaticality of the (b) versions of (1)–(4) was originally attributed to the Subject Condition (see Chomsky 1977a, 108).

(5) *The Subject Condition:*
    No rule can involve positions x and y in
    $\ldots x \ldots [_\alpha \ldots y \ldots] \ldots$
    where α is a subject phrase.

On the assumption that S is a bounding node, the Subject Condition can be subsumed under the Subjacency Condition in at least (1) and (2), in which the *wh* word is extracted from a structure dominated by both S and NP. The Subject Condition can also be subsumed under the Empty Category Principle in these cases since a trace within a subject NP is not c-commanded by the verb and therefore cannot be properly governed.

It is tempting to think that the unacceptability of discontinuous subject phrases might be attributed to properties (perhaps semantic) of subject nominals. However, the ungrammaticality of utterances such as (6), in which the discontinuous phrase is a sentential modifier rather than a subject phrase, suggests that a somewhat more general approach is warranted.

(6) a. According to Bob, John left.
    b. *Who [according to ____] did John leave?

The ungrammatical utterance in (6) shares with (1)–(4) an interesting property: in all cases the discontinuous constituent lies outside the VP. (A comparable observation has been made within TG by Hornstein and Weinberg [1981].) We might suppose, then, that the relevant principle resembles (7).

(7) *The VP Requirement:*
    Discontinuous constituents must lie within VP.

Despite its apparent coverage of the facts, the VP Requirement has a certain ad hoc quality that may well indicate that a generalization has been missed somewhere. On the other hand, it might be worthwhile to explore the possibility that the proposed constraint reflects the interaction of the Subject-Last Requirement (SLR) with certain computational considerations. Thus if the VP is in fact formed first (as required by the SLR), and if "fronted" constituents do place extra strain on working memory (as suggested earlier), we might suppose that there would be some advantage to incorporating these elements into the VP rather than a subsequently formed phrase (e.g., the subject or a sentence modifier). At the very least, we might think that such a state of affairs would constitute the unmarked case that the child would not venture beyond without appropriate experience. Since no such stimulus occurs in English, the VP Requirement would be respected and the desired class of utterances avoided.

Another possibility is that the set of discontinuous constituents allowed by a language is stated as a series of entailments that must be respected in each clause containing a discontinuity. In the case of English, which allows several types of discontinuous phrases, the entailments are those in (8).

(8) discontinuous NP $\supset$ discontinuous PP $\left.\right\}$ $\supset$ discontinuous VP.
    discontinuous S

These entailments ensure that a discontinuous NP, PP, or S entails a discontinuous VP as well. This automatically captures the VP Requirement. Moreover, since a discontinuous NP entails a discontinuous PP, we automatically account for the ungrammaticality of sentences such as *Whose did you see [____ book]?* in which there is a discontinuous NP but no PP. Given the proposals made in chapter 3, the entailments for Polish, French, and Dutch would resemble those in (8′) (ignoring clauses).

(8') *Polish and French:*
   discontinuous NP ⊃ discontinuous VP.
   Dutch:
   discontinuous PP ⊃ discontinuous VP.

This system is apparently as learnable as the other continuity requirements I have posited. Consistent with the proposals and developmental data considered earlier, children learning English would first notice the existence of discontinuous VP constituents, then the existence of discontinuous PPs within discontinuous VPs and finally the existence of discontinuous NPs within discontinuous phrases of the previous two types. Assuming conservative hypothesis formation, only these possibilities would be allowed— just the state of affairs captured by (8). The same scenario would apply to other languages, except that there would be fewer types of discontinuous phrases to manipulate.

"That-Trace" Effects

Still another problem that must be considered at this point relates to the fact that a subject phrase cannot be "extracted" from a clause beginning with a complementizer.

   (9) *Who did John say [that ____ saw Bob]?

(10) *Who did John want very much [for ____ to see Bob]?

(11) *Who were you wondering [whether ____ saw Bob]?

(12) *Who did you ask [if ____ had seen Bob]?

These sentences do not violate the VP Requirement since the discontinuous phrase created by extraction of the subject (the embedded clause) lies within the VP of the S containing it. The restriction illustrated in (9)–(12) also does not involve a prohibition against the extraction of subject phrases in general. As (13) and (14) show, extraction is possible when there is no overt complementizer.

(13) Who did you say [____ saw Bob]?

(14) Who did John want [____ to see Bob]?

Moreover, the restriction manifested in (9)–(12) has no effect on nonsubject phrases, which can be freely extracted from an embedded clause with an overt complementizer.

(15) Who did you say [that Bob saw ____]?

(16) Who did you want very much [for Bob to see ____]?

(17) ?Who were you wondering [whether Bob had seen ____]?

(18) ?Who did you ask [if Bob had seen ____]?

Various approaches to these facts have been adopted over the years within TG. In one of the best-known analyses of this phenomenon, Chomsky and Lasnik (1977) proposed that the offending structures could be ruled out by a filter resembling (19), which prohibits structures in which an overt complementizer is followed by a subject trace.

(19) *The that-trace filter:*
　　$*[_{S'} \alpha [_S t \ldots$
　　where α is not null.

More recent work has attempted to subsume the relevant contrasts under the Empty Category Principle. The key observation is that, while the traces in object position in (15)–(18) are properly governed by the adjacent verb, those in subject position cannot be so governed since they are not c-commanded by the verb. This raises the question of why the subject traces in (13) and (14) are permitted. Discussing this problem, Chomsky (1981) and others have proposed that a trace can be properly governed if it is governed by a coindexed category, including another trace, in COMP. (Two traces are coindexed only if they are both associated with the same moved element.) The relevant portions of the syntactic representations of sentences (9) and (13) resemble (20) and (21), respectively.

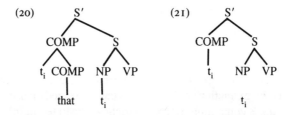

In (21), but not (20), the trace in COMP c-commands and can therefore govern the coindexed subject trace, avoiding a violation of the ECP. (This contrast in the c-command domain of the trace in COMP stems from the fact that the first branching node above it is S' in [21] but COMP in [20].)

This leaves the problem of explaining why sentences such as (22) are acceptable in Spanish.

(22) Quien dijo Juan [que _____ leyó el libro]?
　　who　said John　that　　read the book?
　　"Who did John say read the book?"

Following a proposal by Luigi Rizzi (see Jaeggli 1982), it is often assumed that there is a principled connection between the acceptability of structures such as (22) and the possibility of subject postposing, as illustrated in (23).

(23) a. Juan leyó el libro.
   John read the book
  b. Leyó Juan el libro.
   read John the book

Rizzi suggests that subject postposing precedes *wh* movement in (23), so that the *wh* trace of the subject NP will occur within the VP in a position where it can be properly governed by the verb.

  An alternate proposal, based on work by K. T. Taraldsen, is outlined by Chomsky (1981). The key idea is that Spanish and similar languages allow a trace in subject position to be properly governed by Infl (the verbal agreement marker). Since TG ties proper government of the subject by Infl to the richness of the agreement morphology, this proposal explains why English does not allow this type of government and why violations of the *"that-trace"* filter are apparently restricted to languages that allow null subjects.

  While accounts of *"that-trace"* effects in terms of the ECP are attractive because of their generality, the phenomenon itself is clearly quite narrowly delimited.As noted by Cole (1985) and Engdahl (1985), for instance, the complementizer apparently has no effect on the admissibility of an interpretation for sentence (24), in which *some* has "broad scope" with respect to *every*. (On this interpretation, there is a specific person who everyone believes is at the door.)

(24) Everyone believes (that) someone is at the door.

The significance of this fact within TG is that this interpretation is represented by an operation of quantifier raising in Logical Form, which has the effect of adjoining the NP *someone* to the beginning of the sentence. (See May [1977] for details.)

(25) $[_S$ someone$_i$ $[_S$ everyone believes that t_i is at the door.

This might be expected to occasion a *"that-trace"* effect and render the sentence ungrammatical on the intended interpretation, but this does not happen. This suggests that the effects in question are only manifested in syntactic structure and that the required constraint must somehow reflect this fact.

  One possibility is that the constraint we are considering restricts the combinatorial potential of complementizers, perhaps along the lines of (26).

(26) A complementizer combines with a canonical clause.

Canonical clauses would then be defined as follows.

(27) A canonical clause consists of a adjacent NP and VP.

The definition in (26) makes the desired distinction between the ungrammatical constructions in (9)–(12) and the acceptable sentences in (15) and (16), repeated here.

 (9) *Who did John say [that ____ saw Bob]?

(10) *Who did John want very much [for ____ to see Bob]?

(11) *Who were you wondering [whether ____ saw Bob]?

(12) *Who did you ask [if ____ had seen Bob]?

(15) Who did you say [Bob saw ____]?

(16) Who did John want [Bob to see ____]?

In the ungrammatical structures the complementizer must combine with a noncanonical clause since the subject NP is separated from the VP. In the acceptable sentences, on the other hand, the subject NP and the VP are adjacent in accordance with (26) even though the latter category is itself discontinuous.[3]

Languages such as Spanish would define complementizers as follows.

(28) A complementizer combines with a clause.

Since there is no canonical clause requirement in Spanish, sentences such as (22) will be acceptable. A possible flaw in this proposal is that it fails to draw a principled connection between violations of the "*that*-trace" filter and either rich verbal morphology (null subjects) on the one hand or subject-verb postposing on the other. This may not be as serious as one might think, however. Recent work has identified languages that violate the filter without allowing null subjects (e.g., Dutch; see Maling and Zaenen [1978]), free subject postposing (e.g., Portuguese; see Zubizarreta [1982]), or either (e.g., Scandinavian; see Engdahl [1985]). Although maneuvers can be made to maintain the correlations in these cases, it also seems plausible to suggest that the absence of a link among these phenomena will be confirmed once a broader range of languages is studied.

The learnability of (26) would be ensured if children formulate categorial definitions in the same conservative fashion as syntactic principles. Thus on exposure to complementizers in sentences such as (29) and (30), they would assume only that these elements occur with canonical clauses and not that any S can be introduced in this way.

(29) John said that Harry was late.

(30) John wants very much for Harry to do it.

The findings of an experimental study by Phinney (1981) are consistent with this proposal. Working with eighty-five children between the ages of three and eleven, Phinney designed a series of short stories that were read to the children and followed by questions of the following types.

(31) a. Who did the lion believe [_____ swam in the pond]?
  b. Who did the lion know [that (_____) swam in the pond]?
  c. Who did the horse believe [the lion hugged _____]?
  d. Who did the dog notice [that the rooster kicked _____]?

The stories were designed in such a way that each question could be answered by interpreting the bracketed S as a clausal direct object or an extraposed relative clause. This can be illustrated by considering the story associated with (31b), the structure that is of greatest concern to us.

(32) The lion and the rooster are friends. Yesterday, the lion saw a strange dog swimming in the pond. While the lion was away, the rooster went swimming.

If children interpret the embedded clause in (31b) to be a sentential object, they will answer by saying "the dog" (since this is the animal the lion actually saw swimming in the pond). This answer corresponds to the interpretation in which the embedded clause is noncanonical (because of the fronted *wh* subject). Such a response would indicate that children were not using the complementizer definition I have proposed. If, on the other hand, they take the subordinate clause to be an extraposed relative clause and *who* to be the direct object of the matrix verb *know,* they should respond by saying "the rooster" (since this is the only animal who is known to the lion and who swam in the pond). This latter response would be consistent with knowledge of the complementizer definition since *that* in this case would be a relative pronoun, not a complementizer (see n. 3).

The results from the youngest two groups of subjects (average ages three years, seven months, and four years, nine months) seem to support the prediction I have made (see table 4.1). The crucial scores here are from

Table 4.1

Type	Object Clause Response		Relative Clause Response	
	Group I	Group II	Group I	Group II
(31a) (%)	63	84	17	5
(31b) (%)	5	3	36	52
(31c) (%)	70	89	17	0
(31d) (%)	78	83	12	16

the (b) sentence type, where the children will violate the proposed complementizer definition if they treat the clause beginning with *that* as an object
clause consisting of a nonadjacent NP and VP. Significantly, this happens
very infrequently (5 percent or less). This score is especially impressive in
the light of the fact that children's responses on the other sentence types
indicate that they are quite capable of interpreting discontinuous embedded
clauses. Thus the object clause interpretation for sentence type (a), the
structure most closely resembling (b), is over 60 percent in even the youngest age group. These results suggest that children formulate their complementizer definition in a conservative fashion from the outset and that they
do not allow this element to combine with a noncanonical clause, just as
my proposal would predict.[4]

4.4 Conclusion

According to the proposals made in this chapter, a string of words provided
by the lexicon is assigned a syntactic structure in accordance with the principle "Combine elements," constrained by a variety of independently motivated devices. These range from universal conditions such as the Subject-
Last Requirement to more language-particular mechanisms, including continuity requirements on phrases and clauses, the Adjacency Preference,
and other word order conventions. All these devices are taken to be learnable without the help of innate linguistic principles, in accordance with the
claims developed in this and earlier chapters. Although my approach therefore challenges the familiar claims about special nativism, it shares with
transformational grammar the goal of seeking maximally general grammatical operations constrained by a set of principles that may vary from
language to language in systematic and limited ways. In TG, for example,
much current work assumes the rule "Move category" constrained by
principles referring to proper government, bounding nodes, and other such
notions. This research program is clearly similar in conception to the one I
have been developing, differing from it in the choice of restrictive notions
(proper government and bounding node vs. continuity) and in the per-
ceived role of the genetic endowment (special vs. general nativism).

It would of course be wrong to suggest that there are not substantial
problems with the analyses I have proposed. At the same time, it might
also be a mistake to reject them out of hand. After all, it has taken well
over two decades of collaborative work within TG to develop constraints
like the Subjacency Condition and the Empty Category Principle (ECP),
and even these are still far from problem free (on the ECP, see Lasnik and
Saito [1984]). It is important to bear in mind that there is no finality to the
analyses proposed here. There is a great deal of room for experimentation

within the framework of concepts that I have outlined, and it is to be expected that important adjustments in the proposed principles will be made as work proceeds.

Another matter that deserves comment at this time pertains to an apparent lack of generality in some of my proposals, especially in comparison with the analyses currently being considered within TG. An obvious example of this involves the Empty Category Principle, which appears to do the work of several of the restrictions on discontinuous constituents outlined in the last two chapters. The generality of the ECP in this respect is somewhat deceptive, however, since the major concept that it exploits (proper government) is accompanied by some rather special assumptions. On one approach considered by Chomsky (1981), for example, only verbs and NPs in COMP are potential proper governors for an empty category—hardly an obvious natural class. Moreover, the generality of the ECP is purchased at the expense of very special reanalysis rules that can create complex verbs (see sec. 3.2) and change certain phrasal nodes (e.g., S'-to-S conversion, as discussed in sec. 4.2.1). This is not to say that such maneuvers cannot be motivated within an appropriate framework of assumptions, only that the need for such adjustments must be taken into account when comparing analyses with respect to their generality.

An even more compelling reason for exercising caution in the use of generality as a criterion for evaluating grammars relates to the fundamental assumptions about the human language faculty that claims of this sort require. Even assuming that children ultimately come to formulate maximally general linguistic principles (not an uncontroversial assumption in itself), the assessment of a principle's relative generality must be done with reference to the inventory of concepts available to the language learner. It is quite possible that the most general principle formulable in terms of concepts available to the linguist (e.g., c-command and government) will simply not be available to language learners. On the view I have adopted, for instance, children do not have access to faculty-specific linguistic notions and therefore never consider principles such as the Empty Category Principle. For them, the most general principles are the ones formulated in terms of notions such as continuity, adjacency, precedence, and the like. According to this view of language and learning, then, the principles that I have proposed may well be the maximally general statements that can be made about the phenomena we are considering.

The familiar lesson from recent work in linguistics is that the most fruitful lines of inquiry are those that show promise of providing significant insights into the nature of the language faculty. It is primarily for this reason that TG, with its claims about innate linguistic principles, has provided such an attractive framework for research despite various descriptive shortcomings of the sort discussed in virtually every journal article in the field. I believe that the analyses developed in this and preceding chapters may show a comparable type of promise and that they too point toward a cogent and interesting theory of the language faculty. Moreover, as I have attempted to stress throughout this book, this theory has a rather special character (at least in the light of recent work in linguistics) since it does not posit the existence of innate syntactic principles. I will return to this matter at greater length in chapter 7.

5

ANAPHORIC
DEPENDENCIES

5.1 Anaphoric Dependency

To this point I have largely ignored the status of pronouns in the categorial grammar I am developing. Since such words can satisfy the dependency of verbs on NPs in sentences such as (1), it would seem appropriate to classify them as nominal primaries.

(1) She hurt herself.

A major difference between pronominal elements and other types of NPs is that pronouns can look to another word (called an "antecedent") for the determination of their reference. Thus in (2) the referent of the pronoun *he* can be specified by the NP *Harry*.

(2) Harry said that he was tired.

I will refer to a dependency in which a pronominal element looks to an NP for its interpretation as "anaphoric."

From the earliest work in transformational grammar (TG) it has been assumed that configurational properties of the syntactic representation play a central role in determining the admissibility of anaphoric dependencies. In recent work, the key structural relation is often taken to involve c-command, defined in preliminary form as follows.

(3) *x* c-commands *y* if the first branching node above *x* dominates *y*.

Following pioneering work by Reinhart (1981), it is often assumed that anaphoric dependencies are subject to the following constraint. (This constraint is similar in its effects to principle C of Chomsky's [1981] Binding Theory.)

(4) *The C-Command Principle:*
    A pronoun may not c-command its antecedent.

As a preliminary illustration of how the C-Command Principle works, consider the structure in (5).

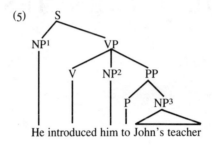

(5)

He introduced him to John's teacher

In (5), NP[1] c-commands both the other NPs since the first "branching node" above it (S) dominates everything else in the sentence. Similarly, NP[2] c-commands NP[3] since the first branching node above it (VP) is higher in the tree than NP[3]. As Reinhart's principle would predict, neither of the pronouns in (5) can look to NP[3] for its interpretation.

Structure (5) contrasts with (6), in which the relative positioning of the NPs permits an anaphoric dependency.

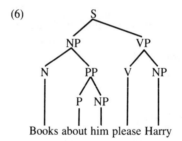

(6)

Books about him please Harry

In (6), the first branching node above the NP *him* (PP) does not dominate the direct object. Since *him* does not c-command *Harry*, the anaphoric dependency is permissible.

Work on anaphora in transformational grammar has provided some of the most spectacular advances in syntactic theory. In addition to various descriptive successes, the characterization of anaphoric dependencies (often called "binding theory") is also thought to have important implications for the study of Universal Grammar. In fact, the basic principles of binding theory (e.g., the C-Command Principle) are routinely assumed to be innately specified, an assumption that has influenced some recent work on language acquisition (e.g., Lust 1980, Solan 1983). In what follows, I will attempt to show that the syntax of anaphoric dependencies can be characterized in terms of principles that exploit the categorial distinctions proposed in earlier chapters rather than notions such as c-command and governing category (the key notion in Chomsky's [1981] version of binding theory). Consistent with the central theme of this book, I will also endeavor to show that the proposed principles can be learned without the help of innate linguistic knowledge.

5.2 The Precedence Constraint

It is not easy to determine the precise role of grammatical principles in the regulation of anaphoric dependencies. Pronoun use is widely acknowledged to reflect a variety of pragmatic and discourse-based principles in addition to syntactic constraints. There is, for example, nothing in the grammar to prevent one from opening a conversation by saying *His mother criticized John,* even though such an anaphoric dependency is extremely unnatural when there is no prior mention of *John* in discourse. Moreover, while virtually all grammatical theories rule out the anaphoric dependency in (1), many people find it to be quite acceptable in a sentence of this length.

(1) He$_i$ has the whole city at his$_i$ disposal, whether John$_i$ admits it or not.

These examples suggest that we must countenance syntactic constraints on anaphora that not only operate in conjunction with extragrammatical principles but may at times be subordinate to them. In what follows, I will take the position that the syntactic contribution to the interpretation of anaphora is extremely simple, consisting essentially of a statement of the conditions under which a pronoun may precede its antecedent. Put another way, I will be assuming that there is a prohibition against a pronoun preceding its antecedent and that the grammar defines the domain of this prohibition. As we shall see, this approach comes close to equaling the descriptive power of analyses that exploit notions far more abstract than precedence.

A key notion in the theory of anaphora that I will be developing is that of "phrasal category," as defined in (2).

(2) The phrasal category for *x* is the minimal phrasal category in which *x* functions as an argument or modifier.

The phrasal categories referred to in (2) are those defined in chapter 1 and restated here.

(3) NP: The maximal nominal category.
   VP: The maximal verbal category.
   AdjP: The maximal adjectival category.
   PP: A secondary or tertiary formed by combining a P with an NP.
   S: The phrase formed by combining two maximal phrasal categories.

Recall that, according to the definitions outlined in chapter 2, arguments are phrases that satisfy a verbal dependency, while syntactic modifiers are phrases that depend on a nominal or verbal category. According to this view, then, we can easily identify the respective phrasal categories of the NPs in (4).

(4)

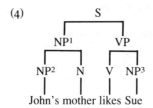

John's mother likes Sue

In (4), the "phrasal category" for NP¹ is S since this is the minimal phrasal category in which it functions as an argument (i.e., combines with the VP that it supports). The phrasal category of NP³, on the other hand, is VP since this is the smallest phrase in which it functions as an argument. (Recall that principles formulated in earlier chaps. require the direct object to be first argument of the verb.) Finally, NP² (a secondary) takes NP¹ as its phrasal category since this is the phrase in which it combines with the nominal element (*mother*) on which it depends.

We can now formulate the following constraint on anaphoric dependencies.

(5) *The Precedence Constraint (PC):*
A pronoun cannot precede an antecedent in its phrasal category.

According to (5), then, the domain for the prohibition against a pronoun preceding its antecedent corresponds to the phrasal category of the former element.

As a preliminary illustration of the effectiveness of the PC, consider the following monoclausal sentences. Here and elsewhere I will use labeled brackets to indicate the phrasal category of the pronoun and will employ coindexing to represent the intended anaphoric dependencies.

(6) *[$_S$ He$_i$ saw John's$_i$ picture.]

(7) *We [$_{VP}$ showed him$_i$ a picture of John$_i$].

(8) *They [$_{VP}$ left her$_i$ in Mary's$_i$ room].

As the bracketing shows, the pronouns in (6)–(8) all occur before the intended antecedent in their phrasal category (S in [6] and VP in [7] and [8]), in violation of the Precedence Constraint. These sentences contrast with the structures in (9) and (10) in which the pronoun precedes an antecedent not in its phrasal category.

(9) [$_{NP}$ Even his$_i$ mother] criticized Harry$_i$.

(10) I showed [$_{NP}$ a picture of him$_i$] to John$_i$.

The Precedence Constraint can easily be extended to anaphoric dependencies involving elements in different clauses within the same sentence. Consider first the contrast exemplified by (11).

(11) a. John$_i$ said [$_S$ that he$_i$ was sick].
    b. [$_{NP}$ His$_i$ mother] said that John$_i$ was sick.
    c. *[$_S$ He$_i$ said that John's$_i$ mother was sick.]

In (11) the PC makes the required distinction between (c) on one hand and (a)–(b) on the other. In sentence (a), the PC does not constrain the anaphoric dependency at all since the pronoun follows rather than precedes its antecedent. In (b), the pronoun precedes an antecedent lying outside its phrasal category and is therefore also compatible with the PC. The pronoun in (c), in contrast, precedes an antecedent within its phrasal category (the matrix S), in violation of the PC.

Sentences such as (11c) also contrast with the structures exemplified in (12).

(12) a. [$_S$ That he$_i$ was late so often] bothered Harry$_i$.
    b. The man [$_S$ who he$_i$ hired] doesn't trust Harry$_i$.
    c. [$_S$ After he$_i$ got home] John$_i$ made supper.

Although the pronouns in (12) all precede the NPs to which they look for their interpretation, none have antecedents within their phrasal category. There is therefore no violation of the PC, and the sentences are acceptable on the intended interpretation.

Consider next the anaphoric dependencies exemplified in (13) and (14).

(13) *Sue [$_{VP}$ told him$_i$ that John$_i$ was going to fail].

(14) *[$_S$ He$_i$ told Sue that Harry$_i$ had gotten home.]

Sentences (13) and (14) are both unacceptable on the intended reading for the usual reason: the pronoun precedes an antecedent in its phrasal category in violation of the PC. What makes these sentences especially intriguing is their relation to (15), which many people find to be quite acceptable (e.g., Reinhart 1981).

(15) Sue saw him$_i$ right after John$_i$ got home.

A promising way to account for the contrast between (13) and (15) would be to assume that temporal clauses combine with S rather than VP. This would result in the fundamental difference between the structures depicted in (16) and (17).

(16) Sue [$_{VP}$ told him [$_S$ that John would fail]].

(17) [$_S$ [$_S$ Sue saw him] [$_S$ after John got home]].

Notice that the NP *John* occurs within the phrasal category of the pronoun (i.e., VP) in (16) but not in (17), in which the adverbial clause lies outside the VP containing the pronoun. This accounts for the apparent contrast in the admissibility of the anaphoric dependency in the two structures.[1]

In addition to accounting for the interpretive facts, the proposed structural difference between the two sentence types has the advantage of receiving independent support from facts pertaining to clause order in English. Notice in this respect that, while a temporal clause can freely occur sentence initially in English, a direct object clause cannot.

(18) After John got home, Sue came for a visit.

(19) ?*[That John was sick], I told Sue.

Assuming that temporal clauses combine with S and object clauses with V, the relative naturalness and frequency of structures such as (18) could be attributed to the fact that there is no need for a discontinuous phrase (since the adverbial clause can combine just as easily with a following S as with a preceding one). Sentences such as (19), on the other hand, will require a discontinuous constituent since the object phrase is separated from the verb with which it must combine. Although such a combinatorial relation is not impossible, as we have seen, it seems reasonable to suppose that its unnaturalness will increase with the complexity of the phrase involved in the discontinuity.

Just as the Precedence Constraint can be extended to multiclausal structures, so it can constrain anaphoric dependencies whose domain is NP. Consider:

(20) a. Harry's$_i$ book about his$_i$ mother.
    b. *[$_{NP}$ his$_i$ book about Harry's$_i$ mother]
    c. [[$_{NP}$ his$_i$ wife's] book about Harry's$_i$ mother]

The crucial contrast in (20) is between (b) and (c). As the bracketing shows, the phrasal category for *his* in (20b) is the entire NP. Since the intended antecedent (*Harry*) also lies within this category, there is a violation of the Precedence Constraint, and the structure is ruled out on the intended reading. In (20c), in contrast, the pronoun functions as a modifier within the smaller NP headed by *wife*. Since this phrase does not contain the intended antecedent, the structure is not in violation of the PC and is therefore acceptable on the intended interpretation.

5.3 The Precedence Constraint versus the C-Command Principle

Thus far, the Precedence Constraint and the C-Command Principle make essentially the same predictions about the admissibility of anaphoric dependencies in the range of structures we have been examining. This is because the first branching node above the pronoun in these structures happens also to correspond to that element's phrasal category. This can be illustrated with the help of sentence (1) repeated from section 5.2.

(1)

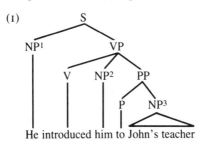

He introduced him to John's teacher

Notice that in (1) the first branching node above *he* is S—its phrasal category on my analysis. Moreover, the first branching node above *him* is VP, also its phrasal category. Since the NP *John* lies within both S and VP, the C-Command Principle and the Precedence Constraint both correctly predict that an anaphoric dependency involving it and either of the pronouns will be impossible.

Significantly, however, there is also a range of cases in which the PC and the C-Command Principle diverge in their predictions about the admissibility of anaphoric dependencies. The first such case is exemplified by the contrast in (2).

(2) a. I [$_{VP}$ showed John$_i$ himself$_i$ in the mirror].
    b. *I [$_{VP}$ showed himself$_i$ John$_i$ in the mirror].

Since the first node above both the reflexive pronoun and its antecedent in these sentences is VP, the C-Command Principle predicts that both should be unacceptable. In contrast, the PC correctly predicts that only the second construction will be ungrammatical since only it contains a pronoun to the left of an antecedent in its phrasal category.

A second contrast between the C-Command Principle and the Precedence Constraint involves structures in which a pronoun is part of a PP, as in (3) and (4).

(3) *Sue sat near him$_i$ at Harry's$_i$ birthday party.

(4) *Sue talked to him$_i$ about Harry's$_i$ exam.

Although the intended anaphoric dependencies here are all inadmissible, the pronoun does not c-command its antecedent in these structures. This is illustrated in (5), corresponding to (3).

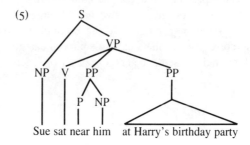

(5)

Sue sat near him at Harry's birthday party

Notice that in (5) the first branching node above the pronominal NP is PP, which does not dominate the intended antecedent. There is therefore no violation of the C-Command Principle, and the anaphoric dependency is incorrectly allowed.

A somewhat different result is obtained in the theory I am developing. According to the view of prepositions outlined in chapter 1, these elements function to convert NPs into secondaries or tertiaries (syntactic modifiers) that can then combine with either a nominal or a verbal element. This means that, within the PP, the NP is neither an argument nor a modifier. Rather it becomes a modifier only after combining with the preposition, and it fulfills its modifier function only when it combines with a verbal or nominal element. According to this view, then, the phrasal category for the NPs combining with a preposition in (3) and (4) above will be, as (6) illustrates.

(6) Sue [$_{VP}$ sat near him at Harry's birthday party].

Since the intended antecedent lies within the phrasal category of the pronoun in (6), there is a violation of the PC, and the sentence is ruled out on the relevant interpretation.

A third range of cases in which the Precedence Constraint and the C-Command Principle diverge in their predictions involves coordinate structures. Consider in this respect a sentence such as (7).

(7) *He$_i$ and Sue visited John's$_i$ mother.

Although (7) is obviously unacceptable, the syntactic structure that would be assigned to this sentence within TG does not reveal any violation of the C-Command Principle.

(8)

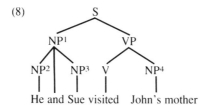

In (8) the first branching node above the pronominal NP is NP^1, which does not dominate the intended antecedent. As things now stand, then, there is no violation of the C-Command Principle. An obvious way around this problem would be to define c-command in a somewhat more complicated way so that the compound NP in (8) is ignored in the search for the first branching node above the pronoun, resulting in the selection of S and a violation of the C-Command Principle.

There is no need to make such revisions in the analysis I am developing. Since the pronoun in (8) functions as neither an argument nor a modifier within NP^1, this cannot be its phrasal category. Rather the phrasal category must be S since this is the phrase within which *he* is joint subject (along with *Sue*). Since the intended antecedent (*John*) also lies within this phrase, the anaphoric dependency will be ruled out by the Precedence Constraint, as desired. A similar result is obtained in sentences such as (9) and (10).

(9) *We [$_{VP}$ saw Sue and him$_i$ in John's$_i$ house].

(10) *We [$_{VP}$ sat between him$_i$ and Sue at John's$_i$ house].

In (9) *him* functions as (joint) direct object within the VP, a phrase containing the intended antecedent in violation of the PC. In (10), on the other hand, the pronoun will function as (joint) modifier after the coordinate NP is converted into a tertiary by the preposition *between* and combines with the verb. The phrasal category for the pronoun is once again the VP, ensuring a violation of the PC.

A fourth set of facts that favor the Precedence Constraint over the C-Command Principle comes from Korean and sentences such as (11), which would presumably be assigned structure (12) in TG. (I base this assumption on a proposal made for Japanese by Saito [1985].)

(11) Caki-rul$_i$ John-i$_i$ piphanha-yess-ta.
    self-Ac John-N criticized
    "John criticized self."

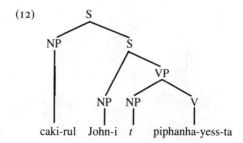

(12)

caki-rul John-i *t* piphanha-yess-ta

Since (12) is grammatical even though the pronoun clearly c-commands its antecedent, it seems necessary to suppose that the admissibility of anaphoric dependencies is determined at a level of syntactic representation (presumably deep structure or logical form) resembling (13).

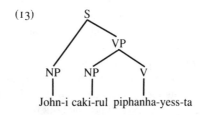

(13)

John-i caki-rul piphanha-yess-ta

A major problem for this proposal comes from sentences such as (14) and (15).

(14) *Caki-eykey$_i$ nay-ka John-ul$_i$ kewul-lo pichwepoyecwu-ess-ta.
     self-Dat I-N   John-Ac mirror in showed
     "I showed John to self in the mirror."

(15) *Caki-rul$_i$ nay-ka John-eykey$_i$ kewul-lo pichwepoyecwu-ess-ta.
     self-Ac I-N   John-Dat mirror in showed
     "I showed John self in the mirror."

The anaphoric dependency in (14) and (15) is inadmissible even though it would be acceptable in (16) or (17).

(16) Nay-ka [$_{VP}$John-ul$_i$ caki-eykey$_i$ kewul-lo pichwepoyecsu-ess-ta].
     I-N   John-Ac self-Dat   mirror in showed
     "I showed John to self in the mirror."

(17) Nay-ka [$_{VP}$ John-eykey$_i$ caki-rul$_i$ kewul-lo pichwepoyecwu-ess-ta].
     I-N   John-Dat self-Ac   mirror in showed
     "I showed John self in the mirror."

Since either (16) or (17) presumably has the configurational properties of the "underlying structure" (depending on whether the dative-accusative or accusative-dative order is basic), their acceptability would appear to under-

mine the claim that the admissibility of anaphoric dependencies in Korean
is determined in deep structure or logical form.

The analysis of these sentences is straightforward in the theory I have
outlined. Assuming that Korean exploits the Subject-Last Requirement
(see chap. 2), (11) and (14) will have the structures depicted in (18) and
(19), respectively. (Recall that the dative does not mark an argument in
Korean: see sec. 2.5.)

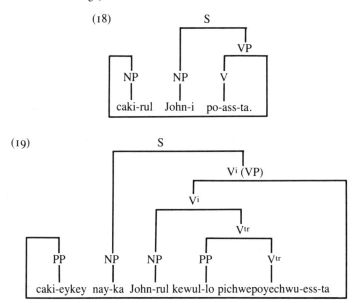

Given these structures, the PC will make the desired distinctions. In (18)
the intended antecedent does not lie within *caki*'s phrasal category (VP),
and there is therefore no violation of the PC. In (19), in contrast, the
intended antecedent is part of the VP (which is once again the pronoun's
phrasal category), creating a violation of the PC and ensuring that the
sentence will be unacceptable. (A broader range of such cases is discussed
in O'Grady [1985a, in press].)

5.4 Pronouns with Nondeterminate Antecedents

It is well known (e.g., Higginbotham 1980, 1983) that anaphoric dependencies involving NPs that do not have specific referents are somewhat
more restricted than those involving prototypical referring expressions
(e.g., proper names and definite NPs). Consider in this respect the following sentences.

(1) a. *[$_{NP}$ His$_i$ mother] loves everyone$_i$.
   b. *The woman [$_S$ he$_i$ works for] despises someone$_i$.
   c. *[$_{NP}$ The picture of him$_i$] pleased each student$_i$.

As the bracketing in (1) indicates, none of the pronouns precedes an antecedent within its phrasal category; yet none of the intended anaphoric dependencies is possible. This contrasts with the situation exemplified in (2), where the antecedent is a referring expression rather than a quantified phrase and the anaphoric dependency is perfectly acceptable.

(2) a. [$_{NP}$ His$_i$ mother] loves Harry$_i$.
   b. The woman [$_S$ he$_i$ works for] despises Harry$_i$.
   c. [$_{NP}$ The picture of him$_i$] pleased Harry$_i$.

Although one might think that the contrast under consideration could be captured simply by stipulating that a pronoun cannot precede an indeterminate antecedent (to use Wasow's [1979] term), this proposal is still not general enough. As the following sentences show, there are also many cases in which an anaphoric dependency is inadmissible even though the pronoun follows a quantified antecedent.

(3) a. *The man [$_S$ everyone$_i$ trusts] betrayed him$_i$.
   b. *The loss of [$_{NP}$ everyone's$_i$ freedom] bothered him$_i$.
   c. *[$_{NP}$ Everyone's$_i$ opinion of the book] amuses him$_i$.

These sentences contrast with the structures in (4), where the intended antecedent is a referring expression and the anaphoric dependency is admissible.

(4) a. The man [$_S$ Harry$_i$ trusts] betrayed him$_i$.
   b. The loss of [$_{NP}$ Harry's$_i$ freedom] bothered him$_i$.
   c. [$_{NP}$ Harry's$_i$ opinion of the book] amuses him$_i$.

One way to account for these contrasts would be to adopt a principle resembling (5).

(5) *The Indeterminate Antecedent Requirement (IAR):*
   A pronoun must occur in the phrasal category of a quantified antecedent.

The IAR automatically rules out the anaphoric dependencies in the sentence types exemplified by (1) and (3) since the pronoun in these structures does not occur in the phrasal category of its antecedent. In (1a), for instance, the phrasal category of the intended antecedent—a direct object—is VP, which does not contain the pronoun. Similarly, in (3a), the phrasal category of the quantified NP is the relative clause (in which it functions as subject), but the pronoun lies outside this phrase, ensuring a violation of the IAR. These structures contrast with the sentences exemplified in (6), all of which comply with the IAR.

(6) a. [$_S$ Everyone$_i$ said that he$_i$ was sick.]
  b. Sue [$_{VP}$ told everyone$_i$ that he$_i$ could go home].
  c. Sue [$_{VP}$ met with each student$_i$ in his$_i$ own home].
  d. [$_S$ Each gun$_i$ and some ammunition was put in its$_i$ owner's locker].

As the labeled bracketing in (6) indicates, the pronoun falls within the phrasal category of the quantified NP, ensuring that the intended anaphoric dependency will comply with the IAR.[2]

Within TG, it is often proposed that a pronoun must be c-commanded by a quantified antecedent (e.g., Higginbotham 1980; Reinhart 1983; and Haïk 1984). However, this analysis encounters problems not associated with the IAR since the anaphoric dependency exemplified by (6c) and (d) is acceptable even though the quantified antecedent seems not to c-command the pronoun. Significantly, however, the pronoun does lie within the phrasal category of the quantified NP in these structures, given our earlier assumptions about the phrasal categories of NPs within PPs and coordinate phrases.

Another advantage of the IAR is that it can be extended without revision to account for the well-known contrasts illustrated in (7) and (8).

(7) a. [$_S$ Who$_i$ lost his$_i$ watch?]
  b. [$_S$ Who$_i$ said he$_i$ was late?]

(8) a. *Who$_i$ did he$_i$ see?
  b. *Who$_i$ did his$_i$ mother criticize?
  c. *Whose$_i$ teacher did he$_i$ say Mary trusted?

If we accept the usual assumption that *wh* phrases belong to the same class of indeterminate antecedents as quantified NPs, the anaphoric dependencies in (7) will comply with the Indeterminate Antecedent Requirement since the pronoun lies within the phrasal category of the *wh* word (as indicated by the bracketing). But what of the sentences in (8)? Assuming as usual that the formation of sentences in English is constrained by the Subject-Last Requirement, a sentence such as (8b) will have a structure resembling (9).

(9)

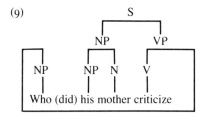

As (9) shows, the pronoun does not occur in the phrasal category of the *wh* phrase (i.e., VP), a fact that renders the intended anaphoric dependency incompatible with the Indeterminate Antecedent Requirement. This contrasts with sentences such as (10) in which the *wh* phrase is in subject position.

(10) [$_S$ Who$_i$ was criticized by his$_i$ mother?]

Another intriguing contrast involving the IAR occurs in sentences such as (11).

(11) a. Who$_i$ did you consult in his$_i$ own home?
     b. Who$_i$ did you tell that his$_i$ car had been stolen?

Under the usual assumptions about the role of the Subject-Last Requirement in the formation of syntactic structure, (11a) will have a representation resembling (12).

(12)

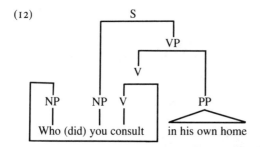

As (12) shows, the phrasal category of the *wh* word—a direct object—is the VP, which also contains the pronoun. The intended dependency therefore complies with the IAR, and the sentence is acceptable. A similar state of affairs manifests itself in (11b). Both these sentences contrast with the structures exemplified in (8) above, in which the pronoun lies outside the phrasal category of the *wh* phrase in a syntactic structure formed in accordance with the Subject-Last Requirement.[3]

A subtle contrast involving the IAR and our assumptions about the architecture of syntactic representations is found in (13) and (14).

(13) ?*Who$_i$ did you report [$_{NP}$ gossip about ____] to his$_i$ wife?

(14) Who$_i$ did you [$_{VP}$ talk to ____ about his$_i$ wife]?

As indicated by the labeled bracketing, the phrasal category for the *wh* phrase corresponds to NP in (13) and VP in (14). Since the pronoun lies within the phrasal category of its intended *wh* antecedent only in the latter case, the first sentence is ruled out by the IAR.

5.5 Blocked Patterns of Forward Anaphora

A particularly intriguing phenomenon involving anaphoric dependencies manifests itself in sentences (1) and (2). (Not all speakers allow the relatively free topicalization needed to obtain the contrasts exemplified in [2].)

(1) a. *Near John$_i$ he$_i$ saw a snake ____.
    b. Near John$_i$ [$_{NP}$ his$_i$ father] saw a snake ____.

(2) a. *Harry$_i$, he$_i$ said Mary liked ____.
    b. Harry$_i$, [$_{NP}$ even his$_i$ father] doesn't like ____.

As things now stand, the Precedence Constraint fails to make the required distinctions since it predicts that all these sentences will be acceptable (since the pronoun does not precede its antecedent). This is the right prediction in the case of (1b) and (2b), where the antecedent does not even lie within the phrasal category of the pronoun. However, it is wrong for (1a) and (2a), whose structures presumably resemble (3) and (4), respectively.

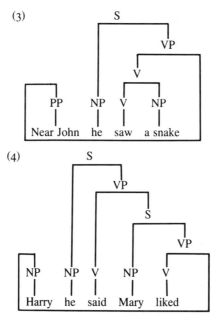

(3)

(4)

In (3) and (4), the antecedent lies within the phrasal category of the pronoun (i.e., within S) but does not follow it in the linear string. There would therefore appear to be no violation of the Precedence Constraint. It is not possible to avoid this problem simply by stipulating that an antecedent cannot occur in the phrasal category of the pronoun (eliminating all refer-

ence to precedence) since this would incorrectly rule out sentences such as
(5) and (6).

(5) Sue [$_{VP}$ returned John's$_i$ book to him$_i$].

(6) Sue [$_{VP}$ showed John$_i$ himself$_i$ in the mirror].

These sentences demonstrate that a pronoun can be preceded by an antecedent in its phrasal category (VP), thereby ruling out the proposed modification of the PC.

  One plausible response to the problem of blocked patterns of forward
anaphora would be to assume that such structures simply do not fall under
the PC and that some additional constraint must be formulated. Although
this is not impossible, I will assume that it is not a desirable step at this
time and that some effort should be devoted to the search for a unified
constraint on anaphoric dependencies. This brings us to the possibility of
reformulating the PC in such a way that it works for (1) and (2). The
possibility that I find most promising and the one that I will pursue here is
that "precedence" involves more than just relative order in the linear
string. The particular idea that I will try to develop is that the Precedence
Constraint is sensitive not to the "linear positions" of the pronoun and its
antecedent but rather to their "combinatorial positions" defined as
follows:

(7) A category's combinatorial position corresponds to the point at which it com-
    bines with another element to serve as an argument or a modifier.

In the case of the structures that do not contain discontinuous constituents,
an element's combinatorial position will correspond to its actual location in
the string. In a sentence such as (8), for instance, the object NP occurs in a
position where it can combine with the adjacent verb, while the subject
occurs in a position that allows it to be attached to the adjacent VP, in
accordance with the usual practice.

(8) [$_S$ The boy [$_{VP}$ read the book]]

Quite a different state of affairs manifests itself in a sentence such (3)
above, repeated here as (9).

(9) *[Near John$_i$] he$_i$ saw a snake ____.

In (9), the NP that the preposition *near* converts into a tertiary must combine with a verbal category. This suggests that its combinatorial position is
in the VP, to the right of the subject phrase.

  Assuming that we interpret the PC along the lines of (10) rather than
(11), sentence (9) will be ungrammatical on the intended interpretation.

(10) The combinatorial position of a pronoun cannot precede the combinatorial position of an antecedent in its phrasal category.

(11) The linear position of a pronoun cannot precede the linear position of an antecedent in its phrasal category.

Notice that in (9) the combinatorial position of the pronoun (the preverbal subject position) precedes the combinatorial position (VP) of an antecedent in its phrasal category, in violation of (10).

Sentence (4), repeated here as (12), provides another illustration of this.

(12) *Harry$_i$ [$_S$ he$_i$ said Mary liked ____].

In (12), the linear position of the pronoun is also its combinatorial position since this element combines with the adjacent VP. In contrast, its intended antecedent (the S-initial NP) combines not with an adjacent phrase but rather with the verb in the embedded clause (of which it is the direct object). This means that its combinatorial position is located within the embedded VP. Since the pronoun not only lies within the phrasal category (S) of the pronoun but also has a combinatorial position that follows that of the pronoun, there is a violation of the Precedence Constraint, and the intended anaphoric dependency is correctly ruled out.

The interpretation of the Precedence Constraint that we are considering also allows us to predict the acceptability of sentences such as (13).

(13) a. Under the boots [$_S$ which John$_i$ bought], he$_i$ found a coin ____.
    b. Near the car which Sue [$_{VP}$ bought for John$_i$], he$_i$ left a note ____.

In (13a–b) there is an S-initial VP modifier whose combinatorial position must lie within the verbal phrase to the right of the subject pronoun. However, neither this PP nor the NP to which the preposition applies is the antecedent in these cases; rather an embedded phrase (the NP *John*) is. Significantly, this NP has its combinatorial position within the fronted phrase since it serves as subject of *bought* in (a) and as modifier in (b). The combinatorial position of *John* therefore precedes that of the pronoun, avoiding a violation of the Precedence Constraint.

A somewhat subtler contrast manifests itself in sentences such as (14).

(14) a. ??Under [$_{NP}$ John's$_i$ boots] he$_i$ found a coin ____.
    b. ??Near [$_{NP}$ John's$_i$ car], he$_i$ left a note ____.

The anaphoric dependencies in (14) should be acceptable since the combinatorial position of the intended antecedent lies within the bracketed NP to the left of the pronoun. Yet many people find the intended interpretations to be extremely marginal. While these sentences are less than fully natural, this does not seem to be the result of structural factors. Thus we can drastically improve the sentences in (14) by adding the intensifier *own,* a modification that does not change the combinatorial position of the antecedent.

(15) a. Under [$_{NP}$ John's$_i$ own boots] he$_i$ found a coin.
    b. Near [$_{NP}$ John's$_i$ own car], he$_i$ left a note.

This suggests that the marginality of (14) is due to nonsyntactic factors that are not of direct relevance to structural principles like the Precedence Constraint.

The grammaticality of sentences such as (13)–(15) points to a significant difference between the proposal I have made and a theory that would seek to apply the Precedence Constraint to ''deep structure'' or some similar level of underlying representation resembling (16).

(16) a. He$_i$ found a coin under the boots which John$_i$ bought.
    b. He$_i$ found a coin under John's$_i$ boots.

If the PC were applied to the representations exemplified in (16), it would incorrectly predict that the corresponding ''surface structures'' [13a] and [14a], respectively) are ungrammatical. This incorrect prediction does not arise in the approach I adopt since the Precedence Constraint applies to ''surface structure,'' ignoring an item's linear position only in cases in which it does not correspond to the point at which it combines with another category (its ''combinatorial position''). Since the S-initial PPs in (13)–(15) are not actually ''returned'' to a position within the VP (although the point at which they combine with a verbal element to form a discontinuous constituent is located therein), their component constituents still occur to the left of a subject pronoun—resulting in the observed patterns of anaphoric dependency (see the discussion of [13] above).

A variant of the deep structure analysis of blocked forward cases would involve assuming that the C-Command Principle is sensitive to the presence of ''traces'' and that it rules out anaphoric dependencies in which the pronoun c-commands either its antecedent or the trace of its antecedent. This correctly rules out structures such as (12) above, repeated here as (12′), while allowing (14a), repeated here as (14a′).

(12′) *Harry$_i$ [$_S$ he$_i$ said Mary liked t$_i$]

(14) a′. [$_{PP}$ Under John's$_i$ boots]$_j$ he$_i$ found a coin t$_j$.

Notice that in (12′) the pronoun c-commands the trace of its intended antecedent (*Harry*). In (14a′), in contrast, the trace corresponds to the fronted PP, not to the intended antecedent of the pronoun, and there is therefore no violation of the C-Command Principle. A problem with this approach is that it incorrectly predicts the grammaticality of (9), repeated here as (9′).

(9') *[$_{PP}$ Near John$_i$]$_j$, he$_i$ saw a snake t$_j$.

In (9'), the trace again corresponds to the PP, not the antecedent of the pronoun, and there is no violation of the C-Command Principle. This problem does not arise in the approach I have adopted since I assume that prepositions simply convert NPs into dependent elements that can then combine with a major category. This allows us to locate the combinatorial position of *John* in (9') within the VP, ensuring the desired violation of the Precedence Constraint. Such patterns contrast with (13)–(15), in which the NP that the preposition converts into a PP is not the intended antecedent.

Another set of contrasts involving the structures we are considering manifests itself in (17) and (18).

(17) *Near Ben$_i$ he$_i$ found a snake.

(18) According to Ben$_i$ he$_i$ found a snake.

Drawing on an earlier proposal by Kuno (1975), Reinhart suggests that there is an important semantic distinction between the sentence-initial PPs in (17) and (18). In particular, it seems that, whereas the PP in (18) provides old information or the background for the assertion made in the rest of the clause, the comparable phrase in (17) provides new information and occurs at the beginning of the clause for purposes of emphasis. Although this contrast is sometimes subtle and hard to formalize, it is correlated in a fairly direct fashion with certain structural phenomena. Thus in the clearest cases of the "background" phrase, the PP is introduced by a "scene-setting" preposition (e.g., *as for* or *according to*) and is an optional component of the utterance. In the clearest case of the emphatic structure, on the other hand, the PP is an obligatory component of the VP (i.e., is part of the verb's subcategorization frame). Sentences (19) and (20) provide examples of this. (The verbs *put* and *dash* both require locative modifiers.)

(19) *Near Ben$_i$ he$_i$ put a cigar ____.

(20) *Against Jane$_i$ she$_i$ dashed a vase ____.

The most obvious way to subsume this contrast into our analysis would be to assume that the sentence type exemplified by (18) has the structure depicted in (21).

(21)

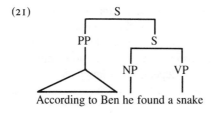

According to Ben he found a snake

As (21) shows, the PP is taken to function as a sentence modifier and is therefore not part of the VP. This means that the intended anaphoric dependency cannot violate the PC since *Ben* is not even part of the pronoun's phrasal category (the smaller S). This contrasts with what happens in (19) and (20), where the PP is part of the VP, leading to a violation of the PC for the reasons outlined earlier.

5.6 Learnability Issues

In keeping with the central thesis of this book, the next step in our consideration of the syntax of anaphora must involve an attempt to establish the learnability of the Precedence Constraint, repeated here as (1). (For the purpose of this discussion. I will set aside constraints specific to indeterminate antecedents.)

(1) *The Precedence Constraint (PC):*
    A pronoun cannot precede an antecedent in its phrasal category.

A major advantage of the Precedence Constraint for a theory of language acquisition is that the notions that it exploits all seem to be readily accessible to the language learner. Precedence, for instance, is a relation that manifests itself outside language and should therefore be available to children independent of grammatical development. Moreover, while the notion "phrasal category" is clearly linguistic in character, it need not be inborn. As noted in earlier discussion, the phrasal categories relevant to the Precedence Constraint are precisely those formed by the combinatorial and categorial mechanisms discussed in the first chapter. Since these mechanisms can apparently be learned without the help of special innate principles, there is nothing here to undermine the thesis of general nativism. There is likewise no challenge to general nativism in the use of arguments and modifiers in the determination of an element's phrasal category since these notions also seem to be the product of linguistic development (see chap. 2).

This leaves us with the problem of motivating the accessibility of the notions "pronoun" and "antecedent." These are almost certainly linguistic notions, but they may still be built on more general concepts. According to the proposals made in section 5.1, for instance, a pronoun-antecedent relation consists of an interpretive dependency in which one element (the pronoun) looks to the other (the "antecedent") for the determination of its reference. Assuming the nonlinguistic character of dependency, at least one component of the notion "anaphoric relation" will be available to children independent of language.

The status of the concept "reference" is somewhat more problematic, and its nonlinguistic base is hard to identify. Bruner (1983) suggests, following Hilary Putnam, that reference is a form of social interaction having to do with the management of joint attention. Related to this proposal is a suggestion by John Lyons (also cited by Bruner [1983]) that "locating in context" (deixis) is the source of reference. If either of these ideas could be developed, they might provide the nonlinguistic basis for reference needed to maintain the thesis of general nativism in this case.

Another possibility is that the roots of reference lie in the more general semiotic ability that is known to be present in even very young children. Along these lines Piaget and Inhelder (1969, 54) have noted that prelinguistic children are capable of various types of nonlinguistic symbolic activity, allowing a piece of wood, for example, to "stand for" an airplane or some other real world object. It is tempting to think that the roots of linguistic reference might lie in this type of nonlinguistic activity. Unfortunately, such examples are little more than suggestive at this time and have not been incorporated into any explicit account of the nonlinguistic origin of reference. It therefore seems necessary to maintain an open mind on this question and to countenance the possibility that very fundamental semantic relations may be the product of quite specific genetic structuring.

Turning now to the character of the experience that is likely to guide the development of the Precedence Constraint, it seems reasonable to suppose that even ordinary speech will contain a reasonable sampling of sentences in which it is clear that one element (what we have been calling a pronoun) looks to another for its interpretation. The observed patterns will presumably include structures resembling (2)–(4).

(2) Harry$_i$ lost his$_i$ watch.

(3) Harry$_i$ said that he$_i$ was late.

(4) His$_i$ mother scolded Harry$_i$.

A slight problem arises at this point since it is not obvious how children would come to realize that the logically possible pattern exemplified by (5) is not acceptable.

(5) *He$_i$ criticized John's$_i$ mother.

Since it is usually assumed that language learners do not take note of the infinitely large set of structures that will be absent from their environment and do not receive systematic feedback about possible errors and misinterpretations, they must have some other way to come to the conclusion that (5) is unacceptable. One possibility is that, as soon as children realize that pronouns are dependent on other elements for their interpretation, they reject all cases of backward anaphora because of the processing difficulties associated with the appearance of a pronoun prior to the element determining its interpretation. In English, of course, there are acceptable instances of backward anaphoric dependencies, and exposure to these would eventually lead children to adjust their grammars so as to allow patterns such as (4). As we will see shortly, the developmental data shed light on precisely how this happens. (I will discuss apparent counterexamples to this proposal from Japanese and other left-branching languages in chap. 7.)

Still another puzzling aspect of the ontogeny of anaphora relates to why children formulate restrictions on backward dependencies in terms of phrasal categories rather than some other, less fruitful, notion. The likely answer to this question lies in the nature of children's linguistic knowledge at the point at which they begin to formulate constraints on anaphoric dependencies (around five years of age, on the average—see below). According to the theory being developed here, children have access to an extremely restricted set of linguistic notions, the most widely used of which pertain to the categories formed in accordance with the combinatorial principles outlined in chapter 1. Given this, it is not surprising that they would try to formulate principles for a novel phenomenon in terms of the categories (NP, VP, S) and relations (precedence, adjacency) that have been the key to earlier grammatical development.

The discovery of the relevance of a pronoun's phrasal category (rather than some other random constituent type) to its interpretation may well be enhanced by the fact that this corresponds to the smallest syntactic unit that can also contain another NP (i.e., a potential antecedent). Thus the phrasal category of a subject pronoun (i.e., S) is the smallest category that can contain that element and another NP; the phrasal category of an object pronoun (VP) is the smallest category that can contain that element and another NP; and so on. Assuming that limitations on working memory influence children's manipulation of syntactic representations, it would not be unreasonable to think that a syntactic constraint on anaphoric dependencies would be formulated in terms of the smallest syntactic unit containing the pronoun and a potential antecedent—its phrasal category.

Further details about how children come to exploit the relevant categorial notions and relations to formulate the Precedence Constraint come from the known facts about the ontogeny of anaphoric dependencies. On the basis of research by Carol Chomsky (1969), Ingram and Shaw (1981), and Lust (1981), it seems plausible to posit the following four steps in the acquisition of the Precedence Constraint. (Following an exhaustive review of the relevant literature, Carden [in press] has independently proposed the same developmental sequence.)

Stage 1:
There are no constraints on anaphoric dependencies. In this stage, even sentences such as (6) and (7) are apparently admitted.

(6) *He$_i$ saw Harry's$_i$ mother.

(7) *He$_i$ said that Harry$_i$ was late.

Stage 2:
Backward dependencies are ruled out in all cases. In this stage even grammatical sentences such as (8) are taken to be unacceptable.

(8) His$_i$ mother likes John's$_i$ car.

Stage 3:
Acceptable and unacceptable cases of backward anaphora are correctly distinguished. In this stage, (8) is permitted, but (6) and (7) are rejected.

Stage 4:
Forward anaphora, hitherto accepted in all cases, is now constrained so as to rule out sentences such as (9).

(9) *Near John$_i$ he$_i$ saw a snake.

Of these putative stages, the fourth is the only one that is likely to be disputed since Lust and Clifford (1982) have claimed that even three- and four-year-old children correctly block coreference in cases such as (9). What Lust and Clifford's data (not included in their 1982 paper but available in unpublished form) actually show is that children between the ages of three and one half and eight allowed coreference in these structures only 18 percent of the time but that they gave responses in which there was disjoint reference in only 19 percent of the cases. The rest of the time, the children either refused to respond or behaved in unexpected ways (taking themselves as referent of the pronoun in 37 percent of the cases, e.g.). I do not see how this response pattern supports the claim that coreference is blocked in such structures. If anything, the results show that the children found the structures used by Lust and Clifford extremely difficult to deal with. (The structures included tokens such as *Under Big Bird, quickly, he threw the choo-choo train.*) This fact surely weakens any conclusions drawn about the children's occasional attempts to interpret the pronouns in these structures.

Because of these problems, I will rely on data collected by Ingram and Shaw (1981) and Taylor-Browne (1983) from children of elementary school age who show no hesitation in responding and do not take themselves as referents of third person pronouns. Significantly, such children typically allow coreference in the constructions we are considering. In Taylor-Browne's study, for example, the sentence *Near Barbie, she dropped the earring* received an interpretation with *she* coreferential to *Barbie* in over 85 percent of the responses given by the ten first-grade children in the study. Similar responses occurred over 70 percent of the time among fourth-grade children ($N = 9$). Such results support the claim that blocked forward patterns of anaphora are mastered at a late point in the language acquisition process (my stage 4).

Another possible objection to the developmental sequence that I have posited is that it does not include a stage in which children allow an anaphoric dependency in sentences such as (10b) but not (10a).

(10) a. *He$_i$ hit the horse after the sheep's$_i$ run.
     b. *The horse hit him$_i$ after the sheep's$_i$ run.

Solan (1983) claims that such a stage occurred in the children (aged five to seven) he studied since they allowed an anaphoric dependency 17 percent of the time in (10a) compared to 39 percent in (b).

Although this difference is statistically significant, it shows only that children prefer coreference somewhat more in one case. It does not show that coreference is blocked in one case but not the other, unless some argument is presented for the view that the criterion for blocked coreference falls between 17 percent and 39 percent. Solan provides no such argument. Interestingly, Ingram and Shaw (1981) suggest that the criterion should be set at 40 percent on the basis of their work with adults. For them, then, only subjects who produce anaphoric responses more than 40 percent of the time are said to allow coreference in a particular structure. On this view both sets of responses in Solan's study would be interpreted as instances of blocked backward anaphora (my stage 2 or later). Carol Chomsky (1969), on the other hand, adopts a much lower baseline, setting her criterion at zero—an assumption that would take both response patterns in Solan's study to exemplify the absence of any constraint on anaphoric dependency (my stage 1).

This suggests that the phenomenon noted by Solan may not reflect the appearance of a new grammatical principle and that it therefore need not be explained by a theory of grammatical development. This is not to suggest that the contrast in question is not interesting or that it should not be carefully studied—only that there is no reason to think that it reflects an important step in the development of the child's grammar.

Assuming the correctness of the developmental sequence I have proposed, we can now proceed to analyze it in terms of the grammatical advances associated with each of the component stages. Significantly, the first three stages in the proposed sequence seem to reflect the step-by-step discovery of the Precedence Constraint. The following principles characterize the first three stages described above.

(11) *Stage 1 (no constraint):*
     A pronoun takes an antecedent.
     Stage 2 (no backward patterns permitted):
     A pronoun cannot precede its antecedent.

Stage 3 (grammatical backward patterns permitted):
A pronoun cannot precede an antecedent in its phrasal category.

The stages outlined in (11) constitute a logical developmental sequence in that each step provides the basis on which the next is built. Stage 1 involves discovery of anaphoric dependencies—an obvious prerequisite for the evolution of constraints on pronoun-antecedent relations. The developmental data suggest that this stage may be very short lived and is often contemporaneous with stage 2 and the use of precedence to rule out all cases of backward anaphora. This is presumably because the processing difficulties associated with backward dependencies arise as soon as children realize that a pronoun must look to an antecedent for its interpretation.

Just as the discovery of anaphoric dependencies (stage 1) is logically prior to the formulation of a constraint on their occurrence (stage 2), so the notion that children initially exploit (precedence) is a prerequisite for the exploitation of phrasal categories that characterizes stage 3. The reason for this is simple: phrasal categories are relevant only to constraints on backward anaphora. (As we have seen, there is no prohibition against a pronoun following an antecedent in its phrasal category.) Until precedence is used to distinguish between forward and backward patterns of anaphora, then, the relevance of phrasal categories to anaphoric constraints cannot be discovered. This explains the relative ordering of stages 2 and 3.

The fourth step in the ontogeny of the Precedence Constraint is the most difficult to understand. It is during this stage that children finally come to distinguish between the cases of forward anaphora represented in (12).

(12) a. According to John$_i$, he$_i$ saw a snake.
     b. *Near John$_i$, he$_i$ saw a snake.

As noted in earlier discussion, this contrast involves a distinction between PPs that function as sentence modifiers (the case in [a]) and those that combine with a nonadjacent verbal element to form a discontinous constituent (the case in [b]). Since the point at which the lexical NP can combine with another phrase (its "combinatorial position") lies within the VP in the latter case, there is a violation of the Precedence Constraint, and the sentence is ruled out on the intended reading.

Two problems confront the child here: determining that some PPs form discontinuous constituents with the remainder of the VP and making the Precedence Constraint sensitive to the combinatorial positions of pronouns and their intended antecedents. Of these two problems, the first is probably the less serious. Not only is there a semantic distinction between PPs modifying S and those modifying VP (see the earlier discussion), but VP modifiers also occur adjacent to the rest of the verbal category the vast majority of the time (e.g., [13]).

(13) John saw a snake near Sue.

Assuming the Adjacency Preference and the Subject-Last Requirement, the type of PP found in (13) will be classified as a VP modifier, ensuring the existence of a discontinuous constituent in sentences such as (12b). The problem here is to determine when and how children come to realize that the sentence-initial PP in (12b) and the postverbal PP in (13) belong to the same semantic class. While I will not try to explain precisely how this takes place, it is conceivable that sentence-initial PPs such as the one in (12a) have a hindering effect. Indeed, it would not be unreasonable to expect children to adopt the initial assumption that all S-initial PPs combine with the adjacent S, in accordance with the Adjacency Preference. This in turn would suppress the contrast between (12a) and (12b), accounting for the late mastery of the blocked patterns of forward anaphora.

This leaves us with the problem of explaining how children come to compute precedence in terms of combinatorial positions rather than location in the linear string. One possibility is that reference to combinatorial positions is a natural consequence of the computation of pronoun-antecedent relations in terms of syntactic structure, which consists of combinatorial relations among words and phrases rather than just a linear string of words. According to the proposals I have made above, the second stage in the ontogeny of anaphora is characterized by a principle that makes reference simply to the linear string (i.e., ''A pronoun cannot precede its antecedent''), but the third stage is marked by discovery of the role played by phrasal categories in constraining anaphoric dependencies. The computation of combinatorial relations entailed by this reference to phrasal categories could be crucial to determining the relevance of combinatorial positions to the syntax of anaphora.

The preceding proposal automatically predicts that the computation of precedence in terms of combinatorial positions cannot occur before the discovery of the relevance of phrasal categories to anaphoric dependencies. As noted earlier, phrasal categories are crucial to the distinction between the blocked and permitted cases of backward anaphora exemplified in (14), while the reference to combinatorial positions is essential to mastery of blocked forward anaphora.

(14) a. $[_{NP}$ The picture of him$_i$] pleased John$_i$.
     b. *$[_S$ He$_i$ saw John's$_i$ picture].

We therefore predict that children will acquire the syntax of backward anaphora before they master the blocked forward cases. As the developmental sequence outlined earlier shows, this is correct.

5.7 The Syntax of Reflexive Pronouns

Thus far I have ignored a contrast that has traditionally been considered central to the nature of anaphoric dependencies, namely, the distinction between "ordinary" pronouns such as *him* and "reflexive" pronouns such as *himself*. As sentences (1) and (2) show, some anaphoric dependencies are possible only if the reflexive form of the pronoun is used, while others are inadmissible with a reflexive pronoun.

(1) a. Harry$_i$ saw himself/*him$_i$.
    b. I showed Harry$_i$ himself/*him$_i$ in the mirror.

(2) a. Harry's$_i$ girlfriend criticized him/*himself$_i$.
    b. The picture of Harry$_i$ pleased him/*himself$_i$.

The existence of this contrast does not challenge the viability of the Precedence Constraint since even reflexive pronouns seem to be subject to this principle. We therefore find contrasts like the following.

(3) *I [$_{VP}$ showed himself$_i$ John$_i$ in the mirror].

(4) I showed [$_{NP}$ a picture of himself$_i$] to John$_i$.

Sentence (3) constitutes a violation of the Precedence Constraint since a (reflexive) pronoun precedes an antecedent in its phrasal category (VP). In this it contrasts with (1), in which the reflexive pronoun follows its antecedent, and (4), in which the reflexive precedes an antecedent lying outside its phrasal category (the NP marked by brackets).

What is clearly needed, then, is not an entirely new treatment of anaphoric dependencies but rather an account of the precise conditions under which a reflexive pronoun can occur. Unfortunately, such an enterprise is fraught with problems caused in part by the fact that the distribution of reflexive pronouns is sensitive to extremely subtle semantic and pragmatic factors. Thus we find sentences such as (5) and (6), in which the reflexive and nonreflexive forms of the pronoun alternate to create very slight differences in focus.

((5) Mary$_i$ keeps a gun near her/herself$_i$ at all times.

(6) John$_i$ doesn't like that picture of him/himself$_i$.

These and other such contrasts have been discussed in detail by Cantrall (1974), Kuno (1975), and Watson (1984).

In what follows, I will concentrate on identifying the syntactic conditions under which the reflexive form of the pronoun is obligatory. I assume that a reflexive is possible in other cases only to the extent that its presence can be motivated by semantic and pragmatic principles that do not concern us here. The key syntactic principle for English seems to resemble (7).

(7) *The Reflexive Requirement (RR):*
The reflexive is obligatory when a pronoun and its antecedent are thematic dependents of the same element.

As a preliminary illustration of how (7) works, consider the following two sentences.

(8) John$_i$ criticized himself/him$_i$.

(9) Sue$_i$ attacked herself/*her$_i$.

In both these sentences, the pronoun and its antecedent receive their thematic role from the same element (the verb). As predicted by the RR, the reflexive form of the pronoun is required. These sentences contrast with structures such as (10) and (11).

(10) *John$_i$ said that Sue criticized himself$_i$.

(11) *The criticism of John$_i$ amused himself$_i$.

In both these sentences the reflexive and its intended antecedent are thematic dependents of different elements (the embedded and matrix verbs in [10] and the verb *amuse* and the noun *criticism* in [11]). Significantly, the reflexive form is not obligatory here; in fact, it is not permitted at all.

The next group of sentences illustrates that the RR also holds in cases in which the pronoun and its antecedent receive their thematic role from the same noun or adjective.

(12) John's$_i$ criticism of himself/*him$_i$.

(13) Sue's$_i$ attack on herself/*her$_i$.

(14) Harry$_i$ is fond of himself/*him$_i$.

Recall that, according to the theory developed in chapter 2, the NPs in (12) and (13) both receive their respective thematic roles from the noun (*criticism/attack*), while those in (14) are thematic dependents of the adjective *fond*. As predicted by the RR, the reflexive form of the pronoun is obligatory in these cases.

A particularly subtle contrast involving the RR is found in (15) and (16).

(15) a. John$_i$ talked to himself/*him$_i$.
 b. John$_i$ thought about himself/*him$_i$.
 c. John$_i$ was criticized only by himself/*him$_i$.
 d. Sue$_i$ pleaded with herself/*her$_i$.

    e. I showed John$_i$ to himself/*him$_i$ in the mirror.
    f. I talked to John$_i$ about himself/*him$_i$.

(16) a. John$_i$ drew the book toward himself/him$_i$.
    b. Sue$_i$ keeps a gun near her/herself$_i$ at all times.
    c. John$_i$ talked to the girl in front of him/*himself$_i$.

As noted in chapter 2, the pronominal NPs in (15) all receive their thematic role from the verb while those in (16) are thematic dependents of the preposition. As the RR would predict, the reflexive form is obligatory only in (15), where the pronoun and its antecedent are both thematic dependents of the verb. In (16), where the pronoun and its antecedent are assigned thematic roles by different elements (the preposition and the verb, respectively), the reflexive is either optional or unacceptable.

    Sentences such as (17) present a possible problem for the RR as it is currently stated.

(17) John$_i$ appears to himself/*him$_i$ to be running well.
       seems

In (17), the reflexive form of the pronoun is obligatory even though it is often assumed that the intended antecedent receives its thematic role from the embedded verb (*run*), not the *seem*-type verb that assigns the experiencer role to the NP in the *to* phrase. This intuition is captured in TG and many other theories by representing *John* as subject of *to be running* in an underlying structure and then "raising" it to the matrix subject position in surface structure.

    While I will make no attempt here to explicate the formation of sentences containing *seem*-type verbs, there are at least two avenues of inquiry that can be explored as far as the reflexivization facts are concerned. First, we could consider the possibility that *seem* and *appear* do in fact assign a thematic role (perhaps "bearer of an appearance") to their subject in (17), just as they must in (18), where there has evidently been no raising. (The existence of such sentences is observed by Lappin [1984].)

(18) John seems as if he is running.

    Alternately, we could explore a more general version of the RR along the lines of (19).

(19) *The Reflexive Requirement (generalized version):*
    The reflexive is obligatory where the pronoun and its antecedent are "terms" of the same element.

We would then take an element's "terms" to be the NPs entering into any type of dependency relation with it. Two types of dependency relation are relevant here: combinational dependency, wherein one element looks to another to provide the argument with which it must combine, and thematic dependency, wherein one element looks to another for its thematic role. Since the subject of a *seem*-type verb satisfies that element's (combinatorial) dependency on an NP, it would count as a term regardless of where it receives its thematic role. Moreover, because the pronoun in the *to* phrase is a thematic dependent of the *seem*-type verb, it too would count as one of its terms, and the generalized RR would correctly predict that the reflexive form is obligatory in sentences such as (17).[4]

To summarize, then, I take the RR to be the only syntactic principle sanctioning the occurrence of reflexive pronouns in English. As noted above, this principle states the conditions under which a reflexive pronoun is obligatory rather than just possible. The appearance of a reflexive in other contexts (e.g., in "picture NPs" and certain types of PPs) is motivated by semantic, pragmatic, and conversational principles of the sort alluded to earlier. The RR is intended to operate in conjunction with the Precedence Constraint, which restricts anaphoric dependencies of all types. Thus sentences such as (20)–(22) all constitute violations of the PC, not the requirement that the reflexive be used when a pronoun and its antecedent are thematic dependents of the same element.

(20) *Himself$_i$ saw John$_i$.

(21) *I showed himself$_i$ to John$_i$.

(22) *I talked to himself$_i$ about John$_i$.

Space does not permit a thorough comparison of the RR with the comparable principles in TG, but a few remarks are in order. The distinction between reflexive and nonreflexive pronouns in TG is assured with the help of the following two principles in the binding theory outlined by Chomsky (1981).

(23) *Principle A:*
An anaphor (reflexive) is bound in its governing category.

(24) *Principle B:*
A pronominal (nonreflexive) is not bound in its governing category.

For a pronoun to be bound, it must have a c-commanding antecedent. Simplifying greatly, we can identify a pronoun's governing category in the cases relevant to our discussion as the minimal NP or S containing it. Thus these principles correctly predict that only the reflexive form of the pronoun is permitted in sentences such as (24).

(25) John$_i$ criticized himself/*him$_i$.

The nonreflexive pronoun in (25) is bound (has a c-commanding antecedent) in its governing category (here S), in violation of principle B.

There are at least two advantages of the RR over principles A and B. First, since the latter principles define binding in terms of c-command. they incorrectly predict that the reflexive pronoun should not be allowed in sentences such as (26).

(26) I talked to John$_i$ about himself/*him$_i$.

Because the intended antecedent *John* is embedded within a PP here, it does not c-command the pronoun. This means that the reflexive pronoun cannot be bound, as required by principle A. This problem does not arise in the theory I have proposed since the pronoun and its antecedent both receive their thematic role from the same element in (26) (the verb *talk*).

Second, because the binding principles of TG stipulate that reflexive and nonreflexive forms of the pronoun are in complementary distribution (one occurring where the pronoun is bound in its governing category and the other where it is not), the cases of free variation restated in (27) and (28) are problematic.

(27) John$_i$ doesn't like that picture of himself/him$_i$.

(28) Mary$_i$ keeps a gun near herself/her$_i$.

Such contrasts are not problematic in the approach I have outlined. Since the pronoun and its antecedent do not receive their thematic role from the same element in these cases, the RR correctly predicts that the reflexive is not obligatory. This sanctions the observed alternations, leaving them to be regulated by nonsyntactic principles.

5.8 Learnability Considerations

In considering the learnability problems associated with the ontogeny of reflexive pronouns, I will focus on the development of the more restrictive version of the Reflexive Requirement (i.e., [7] above). An open question at this time relates to the effect that exposure to optional reflexives such as those in (27) and (28) above has on the language learner's attempts to acquire the RR. I will assume that any effects are minimal. Not only are sentences that allow the alternation quite rare, but it is also known that children favor principles that apply obligatorily within a certain context (see below). This suggests that cases of syntactically free alternation between reflexive and nonreflexive pronouns will be treated separately by language learners.[5]

The major observation that language learners must make about reflexives is that they are required when a pronoun and its antecedent are thematic dependents of the same element. Such a generalization meets at least one of the learnability requirements adopted throughout this book: it exploits concepts (thematic dependency, same) that we can safely assume to be available to children independent of language. (For a discussion of the ontogeny of thematic dependency, see chap. 2.) The major problem is to determine whether the forms of experience to which children have access are rich enough to support formation of the RR. It seems reasonable to suppose that sentences such as (1)–(6) will be common in children's linguistic environment.

(1) Harry hurt himself.

(2) Sue likes herself.

(3) Harry talked to himself.

(4) Sue looked at herself in the mirror.

(5) Sue gave a gift to herself.

(6) Sue's joke about herself was funny.

While (1) and (2) would support the generalization that the reflexive and its antecedent must be syntactic arguments of the same element, (3)–(6) are not consistent with this hypothesis. What these sentences have in common—and what they share with (1) and (2)—is the fact that the pronoun and its antecedent are thematic dependents of the same verb or noun. Such sentences presumably provide the crucial trigger for the RR.

This leaves us with the problem of determining how children come to know that the reflexive form of the pronoun is obligatory in such environments rather than just possible. It has often been noted (e.g., Slobin 1982) that children find it easier to acquire forms that are obligatory in a particular environment than those that are just optional. It is known, for instance, that the optionality of the Japanese direct object marker delays its acquisition with respect to the obligatory accusative suffix of Turkish. This preference for obligatory rules may well be a special case of the predisposition captured by the Conservatism Thesis, since the more restrictive hypothesis is that the reflexive must occur in a particular context, not just that it can occur there. This allows us to assume that children who seek to formulate a hypothesis about the reflexive pronoun in sentences such as (1)–(6) will arrive at the Reflexive Requirement.

The results of a number of recent studies suggest that this is correct. In one of these studies, Otsu (1981) examined the ability of sixty children aged three years, one month, to seven years, one month to understand structures such as (7) and (8).

(7) The elephant next to the hippo tickled himself.

(8) The hippo remembered that the elephant tickled himself.

Otsu found that, from the point at which children can distinguish between reflexive and nonreflexive pronouns, they exhibit a strong tendency to interpret *himself* correctly in both sentence types. These results are compatible with those obtained by Read and Hare (1979), who studied the interpretation of reflexives in the broad range of biclausal structures exemplified in (9).

(9) a. Bert said [$_S$ that Ernie spilled some paint on himself today].
   b. Cookie Monster made [$_S$ Oscar watch himself].
   c. Ernie was sorry [$_S$ Cookie Monster hurt himself].
   d. Oscar wanted [$_S$ Bert to write a short story about himself].

Working with 230 children between the ages of six years, three months, and twelve years, eleven months, Read and Hare found that even the youngest children correctly interpreted the reflexives at rates well above chance. The fact that they did not attain perfect scores from the outset may well be due to the fact that they had not yet mastered the intricacies of the multiclausal constructions used in the experiment (which included causatives and infinitival clauses with overt subjects). In an attempt to control for this, Otsu had his subjects take an imitation task involving biclausal structures in addition to the reflexive interpretation task. Only three of his sixty subjects were able to attain criterion (set at two out of three correct) on the reflexive structures without being able to reproduce the two biclausal structures in the imitation task.[6]

On the whole, then, the studies by Otsu and by Read and Hare suggest that children's initial hypothesis about the interpretation of reflexives is a conservative one. Rather than assuming that a reflexive pronoun can take any NP as its antecedent, they apparently adopt a much more restrictive hypothesis. In particular, they seem to conclude that a reflexive and its antecedent must be thematic dependents of the same verb. They therefore choose the subject antecedent in (7) and the clausemate antecedent in (8) and (9).

Such conservatism should not be language-specific. Indeed, we would expect that, even in languages in which reflexives are not so narrowly constrained in their distribution, children would initially adopt a conservative assumption about their interpretation. Japanese provides us with an opportunity to test this prediction since it does not require that the reflexive and its antecedent be thematic dependents of the same element. A sentence such as (10) is therefore ambiguous.

(10) [$_S$ Harry-wa$_i$ [$_S$ Jane-ga$_j$ zibun-o$_{i,j}$ hihansitato] itta]
    Harry N   Jane N   self Ac   criticized   said
    "John said that Mary criticized self."

Suzuki (1985) tested the comprehension of such sentences in sixty children aged four to eleven. She found that, following a period of random responses among the four-year-old children, there was a sudden increase in responses in which the reflexive was linked to an antecedent in its own clause. The five-year-olds in her study chose this interpretation 83.2 percent of the time, and the percentage of extraclausal antecedents remained low (below 20 percent) until age nine. This is consistent with the view that children's initial response to reflexive pronouns in the monoclausal sentences that presumably predominate in their environment is that these elements must take a specific NP as antecedent (the subject in the same clause). Departures from this initial assumption then occur only in response to the appropriate type of stimulus.

There is some reason to think that children do not formulate an actual hypothesis about reflexive pronouns until a relatively late point in the language acquisition process. Prior to that they exhibit considerable confusion over the distribution of reflexive and nonreflexive pronouns and often appear to interchange them randomly. The studies by Read and Hare (1979) and Otsu (1981) report that younger children (six years of age and younger) sometimes misinterpret the reflexive pronoun in structures such as (11), allowing it to be coreferential with the matrix subject just as the definite pronoun *him* could be.

(11) John said that Harry had criticized himself.

Moreover, Otsu (1981), Wexler and Chien (1985), and Jakubowicz (1984) all report that children also sometimes interpret *him* as if it were a reflexive pronoun. In imitation tasks, they will therefore sometimes replace the definite pronoun by its reflexive counterpart, and they will incorrectly allow *him* to be coreferential with the subject of its own clause in structures such as (12).

(12) John said that Harry had criticized him.

A curious feature of this confusion is that children apparently master the distribution of reflexives before that of ordinary pronouns. Thus it seems that, whereas children can correctly interpret the reflexive from age five and half (and perhaps even younger), they frequently continue to misinterpret the ordinary pronoun by linking it to the intraclausal subject in the examples just considered. Although such results are puzzling, they do not necessarily bear directly on the emergence of the grammar. It is possible, for example, that nongrammatical factors such as memory limitations and empathy effects encourage association of a pronoun with a pragmatically prominent NP (e.g., a subject) in the same minimal clause. Such factors would not interfere with the development of reflexives, which must be interpreted in this way for independent grammatical reasons (i.e., the Reflexive Requirement), but would have a detrimental effect on the interpretation of ordinary pronouns—just the phenomenon reported in the studies we are considering.

5.9 Concluding Remarks

This chapter has been concerned with one of the most challenging and puzzling problems in human language—the nature of the constraints on anaphoric dependencies. The major thrust of my proposals has been that the principles governing anaphoric dependencies exploit very basic syntactic notions (precedence, phrasal categories, thematic dependency) and apply to syntactic representations formed in accordance with the usual combinatorial mechanisms (including the Subject-Last Requirement).

Assuming the viability of the approach to anaphoric dependencies that I have tried to develop in this chapter, there is good reason to think that the proposed principles (the Precedence Constraint and the Reflexive Requirement) will be learnable without the help of innate linguistic knowledge. Not only do the two principles exploit notions and apply to structures that are the product of earlier development, but their emergence can also be traced to a plausible process of hypothesis formation whose intermediate steps involve successively closer approximations to the mechanisms proposed for the mature grammar. I will consider this issue at greater length in chapter 7.

6

EXTRAPOSITION AND QUANTIFIER PLACEMENT

6.1 Introduction

This chapter is concerned with two phenomena that have fallen outside the scope of our discussion to this point, extraposition and quantifier placement. The major thrust of my proposals will be that fundamental properties of these phenomena can be derived from the principles proposed in earlier chapters. Where previous principles do not suffice, it will be shown that the required new mechanisms draw on the same set of notions exploited in the analysis of other phenomena (e.g., syntactic categories, precedence, adjacency, continuity, and so on). If correct, this will confirm the promise of earlier proposals about the nature of syntactic concepts and relations and will provide further support for the thesis of general nativism that I am trying to develop.

6.2 Extraposition from NP

6.2.1 A Preliminary Proposal

According to many conventional analyses, the (b) versions of (1)–(3) are derived from their (a) counterparts by Extraposition from NP, a rule that moves an adjectival PP or relative clause rightward to a position at or near the end of the clause. (Here and elsewhere, the extraposed phrase is placed in brackets, and coindexing is used to indicate the nominal on which it depends.)

(1) a. [$_{NP}$ A review of the new book] appeared.
    b. A review$_i$ appeared [of the new book]$_i$.

(2) a. [$_{NP}$ The man who we knew] left.
    b. The man$_i$ left [who we knew]$_i$.

(3) a. Someone saw [$_{NP}$ a picture of Mary] yesterday.
    b. Someone saw a picture$_i$ yesterday [of Mary]$_i$.

Although formation of the (b) sentences in (1)–(3) is inconsistent with the Adjacency Preference, there is little doubt that the sentence-final PP and the coindexed nominal form an NP in these cases. As sentences such as (4) show, anaphoric elements like *it* and *one* can refer back to these discontinuous strings as if they formed a phrase.

(4) John saw a picture$_i$ yesterday [of Mary]$_i$, and I saw it/one too.

In (4) *it* and *one* take *a picture of Mary* as their antecedent, suggesting that it is a constituent.

The assumption that an extraposed phrase and the nominal on which it depends form a constituent also helps account for an otherwise puzzling fact about the behavior of these structures. As Guéron (1980) has noted, elements that have been extraposed from an object phrase appear to form part of the VP, while those extraposed from a subject phrase do not. The sentences of (5) and (6), whose second conjunct is derived with the help of ''VP fronting,'' illustrate this.

(5) *They said that a book$_i$ would turn up [by Hemingway]$_i$ and [$_{VP}$ turn up by Hemingway], a book did ____.

(6) They said he would find a book$_i$ yesterday [by Hemingway]$_i$ and [$_{VP}$ find a book$_i$ yesterday [by Hemingway]$_i$], he did ____.

Notice that, whereas the extraposed phrase associated with the subject in (5) cannot be fronted with the rest of the VP, the displaced PP associated with the direct object in (6) can. As McCawley (1982a) notes, these facts are what one would expect if an extraposed phrase and the nominal on which it depends form a constituent. This is because displaced elements should be part of the VP only when the nominal with which they combine also is. Since the direct object but not the subject is a component of the VP, only the extraposed phrase in (6) will form part of this constituent. This is precisely what the relevant grammaticality judgments suggest.

A further advantage of the type of discontinuous constituents I have been advocating manifests itself in the contrast between the anaphoric dependencies found in (7) and (8).

(7) ?A man $_i$ visited her$_j$ recently [who was from Mary's$_j$ hometown]$_i$.

(8) *I visited her$_i$ with a man [who was from Mary's$_i$ hometown].

In (7) the bracketed element is part of the subject NP and hence does not occur within the phrasal category of the pronoun (i.e., VP). There is therefore no violation of the Precedence Constraint (repeated here as [9]), and the intended anaphoric dependency is admissible.

(9) *The Precedence Constraint:*
A pronoun cannot precede an antecedent in its phrasal category.

In (8), in contrast, the bracketed phrase combines with the NP *a man* and is therefore part of the VP, the phrasal category of the pronoun. For this reason the intended anaphoric dependency is ruled out by the Precedence Constraint.

A similar contrast has been observed by McCawley (1985).

(10) a. *[$_{NP}$ His$_i$ recantation of Chomsky's$_i$ 1973 theory] finally appeared.
b. *[$_{NP}$ His$_i$ recantation _____] finally appeared [of Chomsky's$_i$ 1973 theory].

The inadmissibility of the anaphoric dependency in (10b) suggests that the extraposed PP is part of the subject NP just as it is in (10a). If this is right, both sentences will be ruled out by the Precedence Constraint since the pronoun would precede an antecedent in its phrasal category (the subject NP).

A final advantage of the analysis of extraposed phrases that I have been considering relates to the predictions that it makes about other languages. A good example of this involves Korean, a language that is subject to the following version of the Continuity Requirement (see chap. 3).

(11) *The Continuity Requirement (Korean):*
Only VPs may be discontinuous.

According to the analysis of extraposition I have proposed, these types of structures should not exist in Korean since they would require the existence of a discontinuous NP. This seems to be a correct prediction, as the ungrammaticality of the following constructions shows.

(12) *Chayk-i$_i$ ecey nawa-ass-ta [mwupep-eykwanhan]$_i$.
book-N yesterday appeared   grammar about
"A book appeared yesterday about grammar."

(13) *Chayk-i$_i$ ecey nawa-ass-ta [nay-ka ssu-un]$_i$
book-N yesterday appeared   I-N wrote REL
"A book appeared yesterday that I wrote."

The variants of English extraposed structures that are used in Korean resemble (14) and (15).

(14) Chayk-i$_i$ ecey nawa-ass-ta—[mwupep-eykwanhan kes-i]$_i$.
book-N yesterday appeared   grammar about thing-N
"A book appeared yesterday—a thing about grammar."

(15) Chayk-i$_i$ ecey nawa-ass-ta—[nay-ka ssu-un kes-i]$_i$
book-N yesterday appeared   I-N wrote REL thing-N
"A book appeared yesterday—a thing that I wrote."

Notice that in (14) and (15) the "extraposed" element has combined with an adjacent noun (kes, "thing") that "refers" back to the subject NP. Since there is no combinatorial relation between the extraposed element and the subject phrase, this NP is not discontinuous, and there is no violation of the Continuity Requirement for Korean.

As with any analysis, the proposals I have made are not unproblematic. One of the most pressing problems involves the fact that English sentences such as (16) appear to violate the VP Requirement (see chap. 4), restated here as (17).

(16) A book$_i$ appeared [about syntax]$_i$.

(17) *The VP Requirement:*
Discontinuous phrases must lie within VP.

The VP Requirement was originally formulated to account for the contrast between (18a), in which a discontinuous NP lies within the VP, and (18b), in which it does not.

(18) a. Who did John see [a picture of ____]?
   b. *Who did [a picture of ____] frighten John?

An obvious difference between the ungrammatical (18b) and the grammatical (16) is that in the latter case the phrase "creating" the discontinuity lies at the end of the sentence. I will take the position that this difference reflects the fact that extraposed phrases are incorporated into the syntactic representation after the rest of the clause has been formed. To account for the difference between (16) and (18b), it is then necessary to assume that the VP Requirement applies only to the formation of clauses and not to the subsequent addition of extraposed elements. Thus (18b) would violate the VP Requirement but (16) would not.

The assumption that extraposed phrases are incorporated into the syntactic representation after the basic clause has been formed has at least two advantages independent of the problem we are considering. A first advantage involves the prediction that independent phrases (i.e., NPs) cannot undergo the type of extraposition we are considering. Consider in this regard a sentence such as (19).

(19) *I read a book about ____ yesterday [syntax].

Assuming that extraposed phrases are incorporated into the syntactic representation only after the rest of the clause has been formed, (19) will be ungrammatical since the direct object phrase contains an element with an unsatisfied dependency (the preposition) and can therefore not be an NP even though such a category is required by the transitive verb. (Recall that according to the Phrasal Category Principle discussed in chap. 1 the NP category contains no elements with unsatisfied dependencies.) Since the verb *read* must combine with an NP, the sentence cannot be formed by the grammar.

A second advantage of the approach we are considering involves sentences such as (20), originally noted by Guéron (1980).

(20) a. Anyone who might be able to help has just left.
 b. *Anyone$_i$ has just left [who might be able to help]$_i$.
 c. *Anyone has just left.

Notice that (20b) is just as ungrammatical as (c), in which there is no relative clause at all. The fact that the principle constraining the occurrence of *anyone* is "blind" to extraposed phrases is suggestive, pointing to the need to distinguish between formation of the basic clause and the incorporation into syntactic structure of extraposed phrases. This is precisely the distinction that my proposal independently makes.

An obvious problem that now arises has to do with how children come to realize that extraposed phrases are incorporated into the syntactic representation after the rest of the clause has been formed. Although I cannot resolve this problem in any definitive way here, part of the answer may lie in the way in which language users compute syntactic representations. One possibility is that strings of words are analyzed from left to right and that combinatorial relations are realized with as much immediacy as grammatical principles such as the Subject-Last Requirement allow. On this assumption, it would not be unreasonable to suppose that, in the case of strings such as *A book appeared last year about syntax,* the first five words are combined in the usual way to form a clause before the "extraposed" PP is even analyzed. This in turn would support the desired conclusion about the point at which extraposed elements are incorporated into the syntactic representations, although it leaves open the question of how the VP Requirement is relaxed.

To summarize, then, I have taken the position that English allows genuine discontinuous dependencies in the case of extraposed elements but that the relevant combinatorial relations are realized only after the rest of the clause has been formed in accordance with the usual principles. Although I will continue to use the terms "extraposition" and "displaced" for purposes of expository convenience, I will not posit a movement transformation and will assume instead that extraposed phrases simply appear in clause-final position in the string, presumably in response to discourse factors that need not concern us at this point. They are then attached to the appropriate nominal by the Combinatorial Principle, in accordance with the assumptions discussed above and the principle to be proposed in the next section.

6.2.2 A Constraint

The major problem that must concern us now relates to the conditions under which a PP or relative clause can combine with a nonadjacent element. The major constraint on this combinatorial operation can be stated as follows.[1]

(1) *The Extraposition Constraint:*
   An extraposed phrase cannot be separated from the phrasal category of the element with which it combines.

Consider in this regard the following sentences, based on structures noted by Ross (1967).

(2) a. [$_S$ [$_S$ That someone who he knew died] was tragic.]
   b. [$_S$ [$_S$ That someone$_i$ died [who he knew]$_i$] was tragic].
   c. *[$_S$ [$_S$ That someone$_i$ died] was tragic [who he knew]$_i$].

In (2), the extraposed phrase is attached to the nominal *someone,* whose phrasal category is the embedded S. Sentence (2b) is therefore acceptable since the extraposed phrase has not been separated from the embedded S. This contrasts with the ungrammatical (2c), in which the extraposed element has been separated from the phrasal category of the NP on which it depends. Utterances like these are to be distinguished from grammatical sentences like (3), in which the phrasal category of the NP on which the extraposed phrase depends (i.e., *someone*) is the all-encompassing matrix S, and there is therefore no violation of our principle.

(3) [$_S$ Someone$_i$ said that it was raining [who had been outside]$_i$].

The Extraposition Constraint manifests itself in a somewhat different way in (4).

(4) a. A review of a book by three authors appeared yesterday.
   b. [$_{NP}$ A review of a book]$_i$ appeared yesterday [by three authors]$_i$.

As Guéron points out, (4a) is ambiguous—permitting a reading in which the three authors produced the review and another in which they produced the book. In contrast, the extraposed structure in (4b) allows only one interpretation, namely, the reading in which *by three authors* is linked to *a review of a book.* Guéron attempts to explain this fact with the help of the Subjacency Condition, noting that the extraposition of a PP from the NP headed by *book* would require movement over two NP boundaries. This is illustrated in (5).

(5) [$_{NP}$ a review of [$_{NP}$ a book by three authors $_{NP}$] $_{NP}$]

No comparable problem arises in cases in which the extraposed phrase originates outside the NP headed by *review,* as (6) shows.

(6) [$_{NP}$ [$_{NP}$ a review of a book $_{NP}$] by three authors $_{NP}$]

On the analysis being developed here, the contrast under consideration will follow from the Extraposition Constraint. Since the phrasal category of *a book* in (4) is the subject NP (in which it serves as syntactic modifier), and since the extraposed element is separated from this phrase, a combinatorial relation between the two is forbidden. However, there is no such problem when the extraposed element combines with the subject NP *a review of a book* within whose phrasal category (i.e., S) it lies.

   Although various problems remain, I will not attempt here to increase the descriptive power of the constraint I have proposed and will turn instead to an examination of the relevant learnability issues.

6.2.3 Learnability Considerations

At the very minimum, the ontogeny of extraposition will have to involve discovery of the conditions under which a modifier can be attached to a nonadjacent element to its left (the Extraposition Constraint). This will entail satisfying the usual three learnability conditions, restated here.

(1) a. Availability of the required concepts.
    b. Availability of relevant experience.
    c. A learning strategy.

Since "extraposed phrase" is simply a cover term for a category that combines with a nonadjacent element to its left, the Extraposition Constraint introduces no concepts that have not already been shown to be available to children. The first learnability condition is thus met. It also seems reasonable to assume that sentences containing extraposed elements will occur with some frequency in the child's linguistic environment, thereby satisfying the second of our conditions. The third condition is more problematic since it raises the question of whether and how children avoid an overgeneralization that would incorrectly allow an extraposed phrase to be attached to any preceding NP, forming sentences such as (2).

(2) *A book about a man$_i$ arrived [who had studied in India]$_i$.

It would be difficult for children to move from such an overgeneralization to the correct form of the Extraposition Constraint since experience presumably provides no information about the ungrammaticality of the utterances (e.g., [2]) that their initial hypothesis would allow.

   What is needed here is a way to ensure that the child's initial hypothesis will be at least as restrictive as the Extraposition Constraint, thereby ensuring that extraposed phrases are not separated from the phrasal category of the element with which they combine. Processing considerations may be relevant to the resolution of this problem since it seems reasonable to think that limitations on working memory would favor an initial hypothesis that preserved the integrity of as many categories as possible. While "extraposition" will necessarily create a discontinuity in the phrase to which the displaced element belongs, the Extraposition Constraint essentially ensures that this is the only category to be so affected. Consider in this regard the following example of extraposition from a subject phrase in an embedded clause.

(3) a. [$_S$ That [$_{NP}$ a man$_i$ _____] appeared [who we knew]$_i$] was not surprising.
b. *[$_S$ That [$_{NP}$ a man$_i$ _____] appeared] was not surprising [who we knew]$_i$.

By requiring that the extraposed phrase not be separated from the phrasal category of the NP with which it combines, the Extraposition Constraint restricts to one the number of discontinuous categories (namely, the subject NP). Were there no such constraint, both the NP and the embedded S containing it would be discontinuous (the case in [3b]).

As another illustration of this point, consider the following sentence.

(4) Sue [$_{VP}$ read [$_{NP}$ a review of a book]$_i$ yesterday] [by several authors]$_i$.

As we have already seen, the Extraposition Constraint allows the extraposed PP in (4) to combine with the NP *a review of a book,* in whose phrasal category (VP) it lies. However, it cannot combine with the embedded NP (*a book*) since it is separated from that element's phrasal category (the direct object NP). By forcing association of *by several authors* with *a review of a book,* the Extraposition Constraint again limits to one (the direct object NP) the number of discontinuous phrases. Were the extraposed PP able to combine with *a book,* this latter phrase as well as the PP and the larger direct object NP containing it would all be discontinuous.

If the preceding proposal is correct, the Extraposition Constraint should characterize the unmarked case for the processing mechanisms, and we would expect it to be adopted as the language learner's initial hypothesis. It would then be retained unless and until experience provided evidence to the contrary (by the Trigger Requirement). Although there seems to be little developmental data bearing on the correctness of this prediction, the results of an experimental study by Otsu and Honda (summarized in Otsu [1981]) are particularly suggestive. Working with sixty children between the ages of three and seven, Otsu and Honda tested their subjects' ability to interpret sentences such as (5). (Notice that the extraposed phrase must be linked to the NP *a cat on a turtle,* not *a turtle.*)

(5) [$_{NP}$ A cat on a turtle]$_i$ popped up [with a ribbon on its neck]$_i$.

Despite the complexity of the test sentences and the strain they undoubtedly put on the children's working memory, Otsu and Honda found that the vast majority (i.e., twenty-seven out of thirty-seven) of the children who were able to deal with multiple PP constructions (as evidenced by performance on an imitation pretest) linked the extraposed phrase to the appropriate NP. Otsu and Honda take these results to indicate that the constraint in question (which they assume to be the Subjacency Condition rather than my principle) is adopted by the child as the initial hypothesis. This is precisely what my proposal predicts in this case.

6.3 Quantifier Placement

6.3.1 Introduction

Among the many "movement" rules that have received extensive attention in the literature on transformational grammar (TG), one of the most perplexing involves the apparent rightward displacement of the quantifiers *each, both,* and *all* in sentences such as (1) and (2). (I use coindexing to indicate the nominal with which the quantifier is "associated.")

(1) a. All/both/each of the men have left.
     b. The men$_i$ have all/both/each$_i$ left.

(2) a. He saw all/both/each of the boys $\begin{cases} \text{twice.} \\ \text{at the same time.} \end{cases}$

     b. He saw the boys$_i$ $\begin{cases} \text{twice each}_i. \\ \text{all/both}_i \text{ at the same time.} \end{cases}$

For purposes of expository convenience, I will refer to an instance of *each, both,* or *all* that lies outside the NP with which it is associated as a "floated" quantifier.

The positions that can be occupied by a floated quantifier are relatively limited in number and seem to fall into two classes.

A. Floated quantifiers that stand alone and must occur prior to a verbal element.

(3) a. The boys$_i$ both/each/all$_i$ left.
     b. The boys$_i$ have both/each/all$_i$ left.
     c. *The boys$_i$ have left both/each/all$_i$.

B. Floated quantifiers that are accompanied by an adverbial element (expressing number in the case of *each* and similarity in the case of *both* and *all*) and that can occur in postverbal position.

(4) The boys$_i$ tried it $\begin{cases} \text{twice each}_i. \\ \text{both/all}_i \text{ at the same time.} \end{cases}$

The traditional view of these structures was that they exemplified a quantifier standing in "apposition" to an NP (see, e.g., Curme 1935, 26–27; and Jespersen 1954, 598). More recently, it has been assumed that the structures in (3) reflect the operation of a rule (or set of rules) that extracts a quantifier (*each, both* or *all*) from an NP and moves it to a position within the VP. Analyses of this sort have been advanced within transformational grammar by Dougherty (1970), Baltin (1982), and others. Disagreement has occurred over whether there are different types of quantifier movement and over whether the required rules refer to grammatical relations such as subject and object or to syntactic categories such as NP and V. (On both these issues, see Postal [1976].)

In recent years, transformationalists have encountered some success in accounting for various properties of quantifier placement in terms of general principles of Universal Grammar (UG). Baltin (1982), for example, has recently argued that certain facts about the positioning of *each* in surface structure can be shown to follow from a general theory of "landing sites." Before that, Fiengo and Lasnik (1976) had noted that the Subjacency Condition can be used to account for the ungrammaticality of sentences such as (5b).

(5) a. [$_{NP}$ The book about [$_{NP}$ each of the men]] was destroyed.
    b. *[$_{NP}$ The book about [$_{NP}$ the men$_i$]] was each$_i$ destroyed.

Notice that movement of *each* in (5a) to yield (5b) would involve extracting the quantifier from a structure dominated by two NP nodes in violation of the Subjacency Condition.

The major thesis that I will attempt to develop here is that the syntax of quantifier placement reflects the operation of the Combinatorial Principle (constrained by the Adjacency Preference) and the Precedence Constraint. The critical assumption underlying this analysis is that floated quantifiers are tertiaries (adverbials) with anaphoric properties. In evaluating the explanatory value of this assumption, I will draw on the somewhat more detailed study of quantifier placement presented in O'Grady (1982).

6.3.2 Floated Quantifiers as Tertiaries

The first claim that I wish to make about floated quantifiers is that they function as tertiaries that combine with an adjacent verbal category rather than an NP. According to this proposal, then, a sentence such as *The boys each left* will have the structure depicted in (1).

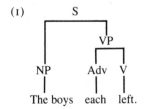

(1)

There are at least two advantages to taking floated quantifiers to be tertiaries that combine with a verbal category rather than secondaries that combine with a nominal. First, there are many sentences such as (2), in which
independent restrictions on the internal structure of NPs would prevent the
quantifier from combining with a nominal (cf. [3]).

(2) The boys have each left.

(3) *Each the boys have left.

Second, if floated quantifiers combine with an NP, we should not find such
elements in languages like Korean that do not permit discontinuous NPs
(see the discussion in chap. 3). In fact, however, such structures are found
in Korean.

(4) Sonyun-tul-i$_i$ Sue-rul motwu$_i$ piphanha-yess-ta.
    boy PL N   Sue-Ac all   criticized.
    "The boys all criticized Sue."

The claim that floated quantifiers function as tertiaries in English is not
without precedent. In fact, Poutsma (1926, 334), Hudson (1970, 236),
Postal (1976. 153n.), and Williams (1982) all make reference to such a
possibility, although none develops the idea. Moreover, Lightfoot (1979,
171f.) has noted that there is some reason to think that floated quantifiers
were adverbs in Old and Middle English, and comparable proposals have
been made for the Romance languages (see Jaeggli 1982, 75). To my
knowledge, however, the possibility that floated quantifiers have the status
of tertiaries in Modern English has never been adequately explored. I will
attempt to remedy this situation by outlining a variety of considerations
that support the view that these elements belong to a subclass of the class of
tertiaries that also includes so-called VP-internal adverbs such as *merely,
scarcely,* and *virtually.* I will begin my discussion by concentrating on
quantifiers that occur preverbally and will then turn my attention to their
postverbal counterparts.

A major advantage of taking floated quantifiers to be tertiaries belonging to a subclass of the *"merely* class" is that we can automatically account for the distributional similarities between these elements and
conventional VP-internal adverbs. As noted above, a floated quantifier
may stand alone in either of the positions indicated by a dash in (5).

(5) The men ____ have ____ shown the boy a book.

Significantly, these are also the positions that can be filled by conventional
adverbs of the *merely* class (see Jackendoff 1972).

(6) a. The men merely/each have shown the boy an old book.
    b. The men have merely/each shown the boy an old book.

Like floated quantifiers, adverbs of the *merely* class cannot stand alone in postverbal position, nor can they appear between the verb and its direct object.

(7) *The men$_i$ have shown the boy an old book merely/each$_i$.

(8) a. *The men$_i$ saw all/each/both$_i$ a book.
   b. *The men saw scarcely the book.

Still another consideration supporting the analysis of floated quantifiers as tertiaries relates to the fact that these elements pattern like adverbs with respect to so-called deletion sites. As Sag (1978) has noted, neither floated quantifiers nor conventional adverbs can occur immediately in front of a "deletion site."

(9) John finished the book in an hour, and his students$_i$ $\begin{cases} \text{all/both/each}_i \quad \text{have} \\ \underline{\quad} \text{ too.} \\ *\text{have} \quad \text{all/both/each}_i \\ \underline{\quad} \text{ too.} \end{cases}$

(10) John virtually finished the book in an hour, and his students $\begin{cases} \text{virtually} \quad \text{did} \\ \underline{\quad} \text{ too.} \\ *\text{did} \quad \text{virtually} \\ \underline{\quad} \text{ too.} \end{cases}$

Other similarities between floated quantifiers and adverbs are examined in O'Grady (1982) and will not be discussed here.

A prima facie departure from the distributional similarity between conventional adverbs and floated quantifiers manifests itself in the fact that the latter type of element can apparently occur between the two postverbal NPs in the double object construction. As (11b) shows, however, other tertiaries cannot occur in this position.

(11) a. I gave the boys$_i$ each/both/all$_i$ the news.
    b. *I gave the boys virtually/scarcely the news.

Fortunately for my analysis, there is good reason to believe that the quantifiers in (11a) are an integral part of the indirect object NP and are therefore fundamentally different from floated quantifiers, which (as we have already seen) occur outside the NP with which they are associated. Notice in this regard that in the passive version of (11a), the quantifier cannot remain in the postverbal position.

(12) a. The boys$_i$ each/both/all$_i$ were given a gift.
    b. *The boys$_i$ were given each/both/all$_i$ a gift.

Equally suggestive is the fact that the only quantifiers occurring after an indirect object are those that are associated with this element. A quantifier associated with a subject NP, for example, cannot occur after the indirect object phrase.

(13) *The men$_i$ gave Mary all/both/each$_i$ a book.

Both these considerations suggest that the quantifier in these cases is an integral part of the NP bearing the recipient role and therefore not a floated element at all.

To this point, my discussion has dealt exclusively with floated quantifiers that occur in preverbal position. However, as noted earlier, these elements can also occur postverbally, provided they are accompanied by an adverbial element (expressing number in the case of *each* and similarity in time, manner, or place of occurrence in the case of *all* and *both*).[2] The sentences in (14)–(15) illustrate this.

(14) a. *The boys$_i$ tried it each/both/all$_i$.
     b. The boys$_i$ tried it $\begin{cases} \text{several times each}_i \\ \text{both/all}_i \text{ at the same time.} \end{cases}$

(15) a. *I saw the boys each/all/both.
     b. I saw the boys$_i$ $\begin{cases} \text{twice each}_i \\ \text{both/all}_i \text{ in the same place.} \end{cases}$

Significantly, other VP-internal adverbs can also occur postverbally under comparable conditions.

(16) a. *The boys tried it scarcely.
     b. The boys tried it scarcely three times.

(17) a. *She saw the boys merely.
     b. She saw the boys merely twice.

In both structure types the element that normally functions as a VP-internal adverb seems to form a constituent with the adjacent adverbial expression, as the "fronted" structures in (18)–(19) illustrate.

(18) a. She saw the boys twice each.
     b. *Twice, she saw the boys each.
     c. Twice each, she saw the boys.

(19) a. She saw the boys merely twice.
     b. *Merely, she saw the boys twice.
     c. Merely twice, she saw the boys.

The fact that the quantifier and the adjacent adverbial must remain together in (18) strongly suggests that they form a phrase, as indicated in (20).

(20) She saw the boys$_i$ [$_{AdvP}$ twice each$_i$].

In (20) *each* combines with the adverbial *twice,* a combinatorial relation made possible by the fact that it is a tertiary.

There is reason to think that floated quantifiers can also combine with adjectival secondaries, as (21) shows.

(21) a. The books$_i$ are [$_{AdjP}$ both$_i$ red].
    b. The men$_i$ were [$_{AdjP}$ each$_i$ exhausted].

This suggests that floated quantifiers have a distributional range identical to that of many conventional tertiaries, providing further support for the view that they are adverbial in character.

In addition to manifesting the full range of combinatorial possibilities associated with tertiaries, floated quantifiers are also characterized by the fact that they do *not* appear in patterns where the Adjacency Preference would require them to combine with a nominal. Thus phrases like (22)–(23) are ill formed—presumably because the floated quantifier is a tertiary and therefore cannot combine with a nominal such as *departure* or *death*.

(22) *The boys' each departure
    (cf. The boys each departed.)

(23) *The soldiers' all death
    (cf. The soldiers all died.)

6.3.3 Floated Quantifiers as Anaphors

It is well known that quantifiers can function as anaphors (pronouns) in sentences such as (1) and (2) where they presumably have the status of primaries (since they occur in argument positions).

(1) The men$_i$ were invited inside and all/both/each$_i$ received an award.

(2) After the men$_i$ had read the book, I asked all/both/each$_i$ a question.

An interesting feature of the anaphoric relation exemplified by (1)–(2) is that the quantifiers require a plural antecedent, as shown by the ungrammaticality of (3)–(4).

(3) *The man$_i$ was invited inside and all/both/each$_i$ received an award.

(4) *After the man$_i$ had read the book, I asked all/both/each$_i$ a question.

Significantly, floated quantifiers also seem to require a plural antecedent, as shown by (5).[3]

(5) a. *The boy$_i$ has all/both/each$_i$ left.
    b. The boys$_i$ have all/both/each$_i$ left.

This fact will follow automatically if we assume that adverbial *each, both,* and *all* exhibit the same anaphoric properties as the corresponding nominals.

A second interesting property of floated quantifiers is that they apparently must occur to the right of their antecedent (hence the use of a rightward movement rule in transformational grammar). Thus whereas (6a) is perfectly acceptable, the same cannot be said of its (b) counterpart in which the floated quantifier occurs to the left of the NP with which it is associated. (Comparable structures are apparently ungrammatical in all human languages, as Baltin [1978] has noted.)

(6) a. Tomorrow, the men$_i$ will each/all/both$_i$ leave.
    b. *Tomorrow, I will each/all/both$_i$ see the men$_i$.

On the analysis being developed here, the ungrammaticality of utterances such as (6b) will follow automatically from the Precedence Constraint, which constrains all anaphoric dependencies.

(7) *The Precedence Constraint (PC):*
    A pronoun cannot precede an antecedent within its phrasal category.

Since floated quantifiers are tertiaries, their phrasal category will correspond to the VP in which they serve as modifiers. The quantifier in structures such as (6b) will therefore precede an antecedent within its phrasal category, in violation of the Precedence Constraint.

An interesting problem with the proposed use of the PC to account for the prohibition against leftward quantifier "movement" stems from the fact that sentences such as (8), from Chomsky (1981, 61), are clearly quite acceptable.

(8) a. He assigned one interpreter each$_i$ to the visiting diplomats$_i$.
    b. One interpreter each$_i$ was assigned to the visiting diplomats$_i$.

Notice that *each* looks for its interpretation to the NP *the visiting diplomats* in (8) even though this element occurs to its right. There are at least two reasons for believing that *each* does not function as a tertiary in these sentences. First, unlike other floated quantifiers, this instance of *each* is apparently part of the adjacent NP headed by *interpreter* and cannot be separated from it. Thus the passive version of (8a) can be only (8b) and not (9), in which *interpreter* and *each* are no longer adjacent.

(9) *One interpreter was each$_i$ assigned to the visiting diplomats$_i$.

Moreover, the type of parenthetical material that can normally occur between a subject and its VP (e.g., "*as you know* clauses") cannot intrude between *interpreter* and *each*. This suggests that the quantifier is part of the NP rather than the VP.

(10) a. *One interpreter, as you know, each$_i$ was assigned to the visiting diplomats$_i$.

    b. One interpreter each$_i$, as you know, was assigned to the visiting diplomats$_i$.

A further indication that the quantifiers in (8) do not function as tertiaries stems from the fact that *all* and *both* cannot occur in this type of structure even though their distribution as floated quantifiers parallels that of *each* in other cases.

(11) a. *They assigned one interpreter all/both$_i$ to the visiting diplomats$_i$.
      b. *One interpreter all/both$_i$ was assigned to the visiting diplomats$_i$.

The use of *each* exemplified in the sentences of (8) seems to resemble that found in structures such as (12) and (13).

(12) He paid two dollars each (for these toys).

(13) Two dollars each is a reasonable price (for them).

In these structures *each* seems to function as an adjectival modifier with the approximate reading "per item" or "apiece." Notice that a comparable interpretation (roughly, "per person") is appropriate in the case of (8), as the paraphrases in (14) show.

(14) a. They assigned one interpreter per person/apiece to the visiting diplomats.
      b. One interpreter per person/apiece was assigned to the visiting diplomats.

Since the phrasal category of an adjectival modifier corresponds to the NP in which it occurs, there will be no violation of the PC in sentences such as (8). As the bracketing in (15) indicates, the NP to which the anaphoric quantifier looks for its interpretation lies outside its phrasal category.

(15) They assigned [$_{NP}$ one interpreter each$_i$] to the visiting diplomats$_i$.

A comparable analysis seems appropriate in the cases exemplified in (16).

(16) a. [$_{AdvP}$ Several times each$_i$], the boys$_i$ climbed the tree.
      b. ?[$_{AdvP}$ Twice each$_i$], I examined the books$_i$.

Recall that, according to our earlier proposal, the quantifier combines with the adjacent adverb of number in these cases. This means that its phrasal category will correspond to the bracketed AdvP within which it functions as modifier. Since the intended antecedent does not lie within this phrase, there is no violation of the PC, and the sentences will be acceptable.

    Although floated quantifiers seem to be subject to the PC just as other types of anaphors are, the interpretive dependencies into which they enter are constrained by additional mechanisms reminiscent of those associated with reflexive pronouns (see chap. 5). For one thing, it is necessary to ensure that floated quantifiers always have an antecedent in their own clause.

(17) a. The boy said [$_S$ that the men$_i$ had each$_i$ left].
    b. *The boys$_i$ said [$_S$ that the man had each$_i$ left].

It is also necessary to make the contrasts exemplified in (18)–(20).

(18) a. The boys$_i$ have each$_i$ left.
    b. She helped the boys$_i$ twice each$_i$.
    c. She gave the boys$_i$ money several times each$_i$.

(19) a. I talked to the boys$_i$ several times each$_i$.
    b. She thought about the boys$_i$ several times each$_i$.
    c. He pleaded with the boys$_i$ several times each$_i$.

(20) a. ?*He ran to the cars$_i$ several times each$_i$.
    b. ?*She played near the boys$_i$ several times each$_i$.
    c. ?*I hit the nail with the hammers$_i$ several times each$_i$.

Although the floated quantifiers and their intended antecedent occur in the same clause in (18)–(20), only the first two sets of sentences are fully acceptable in English. Particularly puzzling is the fact that NPs embedded within a PP can be associated with the quantifier in (19), but not (20). The key to understanding this contrast appears to lie in the notion "thematic dependent" introduced in chapter 2. In particular, notice that the NPs associated with the quantifiers in (19) all receive their thematic role from the verb—just as the argument NPs in (18) do. In (20), in contrast, the NPs associated with the quantifier receive their thematic role from the preposition, not the verb. Thus *the boys* in (19a), for instance, has an addressee-type role rather than the straightforward locative role associated with *the cars* in (20a). It seems reasonable to attribute this contrast to the fact that the verb *talk* determines the thematic role in the former case while the preposition *to,* interpreted in a concrete directional sense, is the source of the NP's thematic role in the second pattern.[4]

The preceding contrasts point toward the need for a principle resembling (21).

(21) *The Floated Quantifier Requirement:*
    A floated quantifier looks for its interpretation to a thematic dependent of the verb in its clause.

Principle (21) will correctly allow the floated quantifier to be associated with the coindexed NP in (17a), (18), and (19) but will disallow the intended anaphoric dependency in (17b) and (20) as well as (22) below, in which the quantifier is associated with a genitive rather than a thematic dependent of the verb.

(22) a. *The men's$_i$ friend has each$_i$ left.
    b. *A friend of the men$_i$ has each$_i$ left.

In addition, constraint (21) also correctly allows two interpretations for sentences such as (23).

(23) The men$_i$ dated the girls$_j$ several times each$_{i,j}$.

In (23) there are two thematic dependents of the verb in the clause containing the quantifier—the subject NP *the men* and the direct object *the girls*. The sentence therefore has two interpretations. On one reading, each man had several dates with various girls, while on the second interpretation, each girl went out on several dates. Thus the second reading, but not the first, is consistent with a situation in which some of the men only went on one or two dates. The ambiguity of this sentence contrasts with the single interpretation associated with (24).

(24) The men$_i$ each$_i$ dated the girls several times.

In (24), the only NP that is eligible to serve as antecedent for the quantifier is the subject phrase *the men*. Since the other NP, *the girls*, follows the quantifier within its phrasal category (VP), an anaphoric dependency is blocked by the PC. This leaves us with the single interpretation indicated by the coindexing in (24).

An interesting consequence of using the Precedence Constraint to rule out a second reading for sentences such as (24) is that we predict a quite different result in languages that differ from English in the ordering of the major constituents in a sentence. Since floated quantifiers belong to the class of tertiaries that occur preverbally in English, and since nonsubject phrases are ordered after the verb, the Precedence Constraint rules out an anaphoric dependency involving an object argument in structures such as (24). In other languages, however, nonsubject arguments can also occur preverbally, thereby opening the possibility of floated quantifiers taking object antecedents. A good example of this comes from Korean, an SOV language, which allows both subject and nonsubject antecedents for the floated quantifier *motwu* (all).

(25) Sonyun-tul-i$_i$ Sue-rul motwu$_i$ piphanha-yess-ta.
     boy PL N   Sue-Ac all   criticized.
     "The boys all criticized Sue."

(26) Nay-ka sonyun-tul-ul$_i$ ecey   motwu$_i$ piphanha-yess-ta.
     I-N   boys PL N   yesterday all criticized
     "I criticized the boys all yesterday."

Notice that, although the "floated" quantifier in (26) has a nonsubject antecedent, there is no violation of the Precedence Constraint since it follows rather than precedes the lexical NP. As one would expect, such sentences become unacceptable if the quantifier appears to the left of an antecedent in its phrasal category.

(27) ?*Nay-ka motwu$_i$ sonyun-tul-ul$_i$ ecey piphanha-yess-ta.
     I-N   all   boys PL N yesterday criticized
    "I all criticized the boys yesterday."

6.3.4 The Learnability Issue

The major claim of the preceding discussion has been that a number of fundamental properties of quantifier placement can be explained if we assume "floated quantifiers" to be tertiaries with anaphoric properties. In considering the learnability problems associated with this proposal, I will concentrate my attention on the way in which the categorial status and anaphoric properties of floated quantifiers might be identified by the language learner.

On the assumption that the Adjacency Preference (the unmarked case of the Combinatorial Principle) and the basic system of categorial contrasts are mastered before acquisition of floated quantifiers begins, the ontogeny of these elements could meet the usual three conditions on learning repeated in (1).

(1) a. Availability of the required concepts.
    b. Availability of relevant experience.
    c. A learning strategy.

The concepts required to identify the categorial status of floated quantifiers (i.e., "tertiary" and "anaphor") will be available to children as the result of the early linguistic development described in previous chapters. The only experience relevant to the acquisition of these new elements will consist of sentences such as (2), in which the floated quantifier combines with a dependent element in accordance with the Adjacency Preference.

(2) a. The men$_i$ have each$_i$ left.
    b. The boys$_i$ tried to read the book twice each$_i$.
    c. They$_i$ are both$_i$ tired.

The generalization that leads to identification of the categorial status of floated quantifiers is presumably based on the following inference.

(3) Floated quantifiers combine with dependent elements.
    Only tertiaries combine with dependent elements.
    Therefore floated quantifiers are tertiaries.

It seems reasonable to suppose that the anaphoric potential of quantifiers will be noted in sentences such as (4).

(4) After the men$_i$ got home, each$_i$ complained of a headache.

The inclusion of quantifiers in the class of categories that can look to another element for their interpretation should automatically make them subject to the major constraint on anaphoric dependencies, the Precedence Constraint.

This leaves us with the problem of explaining the development of the principle governing the interpretation of floated quantifiers.

(5) *The Floated Quantifier Requirement:*
   A floated quantifier looks for its interpretation to a thematic dependent of the verb.

Since the notions "thematic dependent" and "clause" should be familiar to the language learner (see earlier chaps.), our major challenge is to explain how children avoid overgeneralizations that would result in free association of floated quantifiers with antecedents. This would lead to the acceptance of ungrammatical sentences such as (6) and the need to be informed that these utterances are unacceptable.

(6) *The men's$_i$ friend could each$_i$ help.

The most plausible suggestion at this point would seem to be that children make use of the notions "clause" and "thematic dependent" to formulate a conservative hypothesis about the interpretation of floated quantifiers. They would therefore take a sentence such as (7) to indicate only that a floated quantifier can look for its interpretation to a thematic dependent in its clause, not that it can take any NP as antecedent.[5]

(7) She talked to the boys$_i$ several times each$_i$.

Although I know of no data bearing on the development of floated quantifiers, the preceding proposal predicts that children's initial hypothesis should limit the set of potential antecedents to intraclausal thematic dependents of the verb. We would also expect mastery of floated quantifiers to be preceded by acquisition of the Precedence Constraint and the syntax of VP-internal adverbs. Although quantifiers are known to be acquired at a relatively late point (Donaldson and McGarrigle 1974; Roeper and Matthei 1975), I cannot confirm these predictions in a more specific way at this time.

6.4 Conclusion

In this chapter I have been concerned with two "leftward" dependencies, one involving the relation between an extraposed phrase and the nominal with which it combines and the other involving a "floated" quantifier and the NP to which it looks for its interpretation. In both cases, I attempted to show that the required descriptive principles exploit notions that are independently required—phrasal category, continuity, thematic dependency, and precedence. Drawing on the Conservatism Thesis, I also attempted to establish that the emergence of these principles would be a reasonable response to experience in the case of both structure types.

This concludes my examination of individual syntactic phenomena and the associated learnability problems. The time has now come to attempt a synthesis that will draw together the proposals made to this point and provide at least the outlines of a principled theory of language development consistent with general nativism. This is the subject matter of the next chapter.

7

PRINCIPLES AND
PROSPECTS

7.1 Grammar and Learning

For the past twenty years, one of the major preoccupations of linguistic theory has been the search for the innate linguistic principles that supposedly allow children to acquire the grammar of their native language. During this time, it has become clear that any approach to language that accepts transformational grammar (TG) as a model of linguistic competence is also committed to a nativist account of language acquisition. As Chomsky has repeatedly noted (e.g., 1977a, 15), it is completely implausible to believe that the principles and relations exploited in TG could be induced from experience. A comparable position has been articulated for Lexical Functional Grammar (LFG) (Bresnan 1982) and other theories of grammar that purport to provide psychologically real characterizations of linguistic competence.

My position throughout this book has been that there may be learnable grammars but that they consist of categories and principles quite unlike those found in transformational grammar and Lexical Functional Grammar. The major claims that I have made in this area are (*a*) that grammatical categories and principles can be constructed from notions that are not specifically linguistic in character and (*b*) that normal experience provides children with the information they need to form generalizations leading to these grammatical mechanisms. Put another way, I have been claiming that, while the grammar forms a separate cognitive system, the categories and principles needed for language are constructed from notions that are not specifically linguistic in character (e.g., adjacency, precedence, etc.) and that none of the biologically determined structures involved in development are unique to the language faculty. This position contradicts two widely held views within linguistics: the nonreducibility of grammatical notions to nonlinguistic concepts (the autonomy thesis) and the necessity of innate linguistic knowledge (special nativism).

According to the proposals made in earlier chapters, the central notion underlying the construction of a grammar is dependency, which manifests itself in three distinct ways:

a. *Combinatorial dependency:*
   One element looks to another to provide the category with which it must combine.

b. *Interpretive dependency:*
   One element looks to another for its reference.

c. *Thematic dependency:*
   One element looks to another for the assignment of its thematic role.

A significant fact about all three types of dependency is that they involve different aspects of sentence semantics. Under the assumptions outlined in chapter 1, for example, combinatorial dependencies reflect the type of predicate encoded by individual words (cf. the Lexical Projection Principle). Thus, to take one of the most basic categorial contrasts in the grammar, an independent category (e.g., a noun) does not encode a predicate that applies to a linguistically expressed argument, while a dependent category (e.g., a verb or an adjective) does. Other aspects of sentence semantics underlie interpretive and thematic dependencies. Interpretive dependencies, for instance, involve anaphoric relations among the phrases within a sentence, including obligatory coreference and disjoint reference. Thematic dependency, on the other hand, is concerned with the assignment of thematic roles reflecting ontological relations in the world that sentences purport to describe, comment on, and question.

The fact that the dependency relations we have been considering are rooted in sentence semantics is relevant to the language acquisition problem for at least two reasons. First, because of their semantic basis, these dependency notions should be available to children independent of syntactic knowledge. Indeed, it seems reasonable to suppose that these notions are independently involved in the representation of sentence meaning. Thus the interpretation of a sentence such as *Harry blames himself* consists of at least three types of facts: the predicate-argument relation between the verb and its subject and direct object (combinatorial dependency), the thematic roles of agent and patient associated with these phrases (thematic dependency) and the coreference between *himself* and *Harry* (anaphoric dependency). In chapter 1, I suggested that these aspects of meaning are represented in "semantic form," which corresponds to Jackendoff's (1983) conceptual structure—a very general type of mental representation at which linguistic, sensory, and motor types of information are compatible. Since it is widely assumed that children are able to represent the semantic content of sentences independent of language, it is possible to take these notions as the prelinguistic base on which grammatical categories and principles can be constructed. This in turn may help explain how children are able to identify successfully the concepts relevant to the construction of the grammar in a relatively short time.

A second advantage of having crucial grammatical notions grounded in sentence semantics relates to the type of data that will be relevant to linguistic development—namely, sentences. Since sentences not only constitute natural units of communication but also can be very short, they are presumably easy ''chunks'' of information for the child to deal with. Here my position breaks quite sharply with the type of opposition to special nativism found in the work of some radical pragmatists and functionalists. Garcia (1979), Givon (1979), and Bates and McWhinney (1982), for instance, have attempted to circumvent the usual arguments for innate grammatical knowledge by calling into question the need for an independent sentence grammar. In contrast, I have taken the position that the existence of sentence grammar is actually crucial to the development of an alternative to special nativism. The key claim of course is that a sentence grammar built on the type of notions I have proposed can be triggered by highly accessible and simple forms of linguistic experience.

According to the proposals made in preceding chapters, the notion of combinatorial dependency is used to form a basic set of categorial contrasts (N, NP, V, VP, etc.) and principles (the Combinatorial Principle, the Subject-Last Requirement). The syntactic representations formed in accordance with these grammatical devices then play a role in the statement of a variety of other principles, some of which are repeated below.

(1) *The Continuity Requirement (Korean):*
    Only a VP may be discontinuous.

(2) *The Continuity Requirement (Dutch):*
    Only a VP or PP may be discontinuous.

(3) *The Continuous Clause Requirement (Korean):*
    All clauses must be continuous.

(4) *The Independent Clause Requirement (English):*
    Only an independent clause can be discontinuous.

(5) *The Precedence Constraint:*
    A pronoun cannot precede an antecedent in its phrasal category.

(6) *The Reflexive Requirement (English):*
    The reflexive is obligatory when a pronoun and its antecedent are thematic dependents of the same element.

(7) *The Extraposition Constraint:*
   An extraposed phrase cannot be separated from the phrasal category of the
   element with which it combines.

Two points must be made about these principles. First, it should be
obvious that neither these principles nor the syntactic categories to which
they refer (NP, VP, etc.) have counterparts in other cognitive domains.
(There is no equivalent of "noun" in the perceptual faculty and no "Continuous Clause Requirement" in the social faculty.) This is not the claim of
general nativism. Rather the crucial point is that syntactic principles and
categories are formulated in terms of notions (dependency, continuity, adjacency, and so on) that are not specific to the language faculty and are
hence available to the language learner independent of language. Such
notions may well be innately structured themselves, of course, but not by
genetic mechanisms exclusively concerned with language.

Second, it must be acknowledged that none of the principles we have
been considering provides entirely unproblematic coverage of the data in
its domain (any more than the inborn principles that have been posited in
TG do). Likewise, the proposals I have made about learning have not
always been complete or unproblematic. Although I therefore anticipate
the need for important refinements, this does not undermine the viability of
categorial grammar or general nativism. Descriptive perfection has never
been the immediate objective of linguistics or any other discipline. What is
sought rather is some fundamental insight into the research problems that
are considered central to the field. Indeed, it is not unusual for a discipline
to tolerate a (temporary) reduction in descriptive coverage in return for the
promise of a deeper understanding of a significant phenomenon. In the
case of linguistics, the central research problem for the last two decades
has been the "fact" of language acquisition—the emergence of a grammar
in response to limited experience. This has also been my primary concern
in this book, although I have departed from current proposals in claiming
that there are principles of substantial empirical promise that meet learnability conditions consistent with the thesis of general nativism. These conditions require that grammatical concepts be accessible to children through
previous learning or general innate knowledge, that the linguistic environment include relevant forms of experience, and that linguistic principles be
the product of generalization or inference. It is clear that, if such conditions
can be met by principles that even approach adequacy for the phenomena
they are intended to cover, they will provide potentially important insights
into the nature of the human language faculty.

The analyses developed here constitute only the first step in a research
program aimed at characterizing linguistic knowledge and the language
faculty in a manner consistent with the thesis of general nativism. I ac-

knowledge, of course, the existence of gaps in some of the proposals I have made about learnability. Moreover, it is reasonable to expect that further study of grammar and learning will force refinements and adjustments of various sorts. This notwithstanding, the analyses developed in this book support tentative proposals about a variety of important problems in linguistic theory. These problems include the role of generalization in language learning, the motivation for developmental sequences in language acquisition, the marked character of certain constructions, and restrictions on the class of possible grammars. I will discuss each of these issues in turn, drawing on the analyses presented in earlier chapters.

7.2 Issues in Language Learning

7.2.1 Generalization in Language Learning

A recurring theme in this book has been that syntactic categories and principles are the product of learning through generalization. The important role that I have attributed to this type of learning raises two important questions about the language acquisition process.

(1) How are generalizations formed in the face of irregular and apparently contradictory data?

(2) Why do certain types of overgeneralizations not occur?

Let us consider each question in turn.

As noted a number of times in earlier discussion, the key to successful generalization lies in the identification of the correct set of formative concepts. An overly rich initial set of concepts would run the danger of providing the child with too many options from which to choose, thereby compromising the success of the language acquisition process. An overly impoverished set of concepts, on the other hand, would make it impossible for children to form the grammatical principles needed to account for the observed facts of language use. Special nativism offers an obvious and straightforward solution to this problem: the appropriate set of grammatical notions is innately specified. Since this option is not consistent with the thesis of general nativism, other alternatives must be considered in the acquisition theory I am attempting to develop.

The major proposal I have made in this regard is that children must construct grammatical categories and principles on a conceptual foundation that is not unique to language. The key notions of this type that I have identified are dependency, adjacency, precedence, and continuity. As noted above, the first of these notions manifests itself in a variety of ways in the linguistic domain, all of which involve some aspect of sentence

semantics. The other central notions all pertain to fundamental organizational properties of the syntactic representation and presumably constitute
notions that are available for the evaluation of nonlinguistic structures as
well. As proposed in chapter I (sec. 1.5.3), exploitation of these notions
may be enhanced by the child's realization that sentences consist of linear
strings of elements (hence the relevance of adjacency and precedence) and
that some of these elements name predicates that must apply to linguistically expressed arguments (dependency).

Even assuming that children successfully identify the right set of concepts, they still face the problem of forming generalizations that are neither
overly restrictive nor overly permissive. In many cases, their initial generalizations are inappropriate and must be adjusted in response to subsequent
experience. A commonly cited example of this involves the generalization
that all count nouns in English form their plurals with the affix -s. It has
been observed that children pass through a stage in which they produce the
forms in (3) in lieu of those in (4).

(3) foots, sheeps, mans

(4) feet, sheep, men

Errors such as (4) eventually disappear—presumably because children
hear the forms in (4) used in contexts in which they clearly express plurals.
Assuming preference for a one-to-one relation between form and meaning
at the word level (what various authors have called the Uniqueness Principle), exposure to these forms will suffice to trigger the needed changes in
the grammar.

A second, and more serious, type of misgeneralization would involve
the formation of incorrect principles that could not be revised on the basis
of experience. A variety of such potential errors have been considered in
this book, including the possible (but nonexistent) principles outlined in
(5)–(7).

(5) A reflexive pronoun can take any antecedent.

(6) An extraposed phrase can combine with any NP.

(7) Any phrase can be discontinuous.

Such principles would permit formation of sentences such as (8)–(10).

(8) *Harry's$_i$ book pleased himself$_i$.

(9) *[$_{NP}$ A book about our visitor$_i$] arrived yesterday [who lived in India]$_i$.

(10) *Qui avez-vous parlé [$_{PP}$ de ____]?
     Who have you spoken about?

On the usual assumption that children do not receive systematic feedback about the possible unacceptability of their utterances, the adoption of principles (5)–(7) might well be irreversible. Unlike the overgeneralization exemplified in (3) above, these erroneous principles would never be inconsistent with experience since all adult utterances will appear to comply with them. Thus every time children heard a sentence containing an extraposed phrase, they would take it as a vindication of (6) without realizing that the sentence in question was actually complying with a much more restrictive principle (the Extraposition Constraint in [7] of the preceding sec.).

While it is possible to imagine that children might eventually realize that they hear only a subset of the sentences allowed by their overly general principle and make the appropriate adjustment, this is unlikely. Not only does the ability to make such adjustments require a rather remarkable memory capacity (since children would have to remember what they heard over an extended period of time), it might ultimately cause inappropriate modifications to correct principles. Because there is no fixed number of grammatical sentences, children will hear only a subset of the utterances allowed by any principle, including correct ones. If they make the type of adjustments we are considering, they might wrongly try to modify correct principles to restrict them to the set of utterances they actually encounter. This would ultimately undermine the formation of any generalization that goes beyond the observed facts and would make acquisition of a productive set of grammatical rules impossible.

In the light of these considerations, it is perhaps not surprising to discover that children apparently do not make the overgeneralizations exemplified in (5)–(7). This raises the question of how such overgeneralizations are avoided. My approach to this problem has been to adopt the Conservatism Thesis and the Trigger Requirement, restated here as (11) and (12).

(11) *The Conservatism Thesis:*
 Children make use of the available concepts to formulate the most conservative hypothesis consistent with experience.

(12) *The Trigger Requirement:*
 No change is made in the grammar without a triggering stimulus in the environment.

The claim underlying these proposals is that children formulate their initial hypotheses as conservatively as possible and modify them only in the face of contradictory experience.

The Conservatism Thesis constrains the manner in which children formulate linguistic principles, not the way in which they apply them. It therefore does not conflict with the proposal that language learners prefer a principle that operates across the board to one that applies in only some cases. (Such a proposal was made in chapter 1 to help establish the learnability of the Subject-Last Requirement.) Because the latter proposal relates to the functioning of a grammatical principle and not to its formulation, it is not inconsistent with (11). I will therefore continue to take the position that grammatical principles are formulated conservatively but are then applied in the most general manner possible.

The intuition underlying the Conservatism Thesis is found in many approaches to language acquisition, including those associated with transformational grammar. There, it has been observed that insurmountable learnability problems would arise if children did not adopt the most conservative of the options open to them. One such example is discussed by Jakubowicz (1984). She notes that if children assumed that English reflexive pronouns did not require a clausemate antecedent (an option allowed in Japanese), they would incorrectly produce sentences such as *John thinks that Mary likes himself.* Assuming (as usual) that children have no information about the ungrammaticality of the sentences they produce, such errors could not be corrected, and the adult grammar would never be attained. Berwick (1982) attempts to resolve this problem by attributing to the language faculty the Subset Property paraphrased below.

The Subset Property:
Language learners choose the option which allows the smallest number of grammatical sentences.

The Subset Property ensures that children will initially assume a clausemate requirement on reflexives since this allows a smaller range of acceptable sentences than would the assumption that there is no such requirement. Exactly the same effect is achieved by adopting the Conservatism Thesis and the Trigger Requirement, as we shall see shortly.

The role of the Conservatism Thesis and the Trigger Requirement in the theory I have proposed can be illustrated first with the help of the "extraction" facts. A basic problem in the study of *wh* question formation involves ensuring that there will be no generalization from structures such as (13) to (14) and (15) in Korean or from (14) to (15) in Dutch.

(13) Who did you [$_{VP}$ see ____]?
     (grammatical in Korean and Dutch)

(14) What did you [$_{VP}$ work [$_{PP}$ with ____]]?
     (ungrammatical in Korean, grammatical in Dutch)

(15) Who did you [$_{VP}$ see [$_{NP}$ a picture [$_{PP}$ of ____]]]?
     (ungrammatical in Korean and Dutch)

As we have already seen (chap. 3), the undesired generalizations would be avoided in these cases if children proceeded conservatively, taking (13) to indicate only that a VP can be discontinuous and (14) to show only that a PP within a VP can also be discontinuous. The Trigger Requirement would then ensure retention of the appropriate constraint until contradictory evidence was uncovered. This will have the effect of guaranteeing that Korean children will never produce (14) and that Dutch children will not use (15).

A comparable approach will also account for the lack of overgeneralization from (16) to (17) in Korean and from (17) to (18) in English.

(16) Who did John [$_{VP}$ see ____]?
(grammatical in English and Korean)

(17) Who did you say[$_S$ John saw ____]?
(unacceptable in Korean, grammatical in English)

(18) *Who did you walk away [$_S$ after John saw ____]?
(ungrammatical in English and Korean)

According to the Conservatism Thesis, exposure to the discontinuous VP in (16) will not lead to the generalization that other types of phrases (including clauses) can be discontinuous. For this conclusion to be drawn, language learners must be exposed to sentences such as (17)—a structure type that is not found in Korean. This ensures avoidance of the first overgeneralization we are considering. The overgeneralization from (17) to (18) will also be avoided if the Conservatism Thesis is correct. This is because language learners who are formulating hypotheses in a manner consistent with our proposal will take (17) to show only that an independent clause can be discontinuous. There will therefore be no generalization from the discontinuous independent clause in (17) to the discontinuous dependent one in (18) without an appropriate triggering stimulus, something that does not occur in English.

Numerous other examples of conservatism in hypothesis formation were considered in earlier chapters of this book, including the principle that regulates the obligatory occurrence of reflexive pronouns, restated here as (19).

(19) *The Reflexive Requirement (RR):*
The reflexive is obligatory when a pronoun and its antecedent are thematic dependents of the same element.

The RR sanctions the reflexive in (20), in which the pronoun and its antecedent are both thematic dependents of the verb, but not in (21), in which the lexical NP receives its thematic role from the noun *criticism*.

(20) Sue$_i$ criticized herself$_i$.

(21) *Criticism of Sue$_i$ amuses herself$_i$.

According to the proposals I have made, successful identification of the RR comes about because children analyze their experience conservatively. Rather than concluding from (20) that a reflexive pronoun can occur anywhere, they hypothesize that this form occurs where it and its antecedent receive their thematic role from the same element.

In other grammatical domains, conservatism in hypothesis formation might manifest itself in other ways. For example, Baker (1979) suggests that the type of information contained in lexical entries reflects item-by-item learning rather than any type of generalization. Thus a child exposed to the use of *likely* in a "raising" structure such as (22) will not automatically assume that the nearly synonymous *probable* has the same privileges of occurrence.

(22) John is likely to succeed.

(23) *John is probable to succeed.

It would be interesting to explore the possibility that conservatism in the case of lexical development manifests itself in the form of item-by-item learning (i.e., that within the lexicon each entry is treated as a separate category).[1]

The proposal that language learners are uniformly conservative in their hypothesis formation points to the need for further inquiry in a number of areas. Foremost among these is the identification of the precise set of concepts available to the language learner for the formation of syntactic rules and categories. If the approach adopted here is correct, at least the concepts listed in table 7.1 will be available. This list must obviously be treated with some caution since it seems reasonable to expect that refinements and revisions will become necessary as work proceeds. Moreover, it is essential to recognize that not all these concepts will be available to children at the onset of the language acquisition process since some are known to be derived from others (e.g., phrasal categories from lexical categories, lexical categories from dependency contrasts, and so on).[2] These caveats notwithstanding, there seems to be enough promise in the analyses proposed here to warrant further inquiry based on the assumption that table 7.1 provides a reasonable first approximation to the conceptual inventory relevant for the acquisition of syntax.

Another matter that must be assigned priority in future work relates to the nature of the overgeneralizations that are observed in child language. In particular, we must be careful not to formulate the Conservatism Thesis in such a way that attested overgeneralizations are incorrectly ruled out. At this point, our proposal seems to allow overgeneralizations of two sorts.

Table 7.1

Fundamental notions:	Dependency
	Adjacency
	Continuity
	Precedence
Derived notions:	Lexical and phrasal categories (e.g., N, NP, V, VP, etc.)
	Syntactic argument (first, middle, or last)
	Syntactic modifier (adjunct)
	Thematic dependent

First, the child could produce an overgeneralization in cases in which the relevant system cannot be adequately characterized in terms of the grammatical notions listed in table 7.1. An obvious example of this involves plural formation, which children apparently analyze in terms of the syntactic notion "noun" (e.g., "Add -*s* to a noun to form the plural"), not realizing that there are idiosyncratic exceptions (e.g., *feet, sheep*) that must be stated in terms of individual lexical items rather than syntactic categories.

A second type of overgeneralization could occur in cases in which children form their initial hypothesis in an overly conservative manner. A good example of this involves the syntax of anaphora, whose development seems to involve a stage in which all cases of backward pronominalization are ruled out (see sec. 5.6). On the analysis being proposed here, this would result from the child using the notion "precedence" to form an ultraconservative prohibition against all cases of backward anaphora. (For a discussion of why children pass through such a stage, see secs. 5.6 and 7.2.2.) Exposure to patterns of backward anaphora such as *His mother criticized John* leads to a reformulation of this intermediate constraint so that it applies only in the domain corresponding to the pronoun's phrasal category (my Precedence Constraint).

Apparent counterexamples to the Conservatism Thesis will doubtlessly be easy to find, but care must be taken in their analysis. It is important to recognize, for example, that the structures needed to test crucial principles in children's grammars often make special demands on nongrammatical mechanisms. Thus children's understanding of reflexive pronouns, for example, is often tested with the help of multiclausal sentences such as (24).

(24) [$_S$ Harry said [$_S$ that John blames himself]]

Because of the length and complexity of such structures, it is not always clear whether errors should be attributed to an incomplete grammatical principle or to difficulties pertaining to working memory, processing, and the like. Needless to say, only errors of the first type will have any bearing on the correctness of the Conservatism Thesis.

Yet another factor that must be taken into account relates to the problem of determining whether children have actually formulated a grammatical principle. It would not be unreasonable to think, for example, that children who had not yet begun to acquire the reflexive element *himself* might react to such an item in an experimental task by treating it like the phonetically similar definite pronoun *him*. (In fact, Otsu [1981] notes instances of this type of response among some of his younger subjects.) Needless to say, such a response strategy does not indicate that children do not formulate conservative hypotheses about reflexive pronouns. The Conservatism Thesis makes a claim only about the way in which children form hypotheses in response to experience: it makes no prediction about how they will react in experimental settings to elements that they have not yet begun to acquire.

This leaves us with the problem of determining the source of the Conservatism Thesis and the Trigger Requirement. As far as I can see, the only plausible hypothesis here is that they are genetically specified. By itself, this fact does not undermine the thesis of general nativism since it is conceivable that the proposed constraints also manifest themselves outside the language faculty. While this suggestion is not obviously correct, it seems consistent with at least certain developmental facts from other cognitive domains. According to Brainerd (1978), for instance, the general law governing mental growth in Piaget-type theories of cognitive development permits adjustments to mental structures only in response to experience incompatible with currently held hypotheses. There are no spontaneous or untriggered developmental changes. This is precisely the proposal I have made for linguistic development under the rubric of the Trigger Requirement.

The real challenge lies in subsuming the Conservatism Thesis under general nativism. Although generalization is known to play a role in other types of cognitive development (e.g., Cornell 1978), it is much harder to establish the existence of the precise type of conservatism I have posited for language. While generalization in other domains is obviously not unconstrained, claims about conservatism must be made with respect to the use of a specific set of concepts to form the principles of a particular cognitive system. Although I am unable to propose a parallel in which I have confidence at this time, there are hypothetical cases that illustrate the general objective. One example involves "conservation"—the principle stipulating that an object's inherent properties (number, mass, weight, and volume) remain constant despite physical transformations in shape and the like. As is well known (e.g., Odom 1978), children initially do not formulate conservation as a general principle. Rather they begin by noting that the number of objects in a group remains constant despite changes in their physical arrangement. The realization that an object's mass remains the same despite changes in shape emerges about two years later, with conservation in the domains of weight and volume appearing still later. The fact that there is no generalization to conservation in volume from the realization that there is conservation in number is a possible instantiation in a nonlinguistic domain of the conservatism I have posited for grammatical development.

While the situation is not hopeless, it is clear that we must also be willing to consider the "worst-case scenario," which is that for one reason or another the Conservatism Thesis holds only in the language faculty. This is hardly an intolerable result, even for general nativism. While the insight captured by the Conservatism Thesis might be true only of language acquisition, such an innate predisposition would still be quite different from the inborn categories and principles of special nativism in that it constitutes a mechanism for constructing a grammar, not a part of the grammar itself. There is clearly no room for dogmatism here. While I have decided not to adopt as my initial assumption the belief that the language faculty is structured by a rich set of specifically linguistic principles, I noted at the outset that there is no a priori reason why this could not be so. It is important not to lose sight of this fact and to be willing to surrender stronger versions of general nativism as the need arises.

In summary, then, I am proposing that language development complies with the following three principles of learning.

A. Hypotheses are formulated conservatively.
   (The Conservatism Thesis)

B. Hypothesized principles remain stable unless contradicted by experience.
   (The Trigger Requirement)

C. Once formulated, principles apply as generally as possible.

Although innately specified (presumably), these learning principles could well extend beyond the language faculty and may therefore be consistent with the thesis of general nativism.

The proposed learning principles point to various further lines of inquiry, including the need to search for other general principles of learning. Although I cannot deal with this matter here, a number of possibilities are obviously worth considering, including Berwick and Weinberg's (1984) suggestion that the acquisition device is "nonrecursive"—that is, it can work on only one rule at a time. Another area for research relates to the precise type of experience needed to bring about modification in a principle. Especially intriguing here is the possibility that revisions to the grammar require a triggering stimulus that is roughly equal in strength to the forms of experience underlying changes in other cognitive domains. Although there is obviously some potential for interesting work in this area, nothing more can be said about this matter at present and I will therefore set it aside for future consideration.

7.2.2 The Motivation for Developmental Sequences

It is an indisputable fact that certain aspects of language are acquired before others. Thus it is known that active structures are mastered before passives, that the *-ing* ending is acquired before the plural suffix, that adjectives are used before relative clauses, and so on. It is also well known that, in the course of mastering a particular phenomenon, children may adopt successive hypotheses about what the underlying principle is. Developmental sequences have manifested themselves in the phenomena studied here a number of times. We have noted, for example, that *wh* structures such as (1) will emerge before (2) and (2) before (3) (see chap. 3).

(1) Who did John see ____?

(2) What did you work with ____?

(3) Who did you see a picture of ____?

We have also noted that structures such as (1) can be expected to appear before (4) and that the latter construction will be mastered before (5) (in languages like Swedish where these sentences are allowed at all).

(4) Who did Mary say John saw ____?

(5) This is the man who you met someone who likes ____.

Further, it appears that the principle governing pronoun-antecedent relations evolves through the series of steps outlined in (6).

(6) a. A pronoun takes an antecedent.
   b. A pronoun cannot precede its antecedent.
   c. A pronoun cannot precede an antecedent in its phrasal category.

At least three different types of explanation could be offered for this type of phenomenon.

A. *The environmental explanation:*
   Some feature of the linguistic environment (presumably frequency) facilitates the development of certain components of the grammar before others.

B. *The nativist explanation:*
   An innate timetable specifies the developmental sequence.

C. *The grammatical explanation:*
   The nature of the grammatical rules being acquired defines the developmental sequence.

All three of these approaches have been considered in the literature on language learning. Olmsted (1971), for instance, offers an environmental explanation for certain aspects of phonological development. Brown (1973), on the other hand, rejects the environmental explanation in favor of a grammatical explanation in his discussion of morphological development. Nativist explanations are also found in the literature dating back at least to Lenneberg (1967) and are still popular, as exemplified by Chomsky's (1980, 134) view that most of what has conventionally been called learning is actually "growth" and Felix's (1984) proposal that development directly reflects the emergence of innate Universal Grammar (UG).

Of the three types of explanation just outlined, the nativist and environmental accounts are problematic from the perspective I have been developing. The problem with the nativist account, of course, is that it presupposes the existence of innate syntactic mechanisms and is therefore inconsistent with the broader position on learnability that I have adopted. Moreover, in the absence of a serious theory of why the components of UG "emerge" in the posited order, it is hard to see how this type of proposal can explain the facts of development in a satisfying way.

The environmental explanation, on the other hand, seems to encounter serious obstacles of another sort since it begs the question in presupposing the presence of the very structural analysis whose development it is supposedly accounting for. Thus for an environmental explanation based on frequency of occurrence to work in the case of (1)–(3) above, it is necessary to assume that the child will take utterances like these to be manifestations of three separate structure types rather than of a single [*wh* word + S] construction. Otherwise, the putative differences in frequency could have no effect. But the identification of three distinct structure types in these cases seems to presuppose knowledge of the very differences whose acquisition we are trying to explain.

This leaves us with the grammatical explanation, which I will assume relies on the following principle.

(7) *The Developmental Principle:*
   A rule or representation A will emerge after a rule or representation B if A is cumulatively more complex than B.

I define cumulative complexity as follows.

(8) A is cumulatively more complex than B if A involves all the notions that B does plus at least one more.

So stated, the Developmental Principle is relatively uncontroversial since it is hard to imagine an acquisition theory that would predict that more complex structures would be acquired first. The value of the Developmental Principle is therefore contingent on the charaterization of grammatical complexity from which its predictions are derived. The analyses I have proposed allow the Developmental Principle to make the right predictions about acquisitional order for a number of the phenomena we have been considering.

Consider first the problem of explaining why certain types of *wh* questions appear before others. As noted in chapter 3, the three structures exemplified in (1)–(3) above exhibit successively more radical degrees of departure from the computational ideal of continuous constituents. This is illustrated in (9).

(9) a. A discontinuous VP (i.e., [1]).
    b. A discontinuous VP and PP (i.e., [2]).
    c. A discontinuous VP, PP, and NP (i.e., [3]).

Notice that each step in the posited developmental order involves the discontinuous element(s) found in the preceding stage plus one more. As noted in chapter 3, this is a consequence of the type of syntactic representations generated by the grammar. Since discontinuous NPs and PPs must always be within VP, it therefore follows that children must be familiar with discontinuous VPs before they can allow discontinuous PPs or NPs. Similarly, since discontinuous NPs are created by a discontinuity in a component PP, the second step in (9) is logically prior to the third step. This allows a natural explanation for the observed acquisitional order in terms of the Developmental Principle proposed above.

A similar line of inquiry shows promise of explaining the developmental sequence associated with (1) and (4)–(5), repeated here.

(1) Who did John see ___?

(4) Who did Mary say John saw ___?

(5) *This is the man who you met someone who likes ___.

As noted before, (4) differs from (1) in requiring a discontinuous clause since the clause containing the *wh* phrase not only is discontinuous but is also dependent in that it functions as a relative clause rather than an object complement. On the assumption that continuous constituents are preferred by language learners and language users, the three sentences in question might be seen as manifesting the following degrees of departure from the ideal of a continuous clause formed by combining adjacent elements.

(10) a. A continuous clause (sentence [1]).
     b. A discontinuous independent clause (sentence [4]).
     c. A discontinuous dependent clause sentence [5]).

As noted before (chap. 4), this markedness scale seems to reflect degrees of departure from the computational ideal of a continuous clause with no external dependencies. Pattern (10a) complies with this ideal, but (b) and (c) do not since each contains a discontinuous clause. In the case of pattern (c), matters are further complicated by the fact that the discontinuity occurs in a relative clause that already exhibits a dependency on an external element (the head noun *someone*). Once again, then, the relative order of acquisition reflects successively greater degrees of departure from the computational ideal (adjacency and continuity), consistent with the Developmental Principle.

Consider now the different stages in the acquisition of the system of pronominalization as they were outlined in (6) above, restated here.

(6) a. A pronoun takes an antecedent.
    b. A pronoun cannot precede its antecedent.
    c. A pronoun cannot precede an antecedent in its phrasal category.

As indicated in (11), each of these stages presupposes use of certain concepts.

(11) a. Stage 1: Pronoun, antecedent.
     b. Stage 2: Pronoun, antecedent, precedence.
     c. Stage 3: Pronoun, antecedent, precedence, phrasal category.

As noted in chapter 5, each stage requires all the concepts present at the previous stage—plus one more. Moreover, as noted in section 5.6, the relevance of phrasal categories to the syntax of anaphora (stage 3) presupposes the distinction between forward and backward anaphora (stage 2) since phrasal categories are relevant only in the backward cases. Similarly, the forward-backward distinction presupposes discovery of anaphoric relations (stage 1). If this is correct, then, the developmental sequence underlying the syntax of anaphora is internally motivated by grammatical considerations in accordance with the Developmental Principle and need not be attributed to environmental or biological factors.

A similar explanation can be offered for the fact that children apparently learn the basic distributional properties of pronouns before mastering the contrast between reflexives and nonreflexives. As noted in chapter 5, both types of pronoun are subject to the Precedence Constraint.

(12) *The Precedence Constraint.*
    A pronoun cannot precede an antecedent in its phrasal category.

The two types of pronoun are distinguished from each other by the principle repeated in (13), which stipulates the conditions under which the reflexive is obligatory (and the definite pronoun impermissible).

(13) *The Reflexive Requirement:*
   The reflexive is obligatory when the pronoun and its antecedent are thematic dependents of the same element.

Because (13) presupposes the existence of anaphoric dependencies, it follows from the Developmental Principle that the ontogeny of pronoun-antecedent relations will have begun before the contrast between reflexives and nonreflexives mandated by this principle emerges.

The proposed motivation for the development of anaphora is reminiscent of the suggestion made in chapter 1 about the order of emergence of syntactic categories. There it was suggested that the three dependency categories emerge in the order primary > secondary > tertiary thanks to the fact that tertiaries are defined as elements depending on secondaries and secondaries as elements depending on primaries. Since the definition of the latter two categories presupposes the existence of a developmentally prior category, the Developmental Principle will once again predict the acquisitional order. Similar observations were made about the emergence of the verb-adjective contrast as well as the ontogeny of prepositions and copulas, all of which presuppose the existence of NPs.

As noted at the outset, there is an obvious connection between the account of acquisitional order offered by the Developmental Principle and the type of grammar that is taken to characterize the linguistic competence of children and adults. Were we to assume, for instance, that anaphoric relations were governed by Reinhart's principle, which prevents a pronoun from c-commanding its antecedent, the developmental sequence outlined in (6) would presumably have to be characterized as follows.

(14) a. A pronoun takes an antecedent.
    b. A pronoun cannot precede its antecedent.
    c. A pronoun cannot c-command its antecedent.

Notice that (14) shows no signs of cumulative development, suggesting rather a radical change in the child's approach to anaphora between the second and third stages. The same observation could also be made about the developmental order for syntactic categories since many theories are forced to assume a transition from a semantic characterization of these elements (e.g., "nouns are names of things") to qualitatively different formal definitions in terms of abstract syntactic features or distributional properties (for discussion see Pinker [1979]). Examples like these reconfirm the familiar fact that our view of language acquisition is shaped by our understanding of the system being acquired—a recurring theme in this book.

Before closing this section, it is necessary to comment on the position adopted here with respect to the relevance of developmental data for linguistic theory. As I originally noted in section 1.5, I have been maintaining the view that, in cases in which a principle of the adult grammar has been correctly identified, there should be some fairly direct evidence for its emergence in the developmental data. On this view, then, the acquisitional data is just as relevant to the evaluation of grammatical analyses as is data about the form and interpretation of sentences. This in turn implies that an explanatorily adequate theory of grammar not only should account for the observed grammaticality facts by identifying the principles underlying them but should also explain the relevant developmental facts by showing how intermediate stages in the language acquisition process reflect steps in the ontogeny of the proposed principles of adult grammar. Two points must be made about this position.

First, the relation between grammatical theory and developmental data that I have proposed makes sense only if linguistic development is supported primarily by cumulative learning of the sort exemplified in the cases we have been considering. If children could completely restructure their grammar at each step in the language acquisition process as new innately given concepts became available to them, we might well find that intermediate developmental stages did not bear any straightforward relation to the principles composing the final system. Proposals that linguistic development involves wide-scale restructuring are not uncommon in the transformational literature (e.g., White 1981), and they naturally have to be considered. After all, nature does provide us with the example of the caterpillar and the butterfly. Moreover, it seems reasonable to suppose that restructuring is also associated with major milestones in cognitive development (e.g., the transition from preoperational thought to concrete operations in the Piagetian model). At the same time, however, it must be recognized that a great deal of physical and mental growth seems to involve gradual cumulative development and that a fruitful research program might be built around the assumption that it underlies much of language acquisition as well. One of the potentially interesting features of the syntactic analysis that I have tried to develop here is that it seems to be consistent with such a research program.

A second point that must be taken into account when considering my proposal is that there is no more reason to think that every developmental phenomenon bears on the correctness of the grammar than there is to think that every fact about the acceptability of utterances does. Far more than just the grammar is involved in both linguistic performance and linguistic development. Indeed, it is usually assumed that both phenomena reflect the interaction of perceptual strategies, general conceptual knowledge, discourse principles, and pragmatics in addition to sentence grammar. We therefore have no way of knowing, for example, whether *Whom did you sit near?* sounds unacceptable because it violates a rule of the grammar or because it reflects a strange mixture of styles: as Radford (1981) notes, preposition stranding is associated with a casual speech style, while respect for the *who/whom* distinction is normally restricted to formal speech. Countless comparable examples are found in the literature.

The significance of this fact for the study of language acquisition is that we also have no a priori way of knowing whether a particular phenomenon reflects the ontogeny of the grammar or that of some other cognitive system. Fortunately, this fact no more undermines my proposal about the responsibility of linguistic theory to developmental data than it invalidates the relevance of acceptability judgments for the evaluation of grammatical rules. In both cases, recalcitrant facts will have to be examined with a view to determining a possible alternate explanation involving some other cognitive system. Moreover, just as we would become suspicious about a theory of grammar that accounted for only a fraction of the acceptability judgments, so we should exercise caution about a characterization of linguistic competence that accounted for virtually none of the developmental data.

7.2.3 Markedness

It is a well-established fact that not all structures found in human language are equal in frequency or naturalness. Some structures, which are usually referred to as "marked," occur relatively infrequently and seem to involve grammatical devices that are unusual or special in some way. As we have already seen, *wh* questions formed by extraction from PPs and embedded clauses are more marked than those created by "fronting" an argument of the main verb (e.g., [1]).

(1) What did he [$_{VP}$ see ____]?

(2) a. Who did John [$_{VP}$ sit [$_{PP}$ near ____]]?
    b. Who did John [$_{VP}$ see [$_{NP}$ a picture [$_{PP}$ of ____]]]?

(3) Who did Mary say [$_S$ John [$_{VP}$ saw ____]]?

The study of markedness in transformational grammar has yielded some interesting proposals about the status of these structures. According to one suggestion considered earlier, for instance, the relative markedness of (2) and (3) follows from the Empty Category Principle (ECP), which requires all traces to be "properly governed." On the assumption that prepositions are not proper governors, sentences such as (2a) and (2b) must undergo a special reanalysis rule that creates the "complex verbs" *sit near* and *see a picture of*. These complex verbs can then properly govern the trace left by *wh* movement, satisfying the ECP. In the case of (3), on the other hand, the key to compliance with the ECP lies in the removal of the S' boundary (a maximal phrasal category) that separates the trace in the embedded COMP from the matrix verb *say* (cf. [4]).

(4) [$_{S'}$Who [$_S$ did Mary say [$_{S'}$ *t* [$_S$ John saw *t*]]]]

Assuming that these sorts of reanalysis have a marked status within innate Universal Grammar, the proposed analyses will correctly capture the unusual character of structures such as (2) and (3).

While there is obviously nothing inherently wrong with attributing markedness to specific innate mechanisms, it also seems plausible to consider other possibilities. In many instances, for example, the proposals that I have made allow extragrammatical factors to play a role in determining markedness. A good example of this involves the markedness facts pertaining to (1)–(3) above, all of which contain discontinuous phrases of various types, according to the analysis I have proposed. As noted in earlier discussions of the Continuity Requirement in chapter 3 and the Continuous Clause Requirement in chapter 4, it is not unreasonable to think that processing considerations favor structures in which strings of words are mapped onto continuous constituents. Indeed, this assumption has often been adopted in the literature on psycholinguistics (e.g., Wanner and Maratsos 1978) and language acquisition (Slobin 1972). A continuity preference of this sort supports predictions about markedness based on the types of phrases and clauses that can be discontinuous. This is illustrated by the "markedness hierarchies" in (5) and (6), repeated from above.

(5) a. A discontinuous VP.
      (i) Who did John [$_{VP}$ see ____]?
   b. A discontinuous VP and PP.
      (ii) Who did John [$_{VP}$ sit [$_{PP}$ near ____]]?
   c. A discontinuous VP, PP, and NP.
      (iii) Who did John [$_{VP}$ read [$_{NP}$ a book [$_{PP}$ about ____]]]?

(6) a. A continuous clause.
      (i) Who did John [$_{VP}$ see ____]?
   b. A discontinuous independent clause.
      (ii) Who did John say [$_S$ Sue liked ____]?
   c. A discontinuous dependent clause.
      (iii) This is the man who John met someone [$_S$ who knows ____].
         (grammatical in Swedish)

Other examples of the influence of extragrammatical factors on markedness have been raised throughout this book. One of the most intriguing
such cases involves backward anaphora, which is heavily constrained in
English and is not even found in some languages (Solan 1983). I have
tentatively attributed the marked character of such interpretive dependencies to the problems associated with processing a pronoun that occurs before the element to which it looks for its interpretation. This idea has been
challenged in recent work by Lust (1983), who claims that backward
anaphora is not universally marked and that it is actually preferred in left-
branching languages such as Japanese and Korean. (According to Lust, a
left-branching language places a relative clause before the noun it modifies
and an object clause in front of its verb; the reverse is true of a right-
branching language such as English.)

Lust believes that branching direction is relevant to the syntax of anaphora because of the central role (in TG) of principles that are formulated in
terms of c-command asymmetries. In the light of this, she proposes the
following principle (1983, 141).

(7) *Lust's Constraint on Anaphora:*
    In early child language, the direction of grammatical anaphora accords with the
    Principal Branching Direction of the specific language being acquired.

Lust takes (7) to predict that backward anaphora (i.e., the pattern with the
pronoun to the left of its antecedent) will constitute the unmarked case in
left-branching languages, while forward pronominalization will be preferred in right-branching languages.

In support of (7), Lust cites experimental work that suggests that Japanese children prefer structures such as (8) to (9) in elicited imitation
tasks.

(8) Sumire Ø to tanpopo-ga saku.
    violet Ø and dandelion-N bloom

(9) Inu-wa hoeru-shi Ø kamitsuku.
    dog-T bark and Ø bite

In English, on the other hand, children seem to prefer (10) to (11).

(10) John ate and Ø read.

(11) John Ø and Mary ate lunch.

Lust assumes that these coordinate structures contain a null anaphor
(marked as Ø) corresponding to the understood NP or verb. In accordance
with Lust's prediction, the structures preferred by the Japanese children
have the putative anaphor to the left of its ''antecedent,'' while the reverse
is true in English.

An obvious problem with this work is that the coordinate structures exemplified by (8)–(11) may not contain null anaphors. (Indeed, almost all syntactic theories assume that they do not.) In recent work, however, Lust and Mangione (1983) have attempted to extend the data base for hypothesis (7) to include sentences such as (12) and (13), which almost certainly do contain null pronouns.

(12) Mama-ga   kasa-o otoshita-no, Ø doa-o akeru-to.
    Mama-N umbrella-A dropped Ø door opened when
    "Mama dropped the umbrella when [she] opened the door."

(13) Ø mado-o akeru-to, oneesan-ga kusyami-o shita.
    Ø window-A opened when sister-N sneeze did
    "When [she] opened the window, sister sneezed."

Lust and Mangione (1983) report that Japanese children aged two to five perform significantly better on sentence (13) (the backward case) in an elicited imitation task. According to the Japanese speakers I have consulted, however, sentences such as (12)—which supposedly represent the forward pattern of anaphora—are unnatural since the matrix verb (*otoshita,* "drop") is not sentence final. In contrast, the backward pattern manifests the more natural order, with the matrix verb at the end of the sentence. A second problem is that coreference between a zero pronoun and a subject marked by the nominative suffix -*ga* (rather than the topic suffix -*wa*) is apparently unusual, further increasing the unnaturalness of the structure exemplifying forward anaphora.

In attempting to overcome these difficulties, O'Grady, Suzuki-Wei, and Cho (1986) designed an elicited imitation task that made use of the contrast between sentences such as (14) and (15) in Japanese (exemplified) and Korean. In these sentences, the matrix verb occurs sentence finally, and the intended antecedent of the zero pronoun bears a topic marker.

(14) Erityan-wa nezumi-o mi-ta kara Ø nige-ta.
    Erityan-T mouse -A saw because Ø ran away
    "Because Erityan saw a mouse, [he] ran away."

(15) Ø kutabire-tei-ta kara okaasan-wa ne-tei-ta.
    Ø tired was because mother -T sleeping was
    "Because [she] was tired, mother was sleeping."

Working with 178 monolingual speakers of Japanese and Korean between the ages of four and eleven, we found much higher scores on the imitation of forward patterns than of backward structures (as high as 90 percent vs. 10 percent in some cases). Moreover, reversals in the relative order of the pronoun and its antecedent were common in the backward pattern (20 percent of the responses were of this type) but essentially nonexistent in the forward case. This suggests that backward patterns of anaphora are in fact universally marked, consistent with my proposal.[3]

The cases we have been considering point to possible new avenues of inquiry into markedness in human language. In particular, it seems reasonable to explore the possibility that concepts such as dependency, continuity, adjacency, and precedence constitute the central parameters for cross-linguistic variation and that processing considerations play a major role in determining the unmarked case. Consistent with this idea, I have attempted to characterize the syntax of extraction in terms of constraints on discontinuous phrase types, with the unmarked case involving continuous categories formed by combining adjacent elements. Similarly, I have suggested that the unmarked interpretive dependency has the antecedent preceding the pronoun, again for reasons pertaining to processing. Although it remains to be seen whether these proposals can be extended and refined in satisfactory ways, they seem to provide a promising alternative to current attempts to characterize the same markedness facts in terms of proper government, reanalysis, node deletion, branching direction, and the like.

7.2.4 Restricting the Class of Possible Grammars

The unifying theme of much current work in linguistics is the search for a principled way to restrict the class of possible grammars to which children have access. As noted earlier, it is assumed that, if UG does not provide narrowly restrictive principles, the sheer number of hypotheses available to children would make it impossible for them to "select" the right grammar for their language on the basis of experience. Consider, for example, the difficulties that would arise if children had to decide among the following competing grammars.

(i) Syntactic principles refer to grammatical relations such as "subject" and "object," which are treated as primes rather than defined notions (e.g., Relational Grammar—Perlmutter [1982]; Lexical Functional Grammar—Bresnan [1982]).

(ii) Syntactic rules combine phrases into larger phrases and are linked on a one-to-one basis with semantic rules yielding representations in intensional logic (e.g., Montague Grammar—Dowty [1982]).

(iii) Syntactic principles make use of phrase structure rules, rule schemata, complex symbols, and feature conventions, but no transformations (e.g., Generalized Phrase Structure Grammar—Gazdar [1982]).

(iv) The standard theory of TG (Chomsky 1965).

(v) The extended standard theory of TG (Chomsky 1977a).

(vi) Government and Binding Theory (Chomsky 1981).

It is clearly absurd to think that children could select the appropriate one of these options on the basis of experience alone. As recent work in linguistics has shown, the merits of competing grammatical systems can often be determined only with the help of intricate argumentation based on information about the status of complex and unusual sentences that is simply not available to children. By the argument from poverty of stimulus, it would seem to follow that the relevant type of grammar is innately specified. There is, however, perhaps an alternative. Perhaps none of the options listed above is available to the language learner, who is simply not endowed with the innate ability needed to deal with such rules, relations, and notions. Instead of trying to limit the set of "possible" grammars, then, the goal of linguistic theory would be to find even one grammar that a child could construct from experience drawing only on concepts and cognitive abilities not specific to the language faculty. We can state this thesis as follows.

(1) *The Thesis of General Nativism:*
   There is no innate knowledge specific to the language faculty.

There is no guarantee that this proposal will be viable. Not only might the set of possible grammars still be too large, but it is also conceivable that an adequate grammar simply cannot be constructed without special innate concepts (e.g., c-command, subjacency, proper government, etc.). This may be true, but I do not think that it is obviously true, at least not anymore. Indeed, if the analyses presented in earlier chapters are correct even in their essentials, there is reason to think that notions such as dependency, adjacency, continuity, and precedence can be used to construct the needed linguistic categories and principles. Whether this will be true in general (i.e., for all linguistic phenomena) is naturally an open question and one that should be approached with some caution. Nonetheless, the study of human language might be substantially furthered if a serious effort were made to proceed with the line of inquiry adopted here by exploring the types of principles that would have to be posited for other phenomena on the assumption that children are not endowed with innate linguistic knowledge.

While there are no guarantees of success, a research program based on this idea would seem to have at least as much promise as the practice of taking a transformational grammar as the starting point for inquiry into language acquisition. Arguably, we can have as much confidence in cautious assumptions about the cognitive abilities of an eighteen-month-old child as proponents of TG can have in the psychological reality of the grammar that they propose. In fact, given the current lack of agreement among linguists concerning the content of the adult grammar, it might actually make more sense to reorient the study of linguistic competence

around the specific restrictive assumptions about the language faculty
adopted here.

It is important to note at this point that the (tentative) conclusion that the
language faculty is not structured by innate syntactic principles does not
preclude the possibility that other mental faculties (e.g., the perceptual
faculties) are biologically structured in a special way. Nor does it deny the
possibility that the genetic endowment might play a less direct role in linguistic development, consistent with the thesis of general nativism. In fact,
my view of language learning clearly entails the existence of other cognitive systems and abilities whose organization and composition are presumably the product, in part at least, of genetic structuring. The capacity
for generalization and inference are two obvious examples of this. Other
examples include the putative role of processing considerations in determining markedness as well as the conservative fashion in which children
seem to construct hypotheses, as manifested in their observation of the
Trigger Requirement and their tendency to use the available linguistic concepts to construct the most restrictive hypotheses consistent with experience (the Conservatism Thesis).

Another obvious example of a cognitive system whose organization is
almost certainly subject to significant genetic structuring is semantic form,
which provides a representation of word meanings, combinatorial relations
among these meanings, anaphoric dependencies, thematic roles, and the
like. An interesting recent development in the study of semantic form has
been the suggestion not only that this level of representation is innately
structured but that its properties help determine the configurational features
of syntactic structure. Proposals along these lines have been explored in the
literature on language acquisition (Schlesinger 1982) as well as in Montague Grammar (Dowty 1982) and recent work by Marantz (1984). In Marantz's work, for example, the existence of a VP constituent in syntactic
structure is taken to reflect the operation of the compositional semantics,
which creates a predicate by combining the verb with its complement
phrases.

Although the idea underlying this type of work is an interesting one, it
raises the usual questions about the ontogeny of the principles governing
the organization of semantic form. The apparent (and perhaps correct) response would seem to be that they are the product of special innate structuring. As noted in chapter 2, however, we might be led to a very different
conclusion if we assumed that the relation between syntactic structure and
the compositional semantics is the inverse of what is usually assumed and
that it falls under the "projection principle" outlined in (2).

(2) *The Syntactic Projection Principle:*
    The compositional semantics is a "projection" of syntactic structure.

According to (2), the compositional semantics mirrors the configurational properties of syntactic structure, as determined by the Hierarchical Structuring Requirement and the Subject-Last Requirement.

If (2) is correct, there is no principle of compositional semantics that requires a two-place predicate to combine with its object argument before its subject. Rather the configurational properties of semantic form are determined by a syntactic device (the Subject-Last Requirement) in conjunction with the Syntactic Projection Principle. An interesting consequence of this is that combinatorial relations in the compositional semantics would be shaped by learnable syntactic principles rather than special innate mechanisms. This is obviously a desirable consequence, although its correctness can hardly be maintained with any certainty at this point.

It is important to note at this point that nothing in my approach to language or learning constitutes a return to behaviorism or any other form of empiricism. Not only have I found it necessary to posit innate mechanisms of a general sort for language acquisition and use, I have had no occasion to question the view that linguistic behavior, like other types of cognitive activity, bears the unmistakable marks of human creativity. Rather my objective throughout this book has been to show that, at least within the linguistic domain, the system of rules underlying creative behavior is in large part the result of an equally fascinating phenomenon—the construction of knowledge through the exploitation of general cognitive resources.

Interpreted broadly, the pursuit of this objective is reminiscent of the more general research program undertaken by Jean Piaget and his colleagues in the area of cognitive development. Among the major tenets of Piaget's approach to cognition was the claim that language is in some sense "the product of general intelligence" rather than a specially structured language faculty (see, e.g., Piaget 1980). The evidence that has been adduced in support of this claim is typically weak and bears only indirectly (at best) on questions pertaining to syntactic development. In Piaget's early work, for example, it was noted that children's use of language manifested an insensitivity to the perspective and knowledge of the listener and often appeared devoid of communicative intent. This was taken to reflect the cognitive egocentrism that supposedly characterizes the preschool years. However correct this observation is (it has recently been questioned by Donaldson [1978] and others), there is little connection between it and the developmental facts pertaining to the ontogeny of syntactic categories, anaphora, extraction, and so on.

Recent work has been more to the point and there have been various attempts to show how features of early linguistic behavior might be attributed to properties of general cognitive development (e.g., Bever 1970; Cromer 1970; Sinclair 1971; Slobin 1972; Bates et al. 1977; and Inhelder 1980). Although such links are little more than suggestive, this line of inquiry is probably worth pursuing. Certainly, the thesis of general nativism would predict that children's attempts to acquire language will reflect in some significant way properties of the cognitive structures and principles they use to analyze other types of experience. Precisely what this connection will be, however, remains unclear, and I have not attempted to explore it here.

Some recent work by Curtiss (1982) suggests that the connection may be quite indirect. This conclusion is based on the apparent independence of cognitive development and the acquisition of syntax observed in three clinical reports. One involves a child (the well-known Genie) whose syntactic structures remained quite primitive despite relatively advanced cognitive skills (equivalent to a mental age of 12). The other two reports involve children with seemingly sophisticated syntactic knowledge despite low mental ages (less than four years). From this Curtiss concludes that the acquisition of syntax is not simply one instance of general cognitive development.

This conclusion does not challenge my thesis. On the "generalist" view of syntactic development that I have proposed, acquisition involves the formation of a separate cognitive system (the grammar) localized in a certain part of the brain in response to a specific type of experience. Given this, there is no reason to believe that there would have to be a point-by-point association between the emergence of a grammar and the ontogeny of any other cognitive system. Rather, I have posited a much more basic hypothesis about the relation between the grammar and other mental structures—namely, that the resources on which language learners draw do not include innate concepts or principles specific to the language faculty. It remains to be seen whether this relatively narrow claim can be replaced by more general conclusions about point-by-point similarities between language acquisition and cognitive development. Such a conclusion would be welcome, of course, but I do not think that it is warranted at this time.

7.3 Concluding Remarks

Throughout this book I have been concerned with the dual problem of characterizing the grammar underlying linguistic competence and explaining how children come to discover this system of rules. This type of inquiry necessarily involves reference to three distinct entities: the grammar attained and used by the adult speaker, the language-learning mechanisms that allow acquisition of the grammar, and the input from experience on which these mechanisms operate. The common practice in recent work has been to make use of proposals about the grammar (e.g., that it includes the Empty Category Principle) and the character of experience to draw inferences about the properties of the language faculty (in particular, that it includes innate syntactic principles). The proposals explored in this book seem to point in a rather different direction. In particular, there seems to be some support for the view that grammars are constructed on a nonlinguistic conceptual base without the help of special innate principles, consistent with what I have been calling the thesis of general nativism. Assuming the cases studied here to be typical, this thesis contradicts much of what is supposedly known about language and learning.

As with any project of the sort I have undertaken, each proposal raises a new series of questions and issues that cannot always be immediately resolved. Probably the most urgent matter of this sort has to do with how children select the notions in terms of which they form generalizations in response to experience. As I have noted a number of times in earlier chapters, it does not suffice to show that a particular principle could emerge through the analysis of experience in terms of particular concepts (dependency, continuity, etc.). Because even very young children presumably have access to quite a broad range of concepts, it is also necessary to explain how they come to choose just the right subset of notions needed to formulate linguistic principles. Special nativism has a very simple and elegant solution to this problem: the appropriate set of concepts is innately specified in advance. I have tried to develop an alternative to this idea by proposing that children formulate their initial hypotheses in terms of dependency because of this notion's roots in the primitive sentence meanings language learners presumably entertain. From this foundation various contrasts are noted, leading to the formation of syntactic categories and combinatorial principles. The resulting syntactic representations then provide the basis for the formulation of principles that refer to syntactic "objects" such as phrasal categories, discontinuous phrases, and the like. Even allowing for the problems that remain, this is a promising beginning.

It is hard to feel optimistic about a challenge to beliefs as basic to a discipline as those concerning Universal Grammar and special nativism are to linguistics. Progress in science is usually contingent on the willingness of a significant number of researchers to take certain basic empirical assumptions for granted and to pursue the resultant line of inquiry to its conclusion. Nothing that I have proposed is intended to dissuade people from continuing with the traditional research program. Rather my goal has been to open some new lines of inquiry by exploring the promise of a different set of possibilities. I hope that it is not too optimistic to think that these alternate ideas about grammar and learning might have a contribution to make to our understanding of the human language faculty.

NOTES

1. This is not the place to attempt an introduction to transformational grammar. Readers who are unfamiliar with work in this area should consult Radford (1982).

2. In many languages (e.g., Korean) the NPs with which a verb combines need not be overtly expressed. Consider:

(i) Ilg-ess-ta
    read past decl.
    (Someone) read (something).

Following much recent work (e.g., Huang 1982), I will assume that the NPs with which the verb combines in (i) are phonetically null. We can therefore maintain that the Korean verb expresses a function that applies to other linguistic categories (even though these are not always overtly realized) and that it is therefore a dependent element like its English counterpart.

3. In French, phrases such as *un petit* ('a small one') are acceptable (cf. English *the poor*). I will assume that in these cases the adjective either has been nominalized or is accompanied by a null nominal category.

4. Stated technically, this has the effect of ruling out functional composition and allowing only functional application. This restriction seems appropriate for the range of structures considered here. However, it may ultimately have to be relaxed to account for other types of structures.

5. It is conceivable that we will also have to allow the existence of such operations where there is no overt sign of a categorial modification. In a sentence such as *He ran three miles*, for instance, it seems plausible to think that the postverbal NP has been converted into a tertiary (adverbial) that is capable of combining with the intransitive verb *ran*. Similarly, languages that allow a predicative NP to combine with a nominal without a mediating copula (cf. Russian *mal' čik* [(The) boy (is a) student]) may be able to convert NPs into secondaries without the help of an overt category-changing element.

6. An alternate way to capture this intuition would be to have the SLR stipulate that the NP that combines with VP must be marked as subject. In many versions of categorial grammar the rules for assigning morphological and positional features

211

are linked to combinatorial operations in this way. I discuss a proposal along these lines by David Dowty in chap. 2.

7. Children make extremely few categorization errors in acquiring lexical items. I have nothing to say here about how errors of this type might be corrected. However, Pinker (1984, 113) discusses this issue and makes some proposals.

8. I reject the possibility that the word *go* in such a structure is a (one-word) S rather than a V. I take the position that children's utterances must be interpreted conservatively and that a sentential structure (by definition, the phrase formed by combining an NP and a VP) should not be posited where there is no direct evidence for it.

9. Cho (1981) reports comparable findings for Korean. However, Bloom (1970) suggests that the agent-object class may be productive in the speech of some English children. A problem with this claim is that it is not clear that children are actually attempting to combine two nominals to create a larger phrase in these cases. As Braine (1974) has noted, it may well be that they are simply juxtaposing words to describe salient features of the situation they are commenting on.

Chapter 2

1. I will not attempt to address the issue of how children acquiring ergative languages recognize that the subject of a transitive verb and the subject of an intransitive verb are instances of the same grammatical relation despite the fact that they have different case markers. This problem is considered at length in a manuscript on grammatical relations that I am currently preparing.

2. There are some problems for this claim, as shown by the sentences in (i) where the subject does seem to play a role in determining the thematic role that will be assigned to the direct object.

(i) a. Harry hit the student.
   b. An idea hit the student.
   c. A storm hit the town.

Marantz suggests without elaboration that interpretation of the thematic role associated with the direct object in (b) and (c) involves metaphor.

3. In some sentences, there may be no a priori way to determine whether a particular NP is associated with an actor-type role or with a theme-type role. It is not clear on a priori grounds, for instance, whether the subject NP in the following sentences is "active" enough to be associated with the actor class.

(i) a. The coach turned into a pumpkin.
   b. The ball bounced across the room.
   c. The pressure increased.
   d. The shirt shrank in the wash.
   e. The glue stuck to his clothes.
   f. The boy slept soundly.

Decisions about the classification of the relevant roles in these sentences may have to be made on language-particular grounds by observing whether they pattern with actor roles or theme roles with respect to grammatical rules that are sensitive to this distinction. This would be an instance of the bootstrapping phenomenon discussed in the previous chapter.

4. I make no attempt here to determine which, if any, larger class includes these thematic roles.

5. Somewhat surprisingly, the five-year-olds did equally well on both types of verbs, leading Marantz to conclude that they have acquired abstract GRs that are not linked in any way to specific thematic roles. This in turn would entail the rejection of the Mapping Filter for simple declarative sentences, contrary to what I am claiming. Before Marantz's conclusion can be accepted, it must be shown that the five-year-olds really acquired the new verb forms (i.e., would use them spontaneously in a nonexperimental setting) and that they took them to mean what Marantz intended. Thus if *pume* were taken to mean "bounce on," for instance, *The book is puming Larry* would in fact comply with the Mapping Principle. Neither of these requirements was met in Marantz's experiment.

6. I ignore here passives like *This bed has been slept in* in which it is plausible to assume that the intransitive verb has been transitivized by a reanalysis process of some sort that incorporates the preposition into the verb, creating a dependency on a t-argument.

7. I make no attempt here to relate the structures exemplified in (i) and (ii).

(i) The ship sank.

(ii) The enemy sank the ship.

One possibility is that there is a rule "Add an a-argument" that would create the lexical entry in (iv) from (iii).

(iii) V: NP_t

(iv) V: NP_a NP_t

The Mapping Filter would then ensure that the a-argument is encoded as subject, as desired. Application of Passivization to (iv) would yield (v), corresponding to the sentence *The ship was sunk by the enemy.*

(v) V: NP_t ({by NP_a})

8. This mapping relation is not necessarily one of isomorphism, however. In Marantz's (1984) grammar, for instance, there is a semantic entity corresponding to the verb and its logical object (t-argument) even when they do not form a syntactic phrase (as in passives).

Chapter 3

1. For discussion of discontinuous constituents in transformational grammar, see McCawley (1982a), Zubizarreta and Vergnaud (1982), and Higginbotham (1983).

2. For discussion of the Projection Principle and categorial grammar from a different perspective, see Huck (1984) and the reference cited there.

3. Hornstein and Weinberg (1981) suggest that extraction from a temporal PP is impossible, as (i) supposedly shows.

(i) *What time did they arrive at ____?

However, I find extraction from a temporal PP to be perfectly acceptable in many cases. Consider:

(ii) What inning did they score in ____?

(iii) How many days has he waited here for ____?

(iv) What time will you be here by ____?

4. Following Liejiong and Langendoen (1985), I assume that topicalized structures such as (i) contain a phonetically null pronoun in the VP and hence do not involve discontinuous constituents.

(i) Lisi [Zhangsan kanjian-le *pro*]

　　As for Lisi, Zhangsan saw [him].

5. In order to simplify, I have deliberately ignored cases such as (i), in which a (predicative) AdjP is discontinuous.

(i) Of whom does Harry seem [$_{AdjP}$ fond ____]

I assume that discontinuous AdjPs are equal in markedness to discontinuous VPs. We therefore find that in languages such as Dutch, which allow discontinuous VPs but not NPs, sentences such as (ii) and (iii) are acceptable.

(ii) Met wie is hij ____ gelukkig?
　　"With whom is he happy?"

(iii) Op wie is John ____ verliefd?
　　"Of whom is John enamored?"

I also deliberately ignore complications stemming from the possible grammaticality of nonstranded structures such as (iv) in Dutch.

(iv) Van wie hebt je [$_{VP}$[$_{NP}$ een foto ____]] gezien]?
　　Of whom have you　a picture　　seen
　　"Of whom have you seen a picture?"

If grammatical, this sentence would suggest that Dutch allows either a discontinuous PP or a discontinuous NP (cf. [14]), but not both.

6. Many of the early *wh* structures reported in the literature (e.g., Menyuk 1969) do not contain verbs and hence have no discontinuous constituents at all. This is exemplified in (i).

(i) Where Daddy?

(ii) What that?

The early appearance of such structures therefore does not jeopardize my claim that discontinuous constituents do not appear until the fundamental organization of syntactic structure has been mastered.

Chapter 4

1. A problem for this analysis is that it is possible to "extract" from some [*to* VP] structures that are considered to be adverbial phrases.

(i) Who did John stay [to see ____]?

However, extraction from nonfinite adverbial clauses is not permitted in general.

(ii) *What did John die [after eating ____]?

(iii) *Which meeting did John deceive Tim [while attending ____]?

2. The status of some sentences resembling (25b) is somewhat harder to determine. Consider, for example, (i).

(i) ??Who was the job good enough [for us to offer it to ____]?

I will follow Chomsky (1977b, 102) in assuming that (i) is marginal and that nothing can be concluded from it.

3. Sentences like (i) provide an apparent problem for all analyses of the contrast we are considering.

(i) This is the dog [$_S$ that frightened Harry].

I will assume that the element *that* is a relative pronoun here and not a complementizer. Comparable assumptions are frequently made within TG.

4. Incorrect responses to structure (31b) actually seem to increase with age, rising as high as 40 percent in grade 2 and remaining over 20 percent for adults. At no time, however, was the incorrect response dominant for any group. I have no explanation for why this increase occurs.

Chapter 5

1. A problem with this proposal is that it predicts the acceptability of (i), apparently incorrectly.

(i) [$_S$ He$_i$ saw me] after Harry$_i$ got home.

It may be significant that sentences such as (i) do occur in natural speech. The following sentence, for instance, was used by a commentator on a nationally televised football game and sounded extremely natural in context.

(ii) They$_i$ have not been off to this kind of start since 1942 when the Bears$_i$ were 7 and 0.

Indeed Carden (1982) reports that sentences such as these are about as frequent as the seemingly more acceptable (15). (The completely ungrammatical [13] and [14] are less frequent.) It might be worthwhile to explore the possibility that pragmatic or discourse factors rather than a grammatical constraint prohibit the pattern in (i). (On this, see McCray [1980].)

2. A problem here is that the anaphoric dependencies in (i)–(iii) may be possible even though the pronoun lies outside the phrasal category of its antecedent.

(i) ?[$_{NP}$ Every boy's$_i$ mother] thinks that he$_i$ is a genius.

(ii) ?[$_{NP}$ Everyone's$_i$ wife] trusts him$_i$.

(iii) ?[$_{NP}$ Everyone in some city$_i$] hates it$_i$.

Higginbotham (1980) claims that such sentences "seem acceptable" to him, although he admits that others find them marginal. I will assume the latter judgments.

3. A problem for this proposal stems from sentences such as (i) and (ii), which are apparently acceptable for some people (see Higginbotham [1980]; and n. 2 above).

(i) [$_{NP}$ Whose$_i$ mother] trusts him$_i$?

(ii) [$_{NP}$ Which picture of which man$_i$] pleased him$_i$?

4. A comparable analysis seems appropriate in cases such as (i).

(i) John$_i$ expects himself/*him$_i$ to be chosen.

Following Bresnan (1982), I will take the position that the pronominal NP in (i) is the syntactic object of *expect*, even though it apparently receives its thematic role from the embedded verb *choose*. Since objects satisfy combinatorial dependencies of the verb, the pronoun would count as a "term" of *expect* and would therefore have to be reflexive if its antecedent is *John* (the subject argument and a thematic dependent of *expect*). The obligatoriness of the reflexive in (ii) would then follow from the fact that the pronoun and its antecedent are both thematic dependents of the verb *choose* even though the lexical NP is direct object of the matrix verb.

(ii) I expect Harry$_i$ to choose himself/*him$_i$.

5. However, these alternations might prove problematic for other reasons. If, for instance, children only heard sentences such as *John keeps a gun near himself* and did not realize that the definite pronoun could also occur in these patterns, they would incorrectly assume that the reflexive was obligatory in such cases. This in turn would presumably interfere with the formulation of the Reflexive Requirement since the reflexive and its antecedent in these cases are not thematic dependents of the same element.

6. The actual figures from Otsu's experiment on reflexives are as follows.

	Imitation Task	
	Pass	Fail
Comprehension test:		
Pass	24	3
Fail	12	21

Although twelve children passed the imitation task but failed the reflexive interpretation test, Otsu takes these results to indicate that children know how to apply the binding principles as soon as they master biclausal structures. He takes this as evidence for the view that the binding principles are innate. As far as I can see, these results show only that the vast majority of children do not apply the principles for reflexive interpretation correctly before learning the relevant facts about clause structure (hardly a surprising conclusion). Moreover, for at least twelve of Otsu's sixty subjects, there is a delay between the two discoveries. I see no support here for special nativism.

Chapter 6

1. There are also a number of semantic constraints on extraposition that Guéron (1980) tries to analyze in terms of focus. Since these constraints have nothing to do with dependency relations, I will not deal with them here.

2. The fact that *each* occurs with a number expression may well relate to the common observation that it has a "distributive" meaning and can serve in an "individuating function" (Kruisinga 1932, 269; Curme 1935, 52; Dougherty 1970, 3). The elements *all* and *both*, on the other hand, are often said to have "unifying power" (e.g., Jespersen 1954, 595)—a fact that helps explain why they combine with phrases expressing similarity.

3. However, floated *all* can also be associated with a mass noun, as (i) shows.

(i) The linen$_i$ has all$_i$ been washed.

I am grateful to J. D. McCawley for this observation.

4. Some speakers apparently find (19) and (20) equally acceptable, a fact that suggests that they do not adopt principle (21). I assume that for these speakers some notion other than thematic dependency (perhaps occurrence in the phrasal category of the "antecedent" NP) is relevant to the interpretation of floated quantifiers. An anonymous reviewer notes that sentence (i) seems acceptable.

(i) He jumped over the hurdles$_i$ several times each$_i$.

If the complement NP receives its thematic role from *over* rather than *jump*, (i) would indeed be problematic. However, it is perhaps noteworthy that the preposition is optional here.

(ii) He jumped the hurdles.

This suggests that *over* may not be crucial to the assignment of a thematic role in these cases.

5. Of course, the initial hypothesis could also be narrower than this. If, for instance, children formed their first generalization in response to sentences such as (i), they would presumably restrict the set of eligible antecedents to subject arguments.

(i) The boys$_i$ have each$_i$ left.

Subsequent exposure to sentences such as (ii) would then lead to exploitation of the broader notion "thematic dependent."

(ii) I talked to the boys$_i$ twice each$_i$.

Chapter 7

1. Pinker (1984) notes that this cannot be entirely correct since it is known that children overgeneralize double object and passive constructions in some instances. I discussed this matter briefly in chap. 2.

2. The well-known overgeneralizations associated with the acquisition of word meaning may be manifestations of this phenomenon. Thus it is possible that children who use the word *dog* to refer to all animals are making the most conservative use of the notions available for the formation of word meaning at that point in their development.

3. This does not entail that backward patterns will never be more frequent than forward ones. Apparently, VOS languages make extensive use of structures such as (i). (These structures comply with the Precedence Constraint since the antecedent lies outside the phrasal category of the pronoun.)

(i) $[_S [_{VP}$ saw himself] John]

The existence of such backward patterns of anaphora does not support Lust's prediction since VOS languages are right branching.

REFERENCES

Ajdukiewicz, K. 1935. Die Syntaktische Konnexitat. *Studia Philosophica* 1:1–27.

Baker, C. 1979. Syntactic theory and the projection principle. *Linguistic Inquiry* 10:533–82.

Baltin, M. 1978. Toward a theory of movement rules. Ph.D. dissertation, Massachusetts Institute of Technology.

———. 1982. A landing site theory of movement rules. *Linguistic Inquiry* 14:1–38.

Bar-Hillel, J. 1950. On syntactical categories. *Journal of Symbolic Logic* 15:1–16.

Bates, E., L. Benigni, I. Bretherton, L. Camione, and V. Volterra. 1977. From gesture to the first word: On cognitive and social prerequisites. In *Interaction, conversation and the development of language,* edited by M. Lewis and L. Rosenblum. New York: Wiley.

Bates, E., and B. McWhinney. 1982. Functionalist approaches to grammar. In *Language acquisition: The state of the art,* edited by E. Wanner and L. Gleitman. New York: Cambridge University Press.

Berwick, R. C. 1982. Locality principles and the acquisition of syntactic knowledge. Ph.D. dissertation, Massachusetts Institute of Technology.

Berwick, R., and A. Weinberg. 1984. The grammatical basis of linguistic performance. Cambridge, Mass.: MIT Press.

Beukema, F., and T. Hoekstra. 1984. Extraction from *with* constructions. *Linguistic Inquiry* 15:689–98.

Bever, T. 1970. The cognitive basis for linguistic structures. In *Cognition and the development of language,* edited by J. R. Hayes. New York: Wiley.

Bloom, L. 1970. *Language development: Form and function in emerging grammars.* Cambridge, Mass.: MIT Press.

Bloom, L., P. Lightbown, and L. Hood. 1975. *Structure and variation in child language.* Monographs of the Society for Research in Child Development, vol. 40, no. 2, serial no. 160. Chicago: University of Chicago Press.

Bolinger, D. 1972. *What did John keep the car that was in? *Linguistic Inquiry* 3:109–14.

Borsley, R. 1983. A note on preposition stranding. *Linguistic Inquiry* 14:338–43.

Braine, M. 1974. Length constraints, reduction rules and holophrastic phrases in children's word combinations. *Journal of Verbal Learning and Verbal Behavior* 13:448–57.

Brainerd, C. 1978. Learning research and Piagetian theory. In *Alternatives to Piaget: Critical essays on the theory,* edited by L. Siegel and C. Brainerd. New York: Academic Press.

Bresnan, J. 1982. The passive in lexical theory. In *The mental representation of grammatical relations,* edited by J. Bresnan. Cambridge, Mass.: MIT Press.

Brown, R. 1973. *A first language: The early stages.* Cambridge, Mass.: Harvard University Press.

Bruner, J. 1983. *Child's talk: Learning to use language.* New York: Norton.

Cantrall, W. 1974. *Viewpoint, reflexives, and the nature of noun phrases.* The Hague: Mouton.

Carden, G. 1982. Backwards anaphora in discourse context. *Journal of Linguistics* 8:361–87.

———. In press. Blocked forwards coreference: Theoretical implications of the acquisition data. In *Studies in first language acquisition of anaphora: Defining the constraints,* edited by B. Lust. Boston: Reidel.

Cattel, R. 1979. On extractability from quasi-NPs. *Linguistic Inquiry* 10:168–72.

Chierchia, G. 1985. Formal semantics and the grammar of predication. *Linguistic Inquiry* 16:417–44.

Cho, S. 1981. The acquisition of word order in Korean. M.A. thesis, University of Calgary, Department of Linguistics.

Chomsky, C. 1969. *The acquisition of syntax in children from age 5 to 10.* Cambridge, Mass.: MIT Press.

Chomsky, N. 1965. *Aspects of the theory of syntax.* Cambridge, Mass.: MIT Press.

———. 1977a. *Essays on form and interpretation.* New York: North-Holland.

———. 1977b. On *wh* movement. In *Formal syntax,* edited by P. Culicover, T. Wasow, and A. Akmajian. New York: Academic Press.

———. 1980. On cognitive structures and their development: A reply to Piaget. In *Language and learning,* edited by M. Piatelli-Palmarini. Cambridge, Mass.: Harvard University Press.

———. 1981. *Lectures on government and binding.* Dordrecht: Foris.

———. 1982. *Concepts and consequences of the theory of government and binding.* Cambridge, Mass.: MIT Press.

Chomsky, N., and H. Lasnik. 1977. Filters and control. *Linguistic Inquiry* 8:425–504.

Clark, H., and E. Clark. 1977. *Psychology and language.* New York: Harcourt, Brace, Jovanovich.

Cole, P. 1985. Quantifier scope and the ECP. *Linguistics and Philosophy* 8:283–89.

Cornell, E. 1978. Learning to find things: A reinterpretation of object permanence studies. In *Alternatives to Piaget: Critical essays on the theory,* edited by L. Siegel and C. Brainerd. New York: Academic Press.

Cromer, R. 1974. The development of language and cognition: The cognition hypothesis. In *New perspectives in child development,* edited by B. Foss. London: Penguin.

Curme, B. 1935. *A grammar of the English language: Parts of speech and accidence.* Boston: Heath.

Curtiss, S. 1982. Developmental dissociation of language and cognition. In *Exceptional language and linguistics,* edited by L. Obler and L. Menn. New York: Academic Press.

Dixon, R. 1982. *Where have all the adjectives gone?* The Hague: Mouton.

Donaldson, M. 1978. *Children's minds.* London: Fontana.

Donaldson, M., and J. McGarrigle. 1974. Some clues to the nature of semantic development. *Journal of Child Language* 1:185–94.

Dougherty, R. 1970. Grammar of coordinate compound structures. *Language* 46:850–98.

Dowty, D. 1982. Grammatical relations in Montague Grammar. In *The nature of syntactic representation,* edited by P. Jacobson and G. Pullum. Boston: Reidel.

Dowty, D., R. Wall, and S. Peters. 1982. *Introduction to Montague semantics.* Boston: Reidel.

Engdahl, E. 1980. *Wh*-constructions in Swedish and the relevance of subjacency. *Cahiers linguistiques d'Ottawa* 9:89–108.

————. 1985. Interpreting questions. In *Natural language processing,* edited by D. Dowty, L. Karttunen, and A. Zwicky. London: Cambridge University Press.

Erteschik-Shir, N. 1981. More on extractability from quasi-NPs. *Linguistic Inquiry* 12:665–70.

Erteschik-Shir, N., and S. Lappin. 1979. Dominance and the functional explanation of island phenomena. *Theoretical Linguistics* 6:41–86.

Felix, S. 1984. Two problems of language acquisition: An interaction of Universal Grammar and language growth. Typescript. University of Passau, Department of Linguistics.

Fiengo, R., and H. Lasnik. 1976. Some issues in the theory of transformations. *Linguistic Inquiry* 7:182–91.

Flynn, M. 1983. A categorial theory of structure building. In *Order, concord and constituency,* edited by G. Gazdar, E. Klein, and G. Pullum. Dordrecht: Foris.

Fodor, J. 1975. *The language of thought.* New York: Crowell.

Fodor, J., T. Bever, and M. Garrett. 1974. *The psychology of language: An introduction to psycholinguistics.* New York: McGraw-Hill.

Foley, W., and R. Van Valin. 1984. *Functional syntax and Universal Grammar.* London: Cambridge University Press.

French, M. 1984. Markedness and the acquisition of pied-piping and preposition stranding. *McGill University Working Papers in Linguistics* 2:131–45.

Garcia, E. 1979. Discourse without syntax. In *Syntax and semantics,* vol. 12, edited by T. Givon. New York: Academic Press.

Gazdar, G. 1982. Phrase structure grammar. In *The nature of syntactic representation,* edited by P. Jacobson and G. Pullum. Boston: Reidel.

Gentner, D. 1982. Why nouns are learned before verbs: Linguistic relativity versus natural partitioning. In *Language development: Language, cognition and culture,* edited by S. Kuczai. Hillsdale, N.J.: Erlbaum.

Givon, T. 1979. *On understanding grammar.* New York: Academic Press.

Greenfield, P., and J. Smith. 1976. *The structure of communication in child language*. New York: Academic Press.

Guéron, J. 1980. On the syntax and semantics of PP extraposition. *Linguistic Inquiry* 11:637–78.

Haïk, I. 1984. Indirect binding. *Linguistic Inquiry* 15:185–224.

Harris, A. 1981. *Georgian syntax*. London: Cambridge University Press.

————. 1984. Case marking, verb agreement, and inversion in Udi. In *Studies in relational grammar*, vol. 2, edited by D. Perlmutter and C. Rosen. Chicago: University of Chicago Press.

Hawkins, J. 1979. Implicational universals as predictors of word order change. *Language* 55:618–48.

Hayhurst, H. 1967. Some errors of young children in producing passive sentences. *Journal of Verbal Learning and Verbal Behavior* 6:634–39.

Higginbotham, J. 1980. Pronouns and bound variables. *Linguistic Inquiry* 11:679–708.

————. 1983. Logical form, binding and nominals. *Linguistic Inquiry* 14:395–420.

Hildebrand, J. 1984. Markedness, acquisition and preposition stranding: What are children born with? M.A. thesis, University of Calgary, Department of Linguistics.

Hill, J. 1983. Combining two-term relations: Evidence in support of flat structures. *Journal of Child Language* 11:673–78.

Hornstein, N., and A. Weinberg. 1981. Case theory and preposition stranding. *Linguistic Inquiry* 12:55–92.

Huang, J. 1982. Logical relations in Chinese and the theory of grammar. Ph.D. dissertation, Massachusetts Institute of Technology.

Huck, G. 1984. Discontinuity and word order in categorial grammar. Ph.D. dissertation, University of Chicago.

Hudson, R. 1970. On clauses containing conjoined and plural noun-phrases in English. *Lingua* 24:205–53.

————. 1984. *Word grammar*. London: Blackwell.

Ingram, D., and C. Shaw. 1981. The comprehension of pronominal reference in children. Typescript. University of British Columbia, Department of Linguistics.

Inhelder, B. 1980. Cognitive schemes and their possible relation to language acquisition. In *Language and learning*, edited by M. Piatelli-Palmarini. Cambridge, Mass.: Harvard University Press.

Jackendoff, R. 1972. *Semantic interpretation in generative grammar*. Cambridge, Mass.: MIT Press.

————. 1977. *X' syntax: A study of phrase structure*. Cambridge, Mass.: MIT Press.

————. 1983. *Semantics and cognition*. Cambridge, Mass.: MIT Press.

Jaeggli, O. 1982. *Topics in Romance syntax*. Dordrecht: Foris.

Jakubowicz, C. 1984. On markedness and binding principles. In *Proceedings of NELS 14*, edited by C. Jones and P. Sells. Amherst: University of Massachusetts—Amherst, Graduate Linguistic Student Association.

Jespersen, O. 1954. *A Modern English grammar on historical principles,* vol. 7. London: Allen & Unwin.

———. 1965. *The philosophy of grammar.* New York: Norton.

Koster, J. 1978. Conditions, empty nodes and markedness. *Linguistic Inquiry* 9:551–94.

Kruisinga, E. 1932. *A handbook of present-day English,* vol. 2, pt. 2. Groningen: Noordhoff.

Kuno, S. 1973. Constraints on internal clauses and sentential subjects. *Linguistic Inquiry* 4:363–85.

———. 1975. Three perspectives on the functional approach to syntax. In *Papers from the parasession on functionalism,* edited by R. Grossman, L. San, and T. Vance. Chicago: Chicago Linguistic Society.

Lappin, S. 1984. Predication and raising. In *Proceedings of NELS 14,* edited by C. Jones and P. Sells. Amherst: University of Massachusetts—Amherst, Graduate Linguistic Student Association.

Lasnik, H., and M. Saito. 1984. On the nature of proper government. *Linguistic Inquiry* 15:235–90.

Lee, S. W. 1983. Syntax of some nominal constructions in Korean. Ph.D. dissertation, University of Wisconsin—Madison.

Lenneberg, E. 1967. *Biological foundations of language.* New York: Wiley.

Lieber, R. 1983. Argument linking and compounds in English. *Linguistic Inquiry* 14:251–87.

Liejiong, X., and T. Langendoen. 1985. Topic structures in Chinese. *Language* 61:1–27.

Lightfoot, D. 1979. *Principles of diachronic syntax.* London: Cambridge University Press.

Lust, B. 1981. Constraints on anaphora in child language: A prediction for a universal. In *Linguistic theory and language acquisition,* edited by S. Tavakolian. Cambridge, Mass.: MIT Press.

———. 1983. On the notion "principal branching direction": A parameter in Universal Grammar. In *Studies in generative grammar and language acquisition,* edited by Y. Otsu, H. van Riemsdijk, K. Inoue, A. Kamio, and N. Kawasaki. Tokyo: International Christian University.

Lust, B., and T. Clifford. 1982. The 3D study—effects of depth, directionality and distance on children's acquisition of anaphora: An initial report. In *Proceedings of NELS 12,* edited by J. Pustejovsky and P. Sells. Amherst: University of Massachusetts—Amherst, Graduate Linguistic Student Association.

Lust, B., and L. Mangione. 1983. The principal branching direction parameter in first language acquisition of anaphora. In *Proceedings of ALNE/NELS 13,* edited by P. Sells and C. Jones. Amherst: University of Massachusetts—Amherst, Graduate Linguistic Student Association.

McCawley, J. 1982a. Parentheticals and discontinuous constituent structure. *Linguistic Inquiry* 13:91–106.

———. 1982b. *Thirty million theories of grammar.* London: Croom Helm.

———. 1983. Toward plausability in theories of language acquisition. *Communication and Cognition* 16:169–83.

———. 1985. Some additional evidence for discontinuity. Paper presented at the Chicago Conference on Discontinuous Constituents, University of Chicago, July.

McCray, A. 1980. The semantics of backward anaphora. *Cahiers linguistiques d'Ottawa* 9:329–44.

Macnamara, J. 1982. *Names for things*. Cambridge, Mass.: MIT Press.

Macrae, A. 1979. Combining meanings in early language. In *Language acquisition*, edited by P. Fletcher and M. Garman. London: Cambridge University Press.

Maling, J., and A. Zaenen. 1978. The nonuniversality of a surface filter. *Linguistic Inquiry* 9:475–98.

Marantz, A. 1982. On the acquisition of grammatical relations. *Linguistiche Berichte* 80–82:32–69.

———. 1984. *On the nature of grammatical relations*. Cambridge, Mass.: MIT Press.

Maratsos, M. 1982. The child's construction of grammatical categories. In *Language acquisition: The state of the art*, edited by E. Wanner and L. Gleitman. London: Cambridge University Press.

Maratsos, M., and M. Chalkley. 1980. The internal language of children's syntax: The ontogenesis and representation of syntactic categories. In *Children's language*, vol. 2, edited by K. Nelson. New York: Gardner.

Matthei, E. 1979. The acquisition of prenominal modifier sequences: Stalking the second green ball. Ph.D. dissertation, University of Massachusetts—Amherst.

May, R. 1977. The grammar of quantification. Ph.D. dissertation, Massachusetts Institute of Technology.

Mazurkewich, I., and L. White. 1984. The acquisition of the dative alternation: Unlearning overgeneralizations. *Cognition* 16:261–83.

Menyuk, P. 1969. *Sentences children use*. Cambridge, Mass.: MIT Press.

Nelson, K. 1975. The nominal shift in semantic-syntactic development. *Cognitive Psychology* 7:461–79.

Odom, R. 1978. A perceptual-salience account of décalage relations and developmental change. In *Alternatives to Piaget: Critical essays on the theory*, edited by L. Siegel and C. Brainerd. New York: Academic Press.

O'Grady, W. 1982. The syntax and semantics of quantifier placement. *Linguistics* 20:519–40.

———. 1985a. Discontinuous constituents in a free word order language. Paper presented at the Chicago Conference on Discontinuous Constituents, University of Chicago, July.

———. 1985b. Thematic dependency and semantic interpretation. *Canadian Journal of Linguistics* 30:159–77.

———. In press. The interpretation of Korean anaphora. *Language*.

O'Grady, W., Y. Suzuki-Wei, and S. Cho. 1986. Directionality preferences in the interpretation of anaphora: Data from Korean and Japanese. *Journal of Child Language* 13.

Olmsted, D. 1971. *Out of the mouth of babes*. The Hague: Mouton.

Otsu, Y. 1981. Universal grammar and syntactic development in children: Toward a theory of syntactic development. Ph.D. dissertation, Massachusetts Institute of Technology.

Perlmutter, D. 1982. Syntactic representation, syntactic levels and the notion of subject. In *The nature of syntactic representation,* edited by P. Jacobson and G. Pullum. Boston: Reidel.

Perlmutter, D., and P. Postal. 1977. Toward a universal characterization of passivization. In *Proceedings of the third annual meeting of the Berkeley Linguistics Society,* edited by K. Whistler, R. van Valin, C. Chiarello, J. Jaeger, M. Petruck, H. Thompson, R. Javkin, and A. Woodbury. Berkeley: Berkeley Linguistics Society.

———. 1983. Some proposed laws of a basic clause structure. In *Studies in Relational Grammar,* vol. 1, edited by D. Perlmutter. Chicago: University of Chicago Press.

———. 1984. The One-Advancement Exclusiveness Law. In *Studies in relational grammar,* vol. 2, edited by D. Perlmutter and C. Rosen. Chicago: University of Chicago Press.

Peters, A. 1983. *The units of language acquisition.* London: Cambridge University Press.

Phinney, M. 1981. Syntactic constraints and the acquisition of embedded sentential complements. Ph.D. dissertation, University of Massachusetts—Amherst, Department of Linguistics.

Piaget, J. 1980. The psycho-genesis of thought and its epistemological significance. In *Language and learning,* edited by M. Piatelli-Palmarini. Cambridge, Mass.: Harvard University Press.

Piaget, J., and B. Inhelder. 1969. *The psychology of the child.* New York: Basic.

Pinker, S. 1979. Formal models of language learning. *Cognition* 7:217–83.

———. 1984. *Language learnability and language development.* Cambridge, Mass.: MIT Press.

Postal, P. 1976. Avoiding reference to subject. *Linguistic Inquiry* 7:151–91.

Poutsma, H. 1926. *A grammar of late modern English.* Groningen: Noordhoff.

Pullum, G. 1982. Free word order and phrase structure rules. In *Proceedings of NELS 12,* edited by J. Pustejovsky and P. Sells. Amherst: University of Massachusetts—Amherst, Graduate Linguistics Student Association.

Radford, A. 1981. *Transformational syntax.* London: Cambridge University Press.

Rappaport, M. 1983. On the nature of derived nominals. In *Papers in lexical-functional grammar,* edited by L. Levin, M. Rappaport, and A. Zaenan. Bloomington: Indiana University Linguistics Club.

Read, C., and V. Hare. 1979. Children's interpretation of reflexive pronouns in English. In *Studies in first and second language acquisition,* edited by F. Eckman and A. Hastings. Rowby, Mass.: Newbury.

Reinhart, T. 1981. Definite NP anaphora and c-command domains. *Linguistic Inquiry* 12:605–36.

———. 1983. *Anaphora and semantic interpretation.* Chicago: University of Chicago Press.

Roeper, T., S. Lapointe, T. Bing, and S. Tavakolian. 1981. A lexical approach to
    language acquisition. In *Language acquisition and linguistic theory,* edited by
    S. Tavakolian. Cambridge, Mass.: MIT Press.
Roeper, T., and E. Matthei. 1975. On the acquisition of "some" and "all."
    Papers and Reports on the Study of Child Language Development 9:63–74.
Ross, J. 1967. Constraints on variables in syntax. Ph.D. dissertation, Massachuset-
    ts Institute of Technology.
Rothstein, S. 1985. The syntactic forms of predication. Ph.D. dissertation, Mas-
    sachusetts Institute of Technology.
Sag, I. 1978. Floated quantifiers, adverbs and extraction sites. *Linguistic Inquiry*
    9:146–50.
Saito, M. 1985. Some asymmetries in Japanese and their theoretical implications.
    Ph.D. dissertation, Massachusetts Institute of Technology.
Schlesinger, I. M. 1977. The role of cognitive development and linguistic input in
    language acquisition. *Journal of Child Language* 4:154–69.
──────. 1982. *Steps to language.* Hillsdale, N.J.: Erlbaum.
Selkirk, E. 1982. *The syntax of words.* Cambridge, Mass.: MIT Press.
Siegel, M. 1983. Problems in preposition stranding. *Linguistic Inquiry* 14:184–88.
Sinclair, H. 1971. Sensori-motor patterns as a condition for the acquisition of the
    syntax. In *Language acquisition: Models and methods,* edited by R. Huxley and
    E. Ingram. New York: Academic Press.
Slobin, D. 1973. Cognitive prerequisites for the development of grammar. In *Stud-
    ies in child language development,* edited by C. Ferguson and C. Snow. New
    York: Holt, Rinehart & Winston.
──────. 1975. On the nature of talk to children. In *Foundations of language devel-
    opment,* edited by E. Lenneberg and E. Lenneberg. New York: Academic
    Press.
──────. 1982. Universal and particular in the acquisition of language. In *Language
    acquisition: The state of the art,* edited by E. Wanner and L. Gleitman. London:
    Cambridge University Press.
Solan, L. 1983. *Pronominal reference: Child language and the theory of grammar.*
    Boston: Reidel.
Suzuki, Y. 1985. The acquisition of Japanese pronouns. M.A. thesis, University of
    Calgary, Department of Linguistics.
Taylor-Browne, K. 1983. Acquiring restrictions on forward anaphora: A pilot
    study. *Calgary Working Papers in Linguistics* (University of Calgary, Depart-
    ment of Linguistics) 9:75–100.
Wanner, E., and M. Maratsos. 1978. An ATN approach to comprehension. In
    Linguistic theory and pschological reality, edited by M. Halle, J. Bresnan, and
    G. Miller. Cambridge, Mass.: MIT Press.
Wasow, T. 1977. Transformations and the lexicon. In *Formal syntax,* edited by P.
    Culicover, T. Wasow, and A. Akmajian. New York: Academic Press.
──────. 1979. *Anaphora in generative grammar.* Brussels: Story-Scientia.
Watson, G. 1984. Pronouns and prepositional phrases. Ph.D. dissertation, Yale
    University.

Wexler, K., and Y.-C. Chien. 1985. The development of lexical anaphors and pronouns. *Papers and Reports on Child Language Development* 24:138–49.

White, L. 1981. The responsibility of grammatical theory to acquisitional data. In *Explanation in linguistics: The logical problem of language acquisition,* edited by N. Hornstein and D. Lightfoot. London: Longman.

Williams, E. 1982. The NP cycle. *Linguistic Inquiry* 13:277–96.

———. 1983. Semantic vs. syntactic categories. *Linguistics and Philosophy* 6:423–46.

———. 1984. Grammatical relations. *Linguistic Inquiry* 15:639–74.

Zubizarreta, M. 1982. Theoretical implications of subject extraction in Portuguese. *Linguistic Review* 2:79–96.

Zubizarreta, M., and J. Vergnaud. 1982. On virtual categories. MIT Working Papers in Linguistics 4. Cambridge: Massachusetts Institute of Technology.

INDEX